Making Aboriginal Men and Music in Central Australia

Making Aboriginal Men and Music in Central Australia

BY ÅSE OTTOSSON

Bloomsbury Academic
An imprint of Bloomsbury Publishing Plc

BLOOMSBURY
LONDON · OXFORD · NEW YORK · NEW DELHI · SYDNEY

Bloomsbury Academic

An imprint of Bloomsbury Publishing Plc

50 Bedford Square	1385 Broadway
London	New York
WC1B 3DP	NY 10018
UK	USA

www.bloomsbury.com

BLOOMSBURY and the Diana logo are trademarks of Bloomsbury Publishing Plc

First published 2016

British Library Cataloguing-in-Publication Data
A catalogue record for this book is available from the British Library.

ISBN: HB: 978-1-4742-2462-8
ePDF: 978-1-47422-464-2
ePub: 978-1-4742-2463-5

Library of Congress Cataloging-in-Publication Data
A catalog record for this book is available from the Library of Congress.

Typeset by Deanta Global Publishing Services, Chennai, India

Contents

List of illustrations

Acknowledgements

Many people deserve thanks for their participation and support in the research for this book. First of all, a big thanks to all you 'fellas who shared your music and life stories with me, often with a great sense of humour. It has been a privilege, and lots of fun. Special thanks to Stanley Satour for many great conversations about the intricacies of music making in the studio and on stage, Andy Alberts for generously sharing his thoughts and feelings about being Koori and a musician, and Steve Tranter for being a good friend. I want to pay my respect to the families of the musicians who have passed away since I began this project. Some of them appear in the book and I hope it can make you proud of their contributions to the desert music scene.

In the scholarly scene, many good women and men have inspired me with their sharp minds and their generous support in the different phases of the research and in various aspects of my thinking about indigenous, musical and male matters. Genuine thanks to Don Kulick, Ulf Hannerz, Mark Graham, Melinda Hinkson, Francesca Merlan, Alan Rumsey, Stephen Wild, Tony Redmond, Karl Neuenfeldt, Aaron Fox, Kristina Jacobsen-Bia and my many fellow anthropologists in Stockholm, Canberra and elsewhere. I thank Louise, Jennifer, Molly and other people involved at Bloomsbury for their interest in my research and their care when turning it into a book. Thanks, too, for the kind words of the anonymous reviewers.

I would not have been able to complete this work without loyal friends and family. I especially thank Marianne for being the finest listener throughout the years, and Mikaell for his thoughtful and pragmatic advice on how to combine personal convictions and academic work. Finally, I want to thank my mother Minge who passed away unexpectedly when I was in the midst of the research. As long as I can remember, she was striving for the independence that education, lived knowledge of the world and a professional career can provide – a goal that she and many women in her generation were not able or allowed to achieve. I owe a great deal to her and all the women who made it possible for their daughters and granddaughters to create lives on their own terms.

The field research was made possible by grants from Anna Ahlströms och Ellen Terselius Stiftelse, Svenska Sällskapet för Antropologi och Geografi and Humanistiska Samhällsvetenskapliga Forskningsrådet in Sweden.

Preface

Hitch-hiking around remote Australia in 1983, I first arrived in Alice Springs on a freezing July morning. After exploring the surrounding desert ranges for a few days, I returned to the rather dreary-looking town and went looking for a beer. It was a quiet evening in the town centre, with small groups of Aboriginal people sitting on public lawns and keeping warm around smoky camp fires in the dry Todd River bed. I heard music somewhere in the distance. Following the sound, I ended up in front of a sturdy door in a brick-wall on the side of an unsightly shopping-complex building. I stepped inside and found myself in an undecorated barroom. Men and women, most of them Aboriginal, were standing at the bar and in groups around the room. I found the source of the music in a corner of the room where a five-piece, all-male Aboriginal band was playing the final verse of an old Hank Williams number.

The band members looked as if they had blown in from separate worlds and times. The young, brown-skinned singer was dressed in a Bob Marley T-shirt and his reggae dreadlocks were held in place by a headband in the political colours of the Aboriginal flag: red, black and yellow. The rhythm guitarist was a dark-skinned, barefoot man. His shirt and trousers were soiled and torn, his black hair matted and his face showed signs of years living on the grog. The lead guitarist looked part-Indian. In his mid-thirties, he appeared in tight, brand new jeans and a buckle belt, shining cowboy boots, a rodeo-style shirt and a well-worn Akubra, the Australian-style felt cowboy hat. The skinny bass guitar player was the most dark-skinned and the oldest of the band members, maybe in his mid-fifties. He was dressed neatly in a sports jersey, jeans and sneakers – the standard attire of many non-indigenous men in town. The twenty-something drummer showed off his muscles in a black T-shirt with ripped-off sleeves. He looked more like a street fighter than a country music drummer with his mirror sunglasses, a cigarette hanging from his lower lip and scars lining his light brown face and tattooed arms.

With the ease of highly experienced performers, this eclectic combination of black, male-styled guys served out country covers that belonged firmly in the tradition of the honky-tonks I know from southern Texas. The affectionate response from the likewise variously styled and coloured Aboriginal patrons in the pub was similar to that of the people in those Texan bars, too. Just like country was 'our' music for the working-class, red-neck folks I would meet there, this was clearly 'our' blackfella music in Central Australian life worlds.[1]

After emigrating from Sweden to Australia a few years later, I continued to seek out Aboriginal country, rock and reggae gigs across Australia. Apart from truly enjoying the music, I have been drawn to this largely blackfella musical world because of its untidy sociocultural quality and melding of musical and gendered styles that I find both captivating and refreshing. Every performance is a healthy reminder of the futility in trying to fix categorically what others and selves are and can be. They provide a counter-narrative to a globally widespread preoccupation with defining and purifying national, racial, gendered and other forms of being in ways that delimit, and, at times, violate, people's rights to define their experiences and existence in their own terms.

The invigorating 'mongrel' qualities of distinctively Aboriginal ways of being that characterize Aboriginal contemporary music making and events are rarely represented in national public debate or media. The inherently generative social and cultural processes involved in Aboriginal popular music making have not been investigated or theorized much in the substantial anthropological literature in the field of indigenous studies either. Both popular and scholarly representations of, and conceptual approaches to, indigenous and non-indigenous people, practices, experiences and relations largely continue to be cast in terms of two separate and fundamentally different social and cultural realms. The day-to-day reality of constant interaction, interexperience and complex relational dynamic in which indigenous and non-indigenous people from a variety of backgrounds constantly engage does not map neatly onto such bounded notions of difference. Yet, similar to people in multiethnic and indigenous-settler societies around the world, Aboriginal and other Australians purposefully and habitually assert certain forms of distinction in relation to each other. A great deal of time, money and emotions are also invested by indigenous and non-indigenous stakeholders to uphold institutionalized ideas of radical difference between the two categories. This book is interested in the day-to-day experiences and practices underpinning, but also exceeding, such categories of difference and identification. As Jackson puts it:

> Though it is inevitable that many people will always categorize themselves as black and white, colonizer and colonized, traditional and modern, the goal of anthropology is to deconstruct such categorical oppositions by bringing home to us the various reasons they are invoked, the various uses they serve, and the complexity of the lived experience they mask. (1998: 101)

Taking heed of Jackson's advice, I want to bring back to centre stage the complexity and contradictions of the lived experience of contemporary

Aboriginal men. From my detailed ethnographic explorations of the largely male homosocial world of Aboriginal country, rock and reggae music making in Central Australia, this book becomes an argument for conceptual approaches to contemporary Aboriginal male modes of being as intrinsically intersubjective and context-specific processes, in which sociocultural boundaries and categories are at the same time asserted, transgressed and transformed. I develop the analytical concept of 'intercultural mediation' to investigate the social world of Aboriginal music making as an interactional arena in which aspects of a range of local and global forms of practice, imagery, values and ideas about being male, indigenous and musicians are connected and recombined in partial and incomplete ways. In the process, ambivalent and multilayered forms of identifying as Aboriginal and male are continuously created. I will show how such ordinary and 'mongrel' ways of becoming-in-the-world are nevertheless experienced as distinctive, coherent and deeply meaningful.

Conceptually, I begin from an understanding of difference as well as of similarity, and of the ideas, experiences and practices that underpin such definitions, as emerging effects of day-to-day social relations, practices and experiences. In theoretical terms, as outlined in Chapter 1, my core argument aligns with the schools of thought that challenge perceptions of social and cultural boundaries and identities as existing prior to social relations. That is, I understand the desert men's sense of male and blackfella selves and understandings of others as always transformed in social practice, which means they are not stable across time, between different places or over a person's life cycle. How the Aboriginal men identify and define others also produce real and enduring political and economic consequences, injustices and at times great sufferings when they operate within entrenched patterns of structural inequalities informed by race, gender, age and other forms of social locations and categorization.

By following an expressive practice instead of staying put with 'a people', this ethnography invites readers to appreciate music as a dynamic social arena of complex, seemingly incongruous and also joyous Aboriginal cultural expressions and forms of articulating contemporary experiences in ways rarely seen in public debate and academic works. It departs from more common anthropological inquiries into the role and meaning of music in particular Aboriginal language groups or local communities. I am instead interested in what happens when Aboriginal people move within and between different indigenous life worlds with their music practices, and when they move about in settings dominated by a diversity of non-indigenous people and sociocultural orders. Because the most commonly practised Aboriginal music genres in the Australian desert region – country, rock and reggae – are an almost exclusively male activity, the book becomes a journey mainly in the company of men.

Formations of masculinity and indigenous manhood, therefore, also become a central conceptual theme.

As I discuss in Chapter 1, many Aboriginal musicians and the music styles encountered in this book do not always make much sense to a non-Aboriginal audience. Basically, the desert men do not deliver on the privileged and narrow expectations of 'real' and 'authentic' Aboriginal music and people, or as modern rights activists – the two models that dominate mainstream imagery and understandings. My main argument in the book emerges from the ethnographic detailing of indigenous life worlds, expressions and ways of identifying as much more complex and nuanced than such privileged notions allow for. Establishing the rationale for this argument, the second half of the first chapter outlines how contemporary Aboriginal Central Australian life worlds and music styles continue to emerge from more than a century of shared experiences and engagements among a range of indigenous and non-indigenous peoples. It is an ongoing history of appropriations, adjustments, mutual influences, conflicts and mutual 'othering' among the parties involved.

The Aboriginal desert music scene continues to proliferate both as part of, and as a challenge to, partitioned sociocultural orders. Each socio-musical setting also provides its own dynamics for how particular aspects of Aboriginal and male modes of being are remade. To capture this multisided and multisited character of music and identity work, I follow the musicians in four different settings – an Aboriginal recording studio, remote Aboriginal communities, non-indigenous-dominated townships and on tours beyond the musicians' home region. By attending to such site-specific dynamics in which Aboriginal men and music are made, I aim to make visible the greater range of interdependent aspects of the musicians' life worlds, and how these are co-implicated and co-productive in their crafting of changing and 'mongrel' selves as men and Aboriginal.

Mongrel men and music

By using the racially charged concept of 'mongrel' for how indigeneity and masculinity are formed, I wish to highlight the inherently ambivalent and multilayered quality of the processes explored in the coming chapters. At its most neutral meaning, 'mongrel' refers to a dog of mixed breed. The term has subsequently been appropriated and transformed into an indicator of something deplorable or someone despicable. It has taken on particularly offensive meanings as racialized and morally derogatory notions for people of mixed racial heritage, in effect dehumanizing them to the lowest of animal status – a product of sexually and racially indiscriminate dogs.

Like many powerful and racially insulting labels, 'mongrel' has also been appropriated and reinscribed with inverted and self-assertive meanings in indigenous vernacular idioms (e.g. Carter 1988). The Aboriginal musicians frequently resorted to the word 'mongrel' when something frustrated them, like when they could not get their 'mongrel' fingers to play the guitar the way they wanted, or when a 'mongrel' piece of equipment did not work. The men also addressed themselves by the term. 'You mongrel!' one of them would mutter with a sly grin to a colleague who did something they consider characteristically blackfella. In this use, it was an expression of male and blackfella bonding. 'We're just mongrels,' they could agree assertively and, at times, defiantly as they demarcated the integrity of their male, blackfella domain as distinct from both women and whitefellas. I describe in Chapter 6 how the valued mongrel quality also includes something 'too much' – something excessive, untidy and somewhat crude that is beyond whitefella's or women's control. The men variably see this quality as something valued and as a shortcoming. On an occasion when we discussed their use of 'mongrel', I asked a few musicians if they thought it was a positive or negative description of other people. Without hesitation one of them said 'positive!' with a thumbs-up gesture. He then reflected for a moment before adding, 'Well, it can also be the most offensive you'd call another fella,' meaning another blackfella. He thus acknowledged how the racially insulting and stigmatizing powers of the term remain.

It is precisely the contradictory, multilayered and socially specific meanings of the concept 'mongrel' that make it useful for drawing attention to the complex and ambivalent recombination and reinterpretation of multiple and partial meanings that are co-produced in mediating processes over time and place. The transmission, mutation and transformation of meanings – that is, the mediating processes – embedded in notions of 'mongrel' can, therefore, introduce the emerging and untidy dynamics of the formation of indigeneity and maleness explored in the coming chapters. The music the Aboriginal desert men produce is, of course, in themselves 'mongrel cultural forms' (Gilroy 1993: 3), as it is made in a syncretic dynamic in which styles and forms of different regions and cultures of the world have been reworked and reinscribed in diverse, local indigenous life worlds.

The blackfella bar gig I walked in on three decades ago jarred any preconceived ideas I might have had about what Aboriginal music and men should sound and look like. For the blackfella musicians and patrons, however, the 'mongrel' styles of music, indigeneity and masculinity performed were part of their shared, ongoing socio-musical history and ways of identifying. Despite being an ubiquitous feature of indigenous life worlds not only in the Australian desert region, these kinds of music making have not attracted much serious attention from anthropologists, and explorations of contemporary indigenous masculinities are also rare. By attending to these somewhat neglected areas, this book presents the social life of country, rock and reggae music making as an important arena for the articulation and mediation of contemporary ways of being male and indigenous. The ethnographic substance of the book is based on fifteen months of field research, often as the only woman in a company of desert men and musicians, wherever they practised and performed their music and manhood.

Multisited and gendered fieldwork

I drove in to Alice Springs to begin work at the Central Australian Aboriginal Media Association (CAAMA) Music studio in October 2000. Two days later, I was back on the road with a bunch of Aboriginal musicians on a month-long tour. After being baptized into my all-male field by this touring project, I worked at the music studio for eight months, but also took off for the occasional week or two to follow musicians on tour and to performances in other parts of Australia. I got involved in most aspects of the day-to-day studio operation: from administrative and office tasks to assisting in recording projects. I also

MAP 1 *Australian states and relevant locations.*

gained a solid knowledge of localized Aboriginal music styles, and of names of musicians, bands and places, as I was given the task to prepare and detail hundreds of music recordings made in this studio for digital storage.

I subsequently turned my attention to the hinterland music scene and travelled and returned to a number of remote Aboriginal communities to meet up with musicians and participate in music events. I also continued to follow musicians on tour and to music events in the NT and interstate, and came to know a network of music workers who are part of a national indigenous music scene. I conducted interviews with more than fifty musicians and music workers to document their musical and personal biographies and to understand how and why they compose their music and how they perceive themselves as men, blackfellas, performers and instrumentalists. However, the main way in which I learnt about music practices and male relations and aspirations was by being present and part of events as they evolved. This combined method of participation and observation involves using oneself as the medium of research. My own experiences and social locations therefore became central to how I participated, what I could observe and what I was prevented from seeing.

I came to the research as a forty-year-old woman originally from Sweden and an Australian resident since 1989 (now a citizen). I grew up in a large, musical and not very well-off family in a small town dominated by a Volvo car factory and military barracks. Leaving home and supporting myself from the age of sixteen, I worked in a music business and on ships on the North Sea while finishing a college degree externally. My life revolved around music and motorbikes among working-class friends in close-knit, male-dominated groups, and I also travelled extensively through Western Europe. At the age of twenty-two, I left for the big cities and finished a university degree in journalism. I then hitchhiked around Australia for a year. The experience resulted in a fascination with desert environments and a book on Australian people and society (Ottosson 1988). I worked as a journalist for fifteen years, initially as a freelance photo- and radio-journalist specializing in development and human rights in various parts of Asia. After settling in Australia, I covered Australian issues for the Swedish media. In the mid-1990s, I went to Sweden for some work at the national public broadcaster and stayed on for family reasons. This is when I moved over to an academic career in social anthropology, completing a Master's and a PhD. Back in Australia, I settled in Alice Springs, where I have now conducted research and worked for Aboriginal organizations for fourteen years.

Some aspects of these biographical notes made me somewhat 'at home' in my field (Jackson 1989). My familiarity with music practices, all-male working-class socialities, Australian society and deserts, for instance, was soon recognized by the musicians and made me less of a naive stranger.

The fact that English is not my first language was often an advantage among Aboriginal language speakers, perhaps connecting us as non-British and non-colonizers. In a social setting where mature age (ideally) means more respect and authority, my age was mostly an advantage, too, and as most of the men were between thirty and fifty years of age, we shared certain musical influences and memories of world events.

In gendered and racial aspects, I was also an 'other'. Aboriginal Central Australian settings in general are highly gender segregated. I was aware of these conventions but expected the regional music scene to be more gender mixed, as it was in other Australian settings that I had explored. My project thus unintentionally turned out to be rather unconventional, in that a non-Aboriginal woman was studying maleness and hung out with Aboriginal men over a prolonged period. My presence created various degrees of anxiety concerning sex and the protection of gendered domains. Several musicians initially understood me as a sophisticated groupie and I had to negotiate proposals for sexual adventures, but probably less often than if I had been a younger woman. When the musicians realized that I was passionate about music but not necessarily about musicians, our relationship relaxed and friendships developed. Many women and some men on the fringes of the music activities did not make this distinction, though, and I encountered a fair amount of open and covert hostility, especially from women who assumed I was sexually interested in particular musicians. I did not respond much to such (mainly implied) suggestions unless they came from the male musicians, in which case I clarified my independence.

In the light of the above gender aspects, I could rarely socialize openly with individual men in non-musical settings because it could fuel misguided rumours. As a woman seemingly unaccompanied by any man or in the company of women, gig situations were often the most taxing experiences, because I was sexual prey to men in varying states of intoxication and a target for jealous and at times drunken women. I moreover felt I had to choose loyalties and not mingle much with local women. When I initially did so, I felt like a doubly suspect person. The women seemed suspicious of my intentions among the men and expected proof of gendered loyalty in the form of information on what the men were up to. The men's comments implied suspicions that I was indeed 'leaking' information to the women, which made me out as unreliable. My research concerned a highly male-dominated arena of music making and I therefore remained loyal to this domain. I do not know as much about women in my field settings.

My whiteness seemed to be less of a problem for the men, especially when they recognized my working-class background and familiarity with music and all-male sexual bantering. Being non-indigenous did also somewhat 'neutralize' my gendered position. Some men commented that 'a black woman' could never have done a study like mine because they would not let her into their circle. This refers to the gender-segregated organization of regional Aboriginal practices, in which it would be seen as inappropriate for an Aboriginal woman to hang out with men the way I did. Each man would also have to worry about regional Aboriginal restrictions on how to interact with this woman, on the basis of their relative kin, age and marital positions. They therefore envisaged that an Aboriginal woman's presence would cause unwanted tensions between her and particular musicians, between the musicians and her male kin and partner, and among the musicians (because, they said, someone was bound to have a fling with her, which would cause frictions and upset the music work).

My gendered whiteness had implications for how I was perceived by other people, too. Hanging out with musicians before and after gigs, I would occasionally be subjected to derogatory comments from non-indigenous men and women that implied that they saw me as a white woman shopping for black male sex exotica. Indigenous men and women would likewise comment in disapproving terms that defined me as a sexual/racial tourist in their territory. All up, though, the unpleasant experiences that my gender and whiteness produced provided me with valuable insights about the very practices of gender and indigeneity I set out to explore.

As in any research involving a large number of people, the Aboriginal men have shown various levels of understanding my project, and their interest has varied from one person to the next. A few of them read texts and commented on my ideas throughout the project. One or two were reluctant participants from the start. A majority have shown a modest interest. I have done my best to locate and contact the men or part of the bands that appear in the texts and photos. When possible, I travelled to where they were in order to discuss the content, and many of the men contributed insightful comments that shape the final text. I sent texts to those I could not see or who were not interested in meeting up. After reading a draft, a non-indigenous musician was concerned about appearing inflexible and ignorant. It was not how the Aboriginal men or I thought of him. In the final text, I hope it is clear that I focus on interpersonal instances in order to discuss patterns of intercultural dynamics, not to pass judgements about individuals. To respect his integrity, I have removed overtly identifiable features in relevant sections. The responsibility for any unintentional, remaining shortcomings of the descriptions of people and events is entirely mine.

1

Real and imagined Aboriginal music, men and place

A crowd of about a hundred people are making themselves comfortable on picnic rugs and folding chairs on the lawn in front of Stage 3 of the Womadelaide Festival, Australia's most high-profile world-music event. It is staged in the lush grounds of the Botanic Gardens in the South Australian capital, Adelaide (Map 1). During the three-day event, almost 70,000 people will pass through the gates to experience artists and music from most continents on seven stages. A few indigenous Australian artists are usually included in the programme and it is one of these acts people have come to see on Stage 3. At the announced time, a black African woman MC enters the stage and enthusiastically introduces the Benning Brothers from the NT as 'a living legend in their own time'. She informs us that the group was formed in 1958, and because of the racial policies at the time, they were usually marshalled on and off stage by a police man and a welfare officer. 'How times have changed, hey?' she calls out with a triumphant laugh. She introduces the members as 'a family affair' with brothers Barry and Stan and cousin Eric. 'And they've got a number of whitefellas in the background, just to sweeten the juice,' she adds, without naming the drummer, bass guitarist and fiddle player.

The band starts up with a fast-paced, instrumental guitar tune in North American cowboy country style. The non-indigenous bass player immediately launches his body into the beat. The non-indigenous fiddle player, in a purple hippie-style shirt and hair grown long, also gets into a groove, shaking his legs in what looks like an imitation of a traditional Aboriginal dance style. The three Aboriginal men appear in jeans and country and western-style or plain shirts, and they have well-used baseball caps on their heads. They stand very still, only moving their fingers with great speed and skill over the strings, as they churn out catchy guitar picking. They also keep skipping beats in the bars of the songs, a common feature of Aboriginal country and gospel music in central and northern Australia that lends it a characteristic urgent and irregular rhythm pattern. This causes the non-indigenous bass player to fall behind and play the wrong notes all through the performance. The end of the first tune also goes a bit astray when the non-indigenous musicians finish before the actual end, and front man Barry ends up doing the full ending on his own. The audience applauds, shouts and whistles. I see a few bewildered faces, as if people do not know how to react to this rather 'loose' musical act. The performance continues with a mix of classic Hank Williams-style, yearning country love songs that are not always sung in perfect tune, and a few fast tempo, instrumental tunes in the style of 1960s' cowboy film soundtracks. During the upbeat tunes, the non-indigenous bass player gets into a head-banging act and turns laughing and yahooing towards the Aboriginal lead guitarist, trying to get a call-response act going. The Aboriginal guitarist does not respond. In fact, he does not even look at the bass player. He remains very still in a relaxed and seemingly disinterested pose, his face motionless, while completing frenetic guitar solos.

Between songs, the Aboriginal men casually swap bass, rhythm and lead guitars between them, and all through the performance, Barry has a big, broad smile on his face while he keeps calling out 'take it away Eric!' (a cue for guitar solos), 'Andrew, all the way from Tamworth' (a cue for fiddle solos) and 'we're from the Kimberleys, we're the Kimberley boys!' Into the third song, people in the audience begin to leave. As the performance proceeds, more follow them. When the two men beside me, one in a T-shirt printed with the Aboriginal flag and the other in a shirt with traditional Aboriginal patterns, start to gather their things, I look at them questioningly. They shake their heads and say something about 'poor imitation of already bad American country'. When Barry calls out, probably for the tenth time, 'We're from the Kimberleys! We're Kimberley boys!' people start laughing. By the end of the performance, the remaining audience laugh at most things the smiling Barry says or does. The whole act – the country tunes in classic North American style, the Aboriginal men standing absolutely still and looking rather indifferent, the non-indigenous men jumping around like hard rockers, the bass player's continuous mistakes, and Barry's big grin – seems to have turned into some kind of joke for the largely non-indigenous crowd.

After the final song, in which a beaming Barry excels in his characteristic, amazing finger-walking guitar solos, the African MC dances back up on stage. 'Thank you very much for sharing *real* Australia! This is what it's about, isn't it? Fabulous! Very *real* Australians, doing *real* Australian things!'

Framing Aboriginal music and men

The Benning Brothers' performance raises some broader intercultural concerns that frame my explorations of the making of male and Aboriginal modes of being. The Central Australian Aboriginal musicians we meet in the coming chapters primarily create their sense of selves within the blackfella and male realms. My main focus is, therefore, on local dynamics of Aboriginal men's interactions and practices. The Womadelaide performance makes it clear, however, that contemporary indigenous music making and life worlds also always emerge in relation to broader domains of people, ideas and practices. Indeed, in this book, the musical styles practised by the men are a prime example of expressive forms that continue to be made at local, national and global cultural crossroads. It is this 'mongrel' cultural quality that makes these forms of music making especially interesting to explore as 'a medium that mediates, as it were, mediation', in that 'music in global culture … functions as an interactive social context, a conduit for other forms of interaction, other socially mediated forms of appropriation of the world' (Erlmann 1999: 6).

Interactions never take place on equal terms but involve complex negotiations of historically dominant and marginalized versions of legitimate and worthy expressions, representations, practices and identifications. The MC's repeated reference to the 'real' quality of the Benning Brothers is a typical example of how certain privileged notions of 'authentic' Aboriginality are reinforced through a loose essentialism of everyday talk and ways of thinking. It hardly escapes the notice of anybody present that the 'real' she wants us to appreciate refers to the musicians' status as descendants of the indigenous First Peoples of Australia. While we do not expect her to explain what she means by 'real' Australians, she nevertheless engages in, and implicates the Benning Brothers, their music and the audience in, the reiteration of certain pervasive understandings of 'authentic' Aboriginal people and expressive forms. Such notions are represented in the festival programme, too, where the Benning Brothers are described as 'most distinctively the ʼessence of popular Aboriginal Australian music'.

Judging from the many non-indigenous people who leave, the Kimberley musicians' version of 'real' Australia and Aboriginal 'essence' is not easy for them to identify with. What is the Aboriginal essence of playing American country music? Where is the distinctive Aboriginal message in sentimental country song lyrics? Where are the globally recognized musical markers of real, authentic Aboriginality, such as the traditional instruments didjeridu and clap sticks, indigenous languages and lyrics on spiritual, mythical, ancestral themes? Like most of the Central Australian musicians discussed in this book, these Aboriginal performers do not vocalize any recognizable modern and politically activist Aboriginal sentiments about struggling with injustices and disadvantage on the margins of society either. The only glimpse we get of their racial-political location is from the MC's mention of more racist times, followed by her celebratory assertions that these times are now gone, while, we are to presume, something 'real' has survived.

In their appearance, too, the Benning Brothers and the Aboriginal musicians appearing in this book do not exhibit widely recognized signs of traditional 'tribal' or of politically activist Aboriginality. They do not perform with traditional paraphernalia such as painted skin, loin cloths or head-dresses, all of which are included in the now globally established imagery of Australian Aborigines. They do not exhibit any political statements such as the colours of the Aboriginal flag or T-shirts with activist slogans. They are instead modestly dressed like any rural, small-town Australian men.[1] From their style of music and demeanour, these men may seem more or less detraditionalized and Westernized (e.g. Heelas, Lash and Morris 1996). Ultimately, however, they do not fit this bill either. Barry's limited repertoire of verbal expression, for instance, does not exactly fit the image of a successfully assimilated Aboriginal man. Moreover, as performers, the men have not adopted the masculine, often overtly physical and sexually suggestive gestures that are associated with global conventions of country or rock music, and that the non-indigenous band members performed. The Aboriginal men's physically minimalist stage style is a dominant feature also in the Central Australian Aboriginal music scene. Even by the low-key performance standards of global country music or the 'cool' male pose of some rock conventions, these musicians come across as exceptionally bodily modest and even detached. Therefore, people whose tastes and interpretative skills are shaped in global country, rock and reggae conventions may not feel invited to engage with the performers in a shared, intercultural musical experience, which is a raison d'être for events like Womadelaide. The people who do not disengage wholly by leaving Stage 3 instead seem to resort to an alternative congenial interactional genre, that of parody and humour.

A non-indigenous Australian friend of mine came along to Womadelaide. She commented that watching Aboriginal people trying to imitate Western artists and music reminded her of the old minstrel shows. It was quaint and somewhat amusing, she thought, but hardly Aboriginal. Like a majority of people I meet, she expects something else and rather specific from 'real' Aboriginal music, musicians and people in general. Such expectations as well as evaluations and production of indigenous expressive forms have a history in the broader sociopolitical terrain of Australian indigenous issues. Three interrelated processes have been particularly important in shaping this context over the past five decades.

First, since the late 1960s, increased global recognition of indigenous rights and support for indigenous self-determination, combined with a redirection of Australian nationalist sentiments towards multiculturalism and appreciation of ethnic diversity, have resulted in government policies, legislation and funding structures that have underpinned the proliferation of indigenous musical and other artistic production. Secondly, the emergence of a substantial indigenous arts sector, as part of a larger indigenous institutional domain, has essentially been, and continues to be, an intercultural process. That is, like most indigenous organizations and bureaucracies, the creative activities and the organizational structures of indigenous music, media and arts organizations continue to involve a diversity of indigenous and non-indigenous people with different expectations, experiences and beliefs, as well as being circumscribed by changing commercial, political and legal parameters.

Importantly, and as will be made clear throughout the book, by 'intercultural', I not only mean engagements between indigenous and non-indigenous domains. Australian indigenous life worlds and forms of identification are immensely diverse also in a regional setting such as Central Australia. Interactions between people identifying as indigenous, and mutual influences between indigenous intellectual traditions, gendered ideals and expressive forms, may, in other words, be just as intercultural in kind. Moreover, my approach to 'cultural' is as something always already 'inter-'. That is, as human practices, ideas and forms of identification emerge in social encounters and interactions, they are always already socioculturally intermingled and intersubjectively mediated.

From this understanding of intercultural processes, I develop in this book the concept of 'intercultural mediation' as a central analytical tool for exploring the continuous making and re-making of indigenous and male ways of being in the social world of music making. I take mediation to be a socially constitutive process in which coherent senses of selves emerge from peoples' everyday practices and expressive forms. The way in which I apply the concept is meant to bring to the fore the contradictory, ambiguous and ambivalent in the production of still deeply meaningful expressions and coherent experiences of being indigenous and male. With the notion of intercultural mediation, I connect the ways in which male and indigenous practices, desires and identifications operate and how these are experienced and articulated in the different social and musical settings that I investigate. I also use intercultural mediation as a means to connect the various forms of masculinity and indigeneity articulated in broader arenas such as local and global musical, religious and professional domains. It is a means, too, to connect different levels of identification, such as the level of concrete everyday practices and relations, and the more abstract and symbolic levels of identity politics.

My conceptual approach thus resonates with strands of thinking about relational processes beyond pre-existing or bounded categories (e.g. Jackson 1998; Merlan 2005; Sullivan 2006). Nevertheless, and referring to a third broader process shaping today's indigenous expressive cultures and lives, the increased attention paid to indigenous matters has been accompanied by a privileging of rather monocultural understandings that are underpinned by specific notions of 'traditional' and 'authenticity'. These broader shifting terrains are also part of the desert men's life worlds and choices.

Shifting terrains

During the last five decades, indigenous matters have moved from a marginalized, largely ignored periphery to the centre stage of public debate and national identity formation in Australia. The associated reorientations in policy and ideology have been accompanied by a privileging of two different and at times contradictory aspects of indigenous identity formation, that of resistance and that of persistence (Keeffe 1988). In debates over national origins, multiculturalism and Aboriginal land rights, the theme of persistence has become increasingly dominant, involving various notions of 'traditional' culture (e.g. Dodson 2003). When Aboriginal self-determination was introduced as a national policy goal in the early 1970s, it was anticipated that it would empower indigenous people to establish self-managing communities that could regenerate their distinct cultural norms, languages and ancestral connections to their country and kin. A solid body of work has now proved that the very concept of self-determination, as well as the implementation and administration of self-managed indigenous entities, was fraught with difficulties and contradictions from the beginning (Beckett 1985; Cowlishaw 1998; Kowal 2008; Morris 1988; Myers 1985; Rowse 1988, 1998; Sutton 2009). Today, indigenous Australians continue to show up as the statistical category with the lowest levels of income and education and the highest rates of unemployment, infant mortality, imprisonment and endemic health problems (HREOC 2009). The debate about the causes of such disparity continues, as does a plethora of government and non-governmental interventions to get on top of 'failed' and 'dysfunctional' self-governing communities.

However, one unquestionable result of this fading policy era is the emergence of an 'Indigenous Sector' (Rowse 2002: 1): the mushrooming of state-subsidized indigenous bureaucracies, organizations, services and community initiatives. While generating continued segregation of indigenous and non-indigenous realms of activities (Jennett 1987; Morrissey 2003), this sector has also created a legitimate space for the development of certain forms of indigenous agency, including a vibrant arts and music sector.

Prior to the 1960s, indigenous Australian expressive cultural forms were, in the main, categorized and evaluated by criteria for 'primitive art', and the lesser the 'contamination' by European contact, the higher their 'authentic' value (Morphy 1996; Torgovnick 1990). Indigenous creative workers who adopted and adapted contemporary and Western forms of expressions or collaborated with non-indigenous people had a hard time being recognized as artists at all (Mundine 2000). With broader recognition of indigenous rights and increased appreciation of aspects of non-Western cultural practice, this situation has changed dramatically. Hundreds of organizations now provide spaces for the production of indigenous arts, crafts and the performing arts, and the indigenous arts industry generates hundreds of thousands of dollars annually (Altman 2007; Myers 2002).

While indigenous Australians have practised introduced forms of music since the early days of colonization (Clendinnen 2003), these expressive forms, too, were rarely acknowledged or publicly supported in non-indigenous realms before the 1970s. The University of Adelaide took a lead with music training for Aboriginal people at the Centre for Aboriginal Studies in Music, CASM, in 1971 (Ellis 1985; Tunstill 1989). Several successful Aboriginal rock and reggae bands emerged from CASM during the 1980s, including Coloured Stone, Mixed Relations and Us Mob (Castles 1998). Other universities now offer courses in traditional and contemporary indigenous music and in industry skills for indigenous musicians, and indigenous music and instruments are occasionally included in primary school curricula, often as an aid in teaching about indigenous perspectives and social justice (Neuenfeldt 1998a).

Today, indigenous music is performed at arts and culture festivals across the country all year round; for example, the 'Deadlys' annual indigenous music (and sports and community) awards presentation is broadcast nationally, and the Australian national music awards (the ARIAs) and the Australian country music awards commonly include indigenous performers and nominees. Indigenous musicians also often perform at national events such as the Australia Day celebrations as well as high-profile occasions when Australia represents itself to a wider world, such as the 2000 Sydney Olympic Games.

As in multiethnic nationalistic struggles and related quests for identity elsewhere (e.g. Askew 2002; Jamison and Eyerman 1998; Stokes 1994), artistic productions became increasingly important for expressing indigenous rights claims in Australia from the 1960s, and music continues to be integral to indigenous activist events across Australia. Indigenous demands for indigenous-controlled media (Langton 1993a) were rearticulated in the government ethos of self-determination in which 'the central claim was that

Aboriginal people should control the ways in which they are represented; or, as we might say in the 1980s, should control the production and circulation of images about themselves' (von Sturmer 1989: 128). Funding and legislative structures subsequently facilitated the establishment of Aboriginal media associations and radio stations, which have been essential for boosting popular music production (Molnar and Meadows 2001). The pioneer in the field was the CAAMA, incorporated in 1980 in Alice Springs (Batty 2003). CAAMA established the first Aboriginal recording studio and record label in Australia, and is the focus of Chapters 3 and 4.

The profusion of indigenous music, art and media production and the increased appreciation for indigenous expressive culture have, thus, evolved in a dialogic process involving rights activism, government policy, public funding and nationalist sentiments. Indigenous artistic production and the institutions that support and promote it also continue to emerge through intercultural engagements. That is, whether in remote communities or in big cities, indigenous expressive art forms, like the shaping of indigenous life worlds in general, are created in response and resistance to, and in accommodation and collaboration with, a range of local and exogenous expressive traditions, technologies, people and practices (e.g. Anderson and Dussart 1988; Jones 1992; Kurtzer 2003). It is exactly such inherently intersubjective and relational processes of cultural formations that my use of the concept of 'intercultural mediation' is meant to highlight.

Music and identity work as mediation

The concept of mediation has probably been most fully developed within semiotic theory, which has evolved in close interaction with structural linguistics and symbolic anthropology (Lévi-Strauss 1966; Mertz and Parmentier 1985; Peirce 1974; Saussure 1959). Here, mediation is taken as fundamental to the production of meaning in that the semiotic notion of the sign mediates between any object (such as a sound, an existing thing or an event) and the mental representation (the meaningful concept) of it within a particular semiotic system (Mertz 1985). This basic semiotic model has been applied for analysing the production of meaning in a variety of human activities.[2] For instance, the ethnographic study of music as 'language', that is, a semiotic system through which meanings are produced, circulated, communicated and enacted in interpretative, mediating and socially constitutive processes, has developed from semiotic theory (Feld 1974, 1994; Feld and Fox 1994; Samuels 2004; Turino 1999). A source of inspiration for my particular approach is Meintjes' ethnography of a South African recording studio (2003). She uses the concept of mediation to explore how the political (power relations) and the aesthetic (symbolic) operate through each other to produce the affective power of a distinct 'Zuluness' and 'Africanness' (8) in musical styles.

While drawing on literature on music as mediation, my point of departure differs from these texts in some important aspects. First, I do not focus on musical detail or structure and will not analyse music in terms of a semiotic system in which identities and meanings are mediated and produced. As a social anthropologist, my starting point is the social practice, interactions and lived experiences of Aboriginal musicians. I explore how, depending on the socio-musical setting in which the musicians find themselves, and depending on their male, blackfella and musical position in it, different aspects of indigeneity and manhood are emphasized and negotiated as the men articulate their sense of themselves as Aboriginal men and musicians. Secondly, I do not attend to mediation as chains of semiosis of semantic or symbolic meanings apart from socially grounded factors. In the vocabulary of semiotic theory, I take mediation to be indexical; I deal with the mediation of pragmatic meaning that is always dependent on, and embedded in, social practices and interactions.

More importantly, I approach the social realm of Aboriginal music making as 'intercultural mediations' in that it 'connects and translates disparate worlds, people, imaginations, values, and ideas, whether in its symbolic, social or technological form' (Meintjes 2003: 8). Here, mediation is understood as both an intervention and a means of contact, and similar to Fox in his rich ethnography of country music and working-class culture in southern Texas, I see mediation as a process that connects 'the practical and concrete domains of everyday life (work, play, sociability, worship, aggression, sexuality, performance, sound, smell, taste, kinesics) with more abstract domains of memory, historical consciousness, senses of emplacement and displacement, ideologies of class, race, and gender, models of self- and personhood, poetics, theories of emotion, and structures of feeling' (2004: 34).

With this use of the concept of intercultural mediation, I can account for a broad range of socially productive aspects of the Central Australian Aboriginal men's music practice, involving processes of local, national and transnational appropriations and transformations. It involves the embedding of layers and layers of intersubjective experiences into expressive form and through day-to-day practice. The meanings of these layered experiences are not fixed. They are interpreted in many different, ambivalent, contradictory, co-productive and partial ways as they are reorganized and as they re-emerge in different places, relations and practices. Thus, in the course of ongoing socio-musical practice and processes of identification, not only are the already established models for being men and indigenous reaffirmed; these models are also partially co-implicated in the continuous production of new, syncretic and what I have called 'mongrel' meanings and distinctive forms of maleness, indigeneity and music.

Music and identity

Approaching music and identity work as socially constitutive mediations, I build on traditions in ethnomusicology and music anthropology as well as more recent popular music studies and anthropology of indigenous media. Ethnomusicologists and music anthropologists traditionally approached music as mainly reflecting and reinforcing underlying cultural patterns and cohesion of (usually non-Western) societies and seldom recognized music as a generative force that can transform peoples' thoughts, practices or identities beyond their cultural mould (e.g. Blacking 1973).

Ancestral genres of music in Australian indigenous societies provided fertile grounds for studies of such contained cultural difference because song and dance have been the main repositories and modes of transmission of local kin and gender-specific knowledge for indigenous Australians.[3] The songs and the dancing re-enact the actions of ancestral beings that created the particular landscape, language and norms for social practice as any one group knows it. Ancestral music genres, in this way, transfer meaningful norms for appropriate intergenerational, gendered, interpersonal and intergroup relationships, as well as fundamental connections with particular tracts of the country. Hence, any understanding of the cultural specificity of different Aboriginal societies – their social organization, belief systems, attachment to land, repertoire of identifications, kin classifications, use of natural resources and gendered practice – has required the study of their musical traditions.

From the first colonial encounters, as described in the diaries of British First Fleeters (Clendinnen 2003), indigenous Australians have also mimicked, adopted and adapted a range of introduced forms of music. These music traditions have not interested ethnomusicologists or anthropologists much.[4] Most academic writing on 'popular' Aboriginal music has instead been produced in popular culture, music, communication and media studies since the 1980s (e.g. Breen 1989; Dunbar-Hall and Gibson 2004; Hayward 1998b; Mitchell 1996; Neuenfeldt 1994b). Like ethnomusicologists, theorists of popular music worldwide have tried to establish how particular musics enunciate and reflect underlying social structures and relations, but with a focus on sub- or countercultures within larger, usually Western sociocultural formations (Hebdige 1979).

Studies in Australian Aboriginal popular music have likewise been mainly concerned with racial and sociocultural differences, largely leaving intercultural dynamics theoretically undeveloped. Resonating with broader sociopolitical trends, Aboriginal popular music studies usually emphasize one of two approaches. On the one hand, Aboriginal rock, reggae, country and pop are investigated for their 'traditional' content and meanings. The focus may be on the inclusion of ancestral styles of singing and playing, indigenous languages, mythical lyrical themes, traditional instrumentation and styles of appearance. Such studies are mostly carried out among more traditionally oriented peoples in geographically remote and non-urban locations (for instance Corn 1999; Dunbar-Hall 1997; Furlan 2005; Magowan 1994; Neuenfeldt 1993b, 1997). On the other hand, Aboriginal popular music is analysed in terms of a modern activist stance of Aboriginal resistance – a tool for a marginalized, dispossessed and oppressed Black minority to talk back to a white oppressive majority and repressive powers. This approach is more prominent in studies of urban musicians, or in music from remote regions that has had some impact on the broader music industry (Breen 1989; Hayward 1998b; Mitchell 1996; Neuenfeldt 1991, 1996).[5]

More recent theoretical developments in both popular music studies and ethnomusicology have moved away from the structuralist–functionalist and homological approaches, and most scholars now acknowledge that music has a productive role in the formation of social and cultural identification. The focus is increasingly on processes of transnational interplay, migration, borrowing and domestication of musical and sociocultural features (Born and Hesmondhalgh 2000). My approach develops such lines of thought by attending to the multifaceted mediating dynamics of identifications that characterize the Central Australian indigenous music scene.

Many aspects of indigenous Australian life worlds have been investigated by scholars for more than a century, but few have focused on contemporary formations of indigenous masculinities, which I find essential to the production of self-worth and respect among the desert musicians. While I recognize that different kinds and forms of identification such as gender, race, class, sexuality, age and nationality overlap and intersect in complex ways as the musicians deal with their everyday existence, my main focus therefore remains on the mediation of Aboriginal and male forms of identifications.

Men and masculinities

In Central Australia, it is mainly men who write, practice, perform and record Aboriginal country, reggae and rock music making. These styles of music are, in the main, transmitted from older to younger Aboriginal men, who develop individual styles and skills in the company of Aboriginal men. Most people who hang around when musicians practise, rehearse and record music are Aboriginal men and boys. The people who surround and organize the music practices – sound engineers, producers, technicians, roadies – are predominantly men.

This does not mean that women are absent or irrelevant in this musical scene. Aboriginal teenage girls may sing in family bands or other ensembles, but normally quit when they get a serious boyfriend or become mothers. A few adult, local Aboriginal women can occasionally be seen singing on stage at the Aboriginal country music dances in Alice Springs, too. Female relatives may co-write songs with men, and real or imagined women appear in lyrics. Women are present as audiences, fans and at times insistent groupies, and male musicians dedicate songs to female relatives and wives. Aboriginal and non-Aboriginal women also appear in professional roles around the recording and performance of music. During my time in Central Australia, however, I have not come across any adult, local Aboriginal woman who regularly writes and publicly performs these forms of music, who has a core perception of herself as a musician and who is acknowledged as such by others.[6] I will briefly discuss the position and exclusion of women in the all-male domain of the Aboriginal recording studio, but my main focus will be on male relatedness, engagements and experiences.

The overwhelmingly male character of this music scene can be thought of as a strong version of the male-dominated structures and masculinist discourses of popular music cultures and industries described elsewhere (Bayton 1990; Cohen 1991; Finnegan 1989; McClary 1991; Reynolds and Press 1995; Walser 1993; Whiteley and Hawkins 1997). Every music scene is also, and importantly, shaped by being embedded in its own particular sociocultural norms and histories of gender relations. Central Australian Aboriginal societies have historically relied on an intensely homosocial division of men's and women's labour, knowledge, ancestral music practices and daily activities (Bell 2002; Berndt and Berndt 1996; Brock 1989; Hamilton 1980, 1981; Meggitt 1962; Merlan 1988, 1991; Myers 1986; Willis 2003a). Although modified by more than a century of colonial and post-colonial engagements, many Aboriginal settings in Central Australia are still characterized by enduring gender-related restrictions on everyday interpersonal and intergroup relations and interactions. The specific dynamics of the all-male sociality of the Central Australian Aboriginal music scene must be understood partly in such localized gender regimes and associated models of manhood.

My conceptualization of male forms of practice and identification is informed by the interdisciplinary research field of masculinities, within the broader field of gender, sexuality and feminist studies.[7] Connell defines masculinity as 'inherently historical' (1995: 44) and as

> configurations of practice within gender relations, a structure that includes large-scale institutions and economic relations as well as face-to-face relationships and sexuality. Masculinity is institutionalized in this structure, as well as being an aspect of individual character or personality. (Connell 2000: 29)

Like other configurations of sociocultural practice, masculinities are, here, viewed as emerging in particular patterns of power and knowledge, which are investigated in men's studies for the divergent, inconsistent and contradictory meanings they produce about what is understood as masculinity in different relational, place-specific and historical trajectories. The concepts of dominant/ hegemonic and subordinate/marginalized masculinities also emerged for theorizing hierarchical relations among different male modes of being, especially in research on men of ethnic and racial minorities.[8]

Studies of black men, race and masculinities are particularly relevant for this book, and this literature has mainly emerged in North America and Great Britain, focuses mostly on African and Afro-Caribbean men and predominantly discusses Black masculinities in terms of Western historical constructions that justified colonial invasion (e.g. Back 1994; Bederman 1995; Booker 2000; Carby 1998; Clatterbaugh 1990; Kanitkar 1994; Mac an Ghaill 1994; Majors and Manchini Billson 1992). That is, black natives became the necessary primitive contrast and backdrop of a racial 'other' in the promotion of Western civilization (and Christianity) as evolutionary superior. To quote Segal: 'The colonial image of the Black man (and woman), portrayed him (or her) as child-like, emotional, servile, hyper-sexual: the exact antithesis of white manhood' (1990: 173).

As more agency-focused post-colonial theorists have shown, Western colonial categories of representing the 'self' and the 'other' are, in fact, co-produced by such selves and others (e.g. Bhabha 1994; Mitchell 1988; Spivak 1996; Thomas 1991, 1994); colonized people 'themselves engage with, reproduce and manipulate colonial representations, diverting them toward more localized struggles for power, accommodation, or resistance, and nuancing and adding to them in ways that owe little (while remaining in certain respects connected) to their original configurations' (Stokes 2000: 215). The primitivist black male imagery has, for instance, been turned into positive and powerful attributes in Black activist rhetoric and artistic expressions worldwide. Black men being studs with huge penises or possessing innate abilities to express primordial emotions through suggestive erotic musical rhythms and dances are recurring images in global popular culture (Booker 2000: 195; Segal 1990: 169; Wade 2000: 16).

Indigenous masculinities

There is no corresponding body of work on Australian indigenous men, race and masculine imagery to that on black manhood in America and Great Britain. Detailed ethnographic, and theoretically developed, research of contemporary Australian indigenous men's changing self-perceptions and masculine practices is also rare. One exception is Willis' work among Central Australian Pitjantjatjara men that focuses on male sexual health, heteronormativity and concepts of male sexuality and masculinity (Willis 1997, 2003a, b). Also, in the field of health, McCoy (2008) explores the intergenerational shaping of manhood and well-being through deeply embedded values regarding authority with nurturance, autonomy and relatedness in Western Desert societies. Musician and poet Neil Murray's semi-autobiographical book on being a member of the Warumpi Band from Central Australia describes a contemporary all-male Aboriginal world, too, albeit not in a scholarly form (1993). Davis' work on the impact of modernistic political autonomy on masculine identity and subjectivity among Saibaian islanders in the Torres Strait is another rare study of indigenous Australian masculinities (1998).

Male issues are, of course, implied in ethnographic descriptions of traditional practices and norms for male same-sex groupings. Myers' (1986) influential monograph of Pintupi people in Central Australia, for instance, describes male interactional and hierarchical ideals in the development of male maturity, autonomy and authority. Liberman's (1985) study of Aboriginal and intercultural interaction in Central Australia provides useful descriptions of male dynamics of congeniality, and classic works, such as Meggitt (1962) on Warlpiri people and Tonkinson (1974) on Western Desert Jigalong people, describe male power relations and interactional customs, too.[9]

Texts on colonial imagery of indigenous Australian manliness are likewise infrequent. Historians may, however, note early British officials' comments on native men's manly stature, which even gave name to Manly Cove, now a wealthy Sydney beach suburb (Clendinnen 2003: 35). Europeans also paid tribute to native men's prowess in the bush, their tracking and hunting skills and their mastering of skills required in the pastoral industries (Reynolds 2000). In the evolutionary terms in which the natives were commonly conceived, however, such desirable attributes in non-indigenous male pioneers were in indigenous men 'taken as convincing proof that they were less evolved and closer to the animals and, what is more, doomed to disappear from the face of the earth' (Reynolds 2000: 58).

A powerful visual imagery of Aboriginal Australian men was established in the late nineteenth century with the famous publications by Baldwin Spencer and Frank Gillen on Central Australian tribes (Spencer and Gillen 1899, 1904). While their texts on ritual sexual acts and rape conveyed a form of masculinity that did not attract Western readers, their photographs became all the more popular as they were circulated widely in the Western world.[10] The images show bearded, wizened, dusty old desert men in loin cloths, head bands, with spears in hand and gazing out from a stone-age era, or ceremonially painted black men enacting rituals from that same pre-modern time.[11] Similar de-sexualized, traditionalist male images of desert Aborigines appear on present-day postage stamps, dollar coins, postcards and in travel brochures and art catalogues. Not surprisingly, the desert musicians tend to be more attracted to the hyper-sexualized imagery of black American and African manhood than with that of those stone-age men.

A key conceptual argument of mine is that contemporary Aboriginal modes of being men emerge as intercultural mediations involving various blackfella and whitefella models of manhood, which means that non-indigenous masculine models are co-implicated in producing Aboriginal male experiences. The most relevant historical white male types for the Central Australian Aboriginal music scene are those associated with missionaries and the pastoral industry, and to some extent those of miners, colonial officials and police. All those models are variously included in the persistent, albeit changing Australian masculine theme of the white 'Bushman' (Moore 1998; Murrie 1998). Originally drawing on male activities on the largely all-male colonial frontier, and later taking on qualities of the Anzac soldiers (the Australian and New Zealand Armed Corps) in both world wars, this manhood myth includes a tough, physical, inventive, resilient and practical rather than intellectual manly type, unswervingly loyal to his mates, reliable in a crisis but otherwise laid-back and adaptable (Garton 1998; Nicoll 2001; Pringle 1997). In reality, early pioneers frequently depended on the guidance of nameless 'black boys'; Aboriginal men 'who tracked, hunted, foraged and found water, showed him the finer points of bushcraft and taught him about the country' (Reynolds 2000: 9). Many of the qualities used for composing the white Bushman legend, in this way, draw on actual skills of Aboriginal men. Aspects of European men's demeanour and male ideals were also adopted by Aboriginal men as they worked in rural industries, converted to Christianity and went to war as Anzac soldiers (Hall 1989).[12]

Indigenous women seldom appear in frontier tales and bush poetry that solidify the heterosexual, male homosocial white Bushman legend. In reality, non-indigenous women were rare in the bush and it is widely documented how 'rape, concubinage and prostitution of Aboriginal women was endemic in rural areas' (Moore 1998: 45).[13] While Bell's older Central Australian female informants emphasize the independence of women in exercising their own initiative to secure goods or pleasure for themselves (Bell 2002: 98), Aboriginal men would occasionally sanction affairs between their women and non-indigenous men in reciprocal strategies.[14] Non-indigenous men's abuse of such privileges was a common cause of conflicts between settlers and local indigenous men.

The self-declared right of non-indigenous men to have sex with indigenous women, as well as women actively taking control of their own sexuality, has informed notions of Aboriginal men as somewhat emasculated 'weaklings'. Such notions resonate in Black activist explanations for the demise of Aboriginal culture. Leading activist Kevin Gilbert, for instance, lamented how Aboriginal men 'bowed to the demands of stockmen and squatters for "black velvet"' and 'to the fact of his women having to prostitute themselves' (Gilbert 1994: 6). Similar to Black American activist rhetoric, the re-masculinization of Aboriginal Australian men has been presented as crucial in the restoration of a healthy Black society and culture, and of Black male worth and honour (Booker 2000; Carby 1998; du Bois 1982 [1903]; Segal 1990: 182ff).

After the last decades of heightened consciousness and visibility of indigenous realities and political and artistic expressions, representations of Australian indigenous men are more diverse and complex. They nevertheless tend to adhere to the dominant format of either traditional/tribal or modern/activist imagery discussed previously. Similar to non-white male populations in North America and Britain, notions of indigenous Australian masculinity have also become increasingly associated with domestic, sexual and other forms of violence and crimes, as well as alcohol and other drug abuse. In British and North American studies, such associations are commonly analysed in terms of black men's marginalized socioeconomic, political and racial position in society (Booker 2000; Gilroy 1987; Majors and Manchini Billson 1992). Studies in indigenous Australia instead commonly emphasize colonial violence and dispossession to explain present-day problems, or, alternatively, view contemporary forms of violence as a continuation of traditional practices (Atkinson 2002; Bolger 1991; Burbank 1994; Langton 1993b; Macdonald 1988; Memmot et al. 2001).

Masculinities and intercultural mediation

A basic premise for social constructivist masculinity studies is that there are no inevitable or natural connections between actual men, being male, and masculinities. These connections are reproduced as inevitable by particular privileged sets of ideas, practices and institutions in any given time and place. Such anti-essentialist arguments are developed further in Judith Butler's influential thinking of gender-as-performativity (Butler 1990, 1993, 1997a, b). She proposes that there is no subject, no doer, who pre-exists an action. Rather, the subject/doer is continuously created through, and is enabled by, the repeated enaction (performance) of certain norms or 'regulatory regimes'. These regimes acquire authority and take on a quality of inevitability through the recurring, regular repetition over time of certain practices, ideas and values concerning male and female (and other) identities, practices and bodies. While much everyday practice tends to conform to and assert certain ways of being and thinking as 'natural', an understanding of performativity as a reiteration of practice also reveals all action and identity formation as inherently unstable, because it always involves the possibility of 'failure' to repeat; every new action may expose conventions and taken-for-granted norms as not at all natural or inevitable.

Butler's concept of the performative has been criticized for being disconnected from 'the facts of life', that it lacks historical, material and sociological grounding. In some aspects, however, the idea of the formation of identities as reiterative practice resonates with my use of the concept of intercultural mediation. Both notions emphasize the ambiguous, contradictory, multifaceted and emergent processes inherent in identity formations. Both concepts suggest that it is through day-to-day mundane repetition and layering of certain norms and experiences in practice that already socially established sets of meaning are both legitimized and inevitably transformed. The material situation, the dynamics of power relations, or the time and place are never identical. The intention of an action may 'misfire', be misunderstood and responded to in unpredictable ways. And importantly, by adding layers of experiences, every action irreversibly changes the context for renewed action (Goodwin and Duranti 1992).

The notion of the performative and the concept of intercultural mediation become ways to think about musical, indigenous and male practice as emergent, ambivalent and contingent, and not mere reflections or enactments of pre-existing norms for original or 'real', 'authentic' forms of identification. This is not to say that people can reinvent themselves in endless, utterly contingent combinations. As Gilroy argues, 'Whatever radical constructionists may say, it [identity] is lived as a coherent (if not always stable) experiential sense of self. Though it is often felt to be natural and spontaneous, it remains the outcome of practical activity: language, gesture, bodily significations, desires' (1993: 102). Such practical activity is always guided by taken-for-granted conventions and conforms and responds to already established norms.

From this conceptual viewpoint, the relationship between actual men, notions of being male, and ideas and ideologies of masculinity is not inevitable and not wholly arbitrary. It is, in fact, precisely the study of the interaction and particular connections made between actual men and various ideas about being male in any given time, activity, place, occupation and so forth, that can tell us about the practical outcomes for, and lived experiences of, those involved. In this book, my main interest is in the merging of aspects of various models for being men, and in intersections between such male models and varying ways of identifying as Aboriginal. I present the social life of music making as an important medium for connecting and mediating such different ways of being and becoming men and Aboriginal.

My analytical concept of intercultural mediation thus refers to understandings of social engagements that recognize difference while allowing for various kinds and degrees of difference, and for the continuous transfer and transformation of differences as people interact, work and experience together in a shared sociocultural field. Such engagements may be limited to a specific interactive situation and may involve global flows of differing and changing forms of cultural practice and social orientations, as discussed by Appadurai (1991), Hannerz (1996) and others. This brings us back to the problematic and ambiguous 'real' in the Benning Brother's Womadelaide appearance.

Mediating 'Real' Aboriginal men and music

Although indigenous Australian artists and expressive forms that demonstrate certain established markers of monocultural notions of authentic 'traditionality' are essentially intercultural processes, it is nonetheless the case that they are the highest valued by critics and the commercial industry, as well as by scholars, policy makers and the broader society. Artists who overtly incorporate what are seen as non-indigenous aesthetics and gestures are often ignored or criticized for a lack of Aboriginal sentiments or content (Langton 2003; Myers 2002; Sutton 1992). These concerns about authenticity not least articulate tensions between the day-to-day social practices through which more fluid notions of identity are formed and reformed, and the realms of identity politics (Yuval-Davis 2006). While it is important to recognize how the former are always structured by patterns of inequalities and social difference in the broader society, it is equally important to differentiate between the inherently fluid and multilayered processes in which people form their sense of selves as they go about their daily lives, and the necessarily reduced and fixed terms in which difference is cast for particular identity projects.

As Prins (1997) suggests with his notion of 'the paradox of primitivism', and as Ginsburg discusses in terms of a 'Faustian contract' (1991), indigenous peoples cultivate, and actively draw upon, traditionalist imagery for everyday self-fashioning as well as for political counter-strategies of self-representations. Traditionalist rhetoric has, in this way, become a powerful currency in indigenous rights claims, language preservation and cultural activism around the world (e.g. Conklin 1997; Coombe 1997; Hanson 1989; Jackson 1989; Nagel 1996). Indigenous musicians also adapt and rework traditionalist and primitivist stereotypes in response to market expectations and as strategic and aesthetic choices.[15] The paradoxical dilemma for these artists is how, on the one hand, new forms of media have become important means for them to express and assert identity and cultural autonomy, and how, on the other hand, the global spread of such media and communications technology threatens to make irrelevant the very foundations for such identity and autonomy – local languages, imagery, intergenerational relations and respect for ancestral knowledge.

The multifaceted dynamics for reproducing notions of authenticity reappears in the Benning Brothers' performance. Their overtly intercultural form of music does not fit easily within traditionalist imagery. Perhaps this can explain why the MC felt she had to repeatedly emphasize their 'real' Australian quality. That is, in part because of the lack of evident 'authentic' Aboriginal markers, it had to be pointed out that they were, in fact, 'real' Aborigines. She also neglected to properly acknowledge the musical collaboration we, in fact, witnessed. Similar intentional or mere habitual strategies of concealing or playing down non-indigenous collaborators are commonplace. For instance, one of the few internationally famous Aboriginal bands, Yothu Yindi from Yirrkala in northern Australia, always included non-indigenous members and songwriters. These men rarely appear in promotional material, interviews and video clips.[16] The band is mostly presented in all-Aboriginal traditionalist imagery, with happy, ceremonially painted black people in tropical settings with few signs of Western influences (Hayward 1998a; Mitchell 1993).

Considering these developments, the Benning Brothers' appearance seems an anomaly. In previous and later Womadelaide events, it has been rare to see indigenous acts that do not perform traditionalist elements or forge a recognized Black rights agenda. Tellingly, in 1993, a rock band from the south-east was dropped from the programme because 'their music doesn't sound Aboriginal, it sounds Western' (Hollinsworth 1996: 63).[17] From Womadelaide organizers and press reports, I understand that the Benning Brothers were invited after a non-indigenous festival publicist picked up a tape of the band in a Tennant Creek store as she was travelling in the NT.[18] I was left with the clear impression that the festival people saw the band as a kind of happenstance 'discovery' by their publicist of a remote, exotic and somewhat quirky Aboriginal act. In Aboriginal central and northern Australia, country bands like the Benning Brothers have, in fact, been part of daily life since the 1950s. While the MC and the festival programme acknowledged the band's longevity, it was here reinterpreted in traditionalist terms in order to authenticate a 'real' Aboriginal essence that evokes a quality much deeper in real and mythological time.

The audience response indicates that this exercise in neo-authentication partly misfired. Perhaps the gap between what people experienced and what the MC and the festival programme emphasized was just too obvious. Perhaps the festival organizers were too caught up in traditionalist conceptions of all remote, northern Aboriginal people as essentially 'real' and 'tribal' to even check whether the Benning Brothers fit this imagery. Either way, I suggest that it is precisely such 'failed' performances that can expose the privileged notions of 'authentic' people and music as far too limiting for appreciating the multidimensional and diverse contemporary cultural forms indigenous Australian artists articulate and negotiate.

The Benning Brothers' performance also demonstrates the now fairly well-established argument in music anthropology, ethnomusicology and popular music studies that music 'is not the universal language it has sometimes been cracked up to be' (McClary 1991: 25). Musical experiences and activities can certainly bring out momentary feelings of pleasure and understandings as shared beyond social and cultural differences. At the same time, the ways in which we engage and identify, to various degrees, in different ways or not at all, with particular musical pieces, styles, performance conventions and artists are always shaped by our particular biographies and future aspirations. That is, we interpret musical experiences through layers of prior and imagined future engagements with a range of global and local musical and extra-musical ideas, imagery, values, practices and aesthetic traditions. This informs the way we practice music, how we interpret a musical experience and what sense we make of ourselves and others as particular kinds of persons in the process. In other words, music is a fundamentally social practice and experience through which multiple modes of identifying can be simultaneously reflected, reconstituted, mediated and imagined.

Looking at the home region for the desert musicians we meet in the coming chapters, we can better appreciate the intercultural mediation of local and broader aspects of indigenous and male ways of becoming that shape their music and life worlds.

Central Australia

A good way to grasp the vastness, remoteness and variety of Central Australia is to approach it from above. From whatever direction one flies in, the final hours are over dry lands with only scant evidence of human presence – the occasional cattle station homestead or mining operation, and small clusters of housing in Aboriginal settlements. The colour of the desert landscape shifts from pink sand dunes to pale yellow-brown plains and deep-red rocky outcrops. Bushes, trees and desert grasses add nuances of silvery green, often along veins of meandering, mostly dry river systems. Closer to Alice

Springs, the one sizeable town in Central Australia (pop. 27,000), parallel mountain ranges run east–west for hundreds of kilometres like frozen, red waves moving northwards.

On the ground, the country is less accessible. The only bitumen roads in the region are the Stuart Highway that runs north–south through the interior, the roads to the major tourist attractions Uluru and Kings Canyon and the network around Alice Springs. Most remaining roads to Aboriginal communities, cattle stations and mines are poorly maintained gravel with deep sandy washouts and severe corrugation. The fact that much of Central Australia is unfenced cattle country adds to the road dangers as livestock as well as kangaroos, dingo dogs, emu birds, big goanna lizards and wild camels may appear at any time. The desert climate swings between burning hot summers and icy winters, and the average annual rainfall is a mere 287 mm. When rain falls, it usually pours, and roads turn into red mud and are cut off by running creeks and flooded plains.

Geographically, Central Australia covers parts of three Australian states – Western Australia, South Australia and Queensland – and the self-governing NT, not yet a state in the Australian federation (Map 1). This book is mainly set in the southern half of the NT (Map 2).

The NT capital is Darwin (pop. 131,700) on the tropical coast 1,500 km north of Alice Springs. The towns are linked by the Stuart Highway and a railway completed in 2004. The towns in between are Tennant Creek (pop. 3,000) and Katherine (pop. 10,700). Other roadside stops typically consist of a roadhouse with petrol, pub, food and accommodation and camping sites. A few comprise a cluster of homes, a small school, shop, nursing post and police station. South from Alice Springs, the Stuart Highway continues as the only paved road over the state border to South Australia and its capital Adelaide (pop. 1.2 million), 1,500 km from Alice Springs. The only inhabited places along the first 1,200 km are roadhouses and a few nearby settlements.

Twenty-seven per cent of the NT population of 211,945 declared themselves Aboriginal or Torres Strait Islanders in the 2011 Census, compared with 2.5 per cent of the Australian population of 21.5 million. More than forty indigenous languages and dialects are still spoken in the NT and especially remote-living people actively maintain modified ceremonial practices and are guided by traditional norms in many aspects of their lives. Among the twenty-five languages and dialects spoken in the Central Australian region, Arrernte, Warlpiri and Pitjantjatjara dominate with 2,000–3,000 speakers in each group (IAD 2002). Aboriginal language speakers, including many musicians I have worked with, are often multilingual in several Aboriginal languages while their level of Standard English skills varies. A number of Aboriginal people in the region speak English only, including several of the musicians who grew up in towns, many with one non-Aboriginal parent, and also many people of mixed

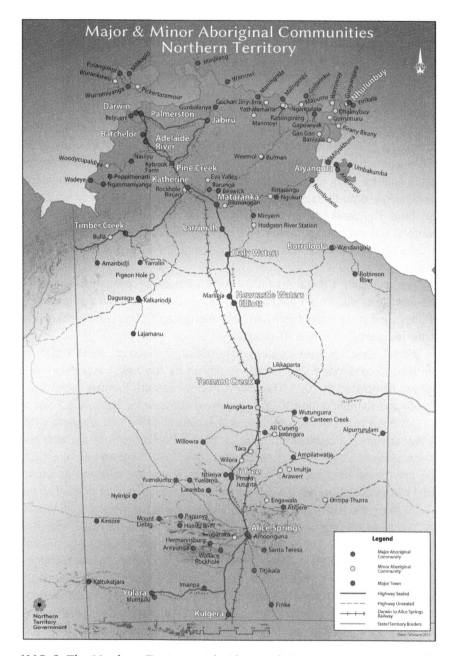

MAP 2 *The Northern Territory with Aboriginal Communities (map provided courtesy NT Dept of Lands, Planning & Environment, © NT of Australia).*

ancestry who were taken away from their Aboriginal families as children under former state policies.

Miscegenation between Aboriginal and non-Aboriginal people has a history as long as colonial settlement and most Aboriginal people in Central Australia have both Aboriginal and some other ancestry. This is not least a legacy of the comprehensive dispersal and relocation of Aboriginal individuals and groups over the last century. Therefore, while the musicians we meet in forthcoming chapters primarily identify with one language group, most of them belong to genealogically complex and geographically scattered kin networks. In any one Aboriginal settlement, though, there is a density of such ties. The biographies of individual musicians further accentuate the proliferating diversity of experience and ways of identifying that emerge from the regional intercultural history.

Indigenous-settler relations and segregation

Central Australia became one of the last colonial frontiers on the Australian continent when the first European explorers arrived in the 1860s. The subsequent construction of a telegraph line from Adelaide to Darwin through the interior in 1870–72 became the single most important factor in the expansion of colonial powers and occupation by non-indigenous people in Central Australia (Donovan 1988). The string of telegraph stations became stops on an overland route for all kinds of newcomers: pastoralists, gold diggers, traders and colonial officers. Among the early arrivals was also a group of German Evangelical Lutherans, 'religious exiles from their home country' (Hill 2002: 46), on a mission to protect and convert 'the natives'. They established Hermannsburg Aboriginal mission in 1877, 100 km west of today's Alice Springs (Map 2), and missionaries of other Christian denominations followed later. Most early missionaries' dual goal was to make Aboriginal people reject their ancestral belief systems while also keeping them away from non-indigenous settlements and the 'evils of civilisation' and its 'moral and spiritual decadence' (Parry and Austin 1998: 17). In this, the Christian administrations were a powerful force in establishing a regional regime of segregation of Aboriginal and other people.

With the more systematic pastoral expansion in the first decades of the twentieth century, retaliatory chains of brutalities and mutual fear between Aboriginal locals and settlers ensued (Austin 1992, 1997). Spears and sorcery proved inefficient against guns, and hunting parties for a single Aboriginal suspect could result in the killing of large numbers of Aboriginal men, women and children (Cribbin 1984). Such killings are still powerful in Aboriginal people's shared memory and feature in newly composed songs, such as Sammy Butcher's sombre, instrumental guitar ballad 'Massacre' (2002) and Clifford Brown's 'Coniston', a country-rock ballad in Warlpiri language.[19] As European dominance became more firmly established, the violence was gradually replaced by a management regime of state and missionary food rationing of Aborigines, not least aimed at keeping them away from white settlements (Rowse 1998). Aboriginal people also gathered in camps on cattle and sheep properties where some of them worked, mostly for food, clothes and other basics (Larbalestier 1988; Markus 1990). Christian and European rural worker models of manhood and gender relations have, thus, co-existed with indigenous norms for more than a century and have been partly adopted and adapted by Aboriginal peoples. As described in Chapter 2, such masculine styles, experiences and sentiments have been mediated especially in Aboriginal desert gospel and country music traditions.

Very few non-Aboriginal women were present in the early decades of colonial settlement, and exploitative as well as voluntary sexual relationships between non-Aboriginal men and Aboriginal women became intrinsic to the regional history (Bell 2002; McGrath 1984). Children born from these liaisons were anomalies in terms of the 'White Australia' ideology which aimed at establishing Australia as a racially pure white nation (Kane 1997; Yarwood 1962). One of the most extreme race segregation policies in Australia was subsequently put in place in the 1920s for 'breeding out the colour' in the NT population (Austin 1997). On the basis of the ideas that Aboriginal people would be genetically 'whitened' in a couple of generations, 'half-caste' children were to be removed from their parents and raised in institutions, and marriages between 'half-castes' and 'full-bloods' were outlawed. The 'half-caste' institution in Central Australia was 'The Bungalow', in operation in various locations around Alice Springs 1914–42 (Austin 1997; Heppell and Wigley 1981; also see Wilson 1997).

By the Second World War, most Aboriginal people in Central Australia had been forcibly moved off their traditional lands or had fled violence and starvation and sought refuge around missions and rationing depots. These centres also attracted people to come voluntarily for food, blankets and tools, and for addictives such as tobacco, tea, sugar and alcohol (Rowse 1998). With the recent Nazi genocide in mind, the rhetoric of eugenics and the ideology of biological absorption were replaced by a 'New Deal' for Aboriginal people: social and cultural assimilation. A network of state settlements modelled on Anglo-Australian towns and way of life was central to the implementation of the new policy in Central Australia (Bell 2002: Wells 1998). The hope was that Aboriginal people would reject their ancestral beliefs and become economically productive citizens if they were trained in Anglo-Australian forms of work ethics, domestic habits and nuclear families (Austin 1997: 18). However, many ancestral activities were, in fact, intensified by the large aggregations of people and the constant food supply provided by the settlements (Long 1964). At the same time, all pre-colonial practices were inevitably modified by the disciplining regimes in each state settlement, just as life in each Christian mission and cattle station produced its own configurations of co-existence and co-production of ways of identifying.

As part of the increased recognition of indigenous rights, Aboriginal rural award wages were introduced in the 1960s, and combined with the rationalization and mechanization of the rural industries across Australia and the Western world, many Aboriginal rural workers and their families were made to leave rural properties. The Australian welfare system expanded at this time to include Aboriginal Australians, and many former workers were left with few other options than to join other welfare recipients in state settlements, missions and non-indigenous towns. Today, the Australian welfare state has come to penetrate most aspects of many Aboriginal people's lives in Central Australia. At the same time, the introduction of the 1976 NT Land Rights Act has seen large areas of land being handed back to Aboriginal claimants (Peterson and Langton 1983).

Aboriginal desert communities

Today, almost half of the land in the NT Central Australian region is held by Aboriginal land trusts, and the governing of state settlements, missions and some cattle station camps has been transferred to Aboriginal community councils.[20] Government grants for cultural restoration have moreover supported the establishment of new settlements closer to people's ancestral lands (Stanley 1989). The thirty or so Central Australian Aboriginal settlements and a large number of family camps (so called 'outstations') are commonly referred to as 'Aboriginal communities', or simply 'bush communities'.[21] Relations within and among these communities underpin a dynamic blackfella hinterland realm that provides a main space for men to establish musical and male reputation.

The largest desert community, Yuendumu, has a population of 800–1,000 people, but most other communities have less than a couple of hundred residents, and outstations may comprise ten to twenty-five people. These numbers may fluctuate considerably with changing seasons and events. Mobility is a recognized aspect of Aboriginal life, and people are on the move both within and between communities, outstations and non-indigenous towns (Taylor and Bell 1994; Young and Doohan 1989). People travel to visit relatives, to do ceremonial and 'sorry' business (funeral practices), to work, for their education, to do time in prison, to receive medical care, to shop, to drink, to play sports, and for various other reasons. Music making also generates mobility. Not only do bush musicians travel between communities and towns to perform and record music; their families and friends also journey to support 'their' bands and participate in musical happenings. Musical experiences, moreover, allow musicians and audiences to move imaginatively between both experienced and imagined places, times and ways of being. Such ideational and physical mobility is a lyrical theme in many local country, rock and reggae songs about ending up in other places and longing to get back home, and about being on the road,[22] describing both events and states of mind.[23]

Aboriginal bush communities are built similar to other small Australian towns, but the houses are usually of lower standard, less well maintained and more overcrowded. In contrast to Western-style domestic orders, yards and house verandas are the main social spaces that people often share with numerous dogs, car wrecks, pieces of junk and strewn rubbish. The socioeconomic dynamic of desert communities differs markedly from that of other Australian towns. They are established without economic rationale and far from mainstream labour markets and commercial activities, and there are few profit-making activities or production of goods for local consumption. The Aboriginal unemployment rate is persistently high, and existing jobs are mainly in council-related and publicly funded jobs at schools and health clinics, or in community development and work-for-unemployment-benefit projects. Some people receive royalty income from mining or tourist operations on their lands, and in some places income is generated by (partly government funded) community art centres. On occasions, such incomes are invested for the benefit of the whole community for carrying out works like installing a dialysis unit or constructing a swimming pool. In the entrenched welfare regime of the desert communities, however, these incomes are often perceived as 'spending money' and used on alcohol, gambling and second-hand vehicles.

Music making is not an important income-generating activity in desert communities. Aspirations to fame and related wealth are certainly part of the globally informed imagery that circulates among the musicians. In practice, such aspirations are adjusted to local circumstances where they cannot expect to be paid for performing in their own or neighbouring communities. When performing at regional Aboriginal festivals or in faraway communities they may ask to be compensated for petrol costs, and sometimes they are. Bands also travel to enter Battles of the Bands competitions in the hope of, and, in some instances, counting on, taking home the prize money which they envisage will pay for the return journey. Plenty of times, of course, they do not win and it may take a few days or weeks to raise the petrol money needed among relatives and friends, or to catch a ride with someone else. Or they may sell an instrument to buy petrol. For some gigs in non-indigenous regional towns like Alice Springs, the musicians are paid with door takings minus sound and staging costs, or a set sum. In either case, each individual usually ends up with anything from a mere twenty-five dollars to maybe a hundred dollars. Bush musicians seldom receive much royalty income from commercially released recordings either. The main market for their recordings is the Aboriginal people in the desert region. Considering how small this population is, and that it is among the poorest in Australia, the fact that musicians receive royalty (which is paid out after production costs have been covered by the sales) is an indication of how highly valued these forms of music are in Aboriginal desert settings.

Desert communities consistently report some of the lowest levels of standard education and the highest rates of illiteracy in Australia, and they struggle with endemic problems, including family conflicts, poverty, chronic diseases, domestic violence, petrol sniffing, neglected children and sexual assaults. To meet these challenges, community associations such as women centres, art cooperatives, media association, youth programmes and law and order teams are formed to assist the vulnerable and the needy, manage community conflicts and strengthen shared cultural values and practices. A majority of desert communities are declared 'dry', which means they have banned alcohol within their boundaries. A problematic consequence of such restrictions is that people leave family responsibilities behind to go and drink in towns, which is a recurrent lyrical theme in desert musicians' repertoires.[24]

Entry to Central Australian Aboriginal land and communities is restricted for outsiders, who need a permit. Most communities still constantly interact with a wide variety of exogenous people, ideas and practices. In Yuendumu, for instance, 10 per cent of the residents are non-Aboriginal. This is the highest proportion in any community, but most communities employ non-Aboriginal people in various managerial positions. Non-Aboriginal tradesmen are also brought in for infrastructure work, and a string of non-Aboriginal researchers, government officials, politicians, educators, musicians, media and art workers, geologists and other professionals have frequented desert communities over many decades. Aboriginal bush people also continue to frequent non-indigenous regional towns, which are Aboriginal settlements in themselves, as they are built on the ancestral land of people who never left.

Alice Springs is the main urban centre in Central Australia. The town was a tiny non-indigenous settlement close to a telegraph station on the overland telegraph line in the 1870s and has now expanded on the lands of the Central Arrernte people, by the MacDonnell Ranges and along the usually dry Todd River.[25] The town grew slowly with periods of marked increase when it became the end station for the railway from the south in 1929 and a base for US and Australian army personnel during the Second World War (Donovan 1988). Tourism underpinned the growth of the town from the 1960s and it now has an international casino, convention centre and a large selection of tourist accommodation and restaurants.

Today, the majority of Alice Spring's residents remain of British and Irish ancestry, but about thirty languages other than English are spoken in homes, some by indigenous people and the rest by both long-time settled and more recently arrived migrants from various parts of Asia, the Pacific, the Middle East, Europe, Africa and North America.[26] The proportion of town residents who identify as indigenous has increased from 15 per cent in 2001 to about 18.6 per cent in 2011. A majority are of mixed Arrernte and non-indigenous ancestry, and indigenous people from cities, towns and remote communities in other parts of Australia have long come to Alice Springs to work, study or visit, too.

The town is also the service hub for the estimated 15,000 remote-living Aboriginal people across the desert region, also beyond the NT (Taylor 2009). The constant coming and going of these 'bush people' provides Alice Springs with a distinct blackfella rhythm. Before Christmas and around school holidays, for instance, large numbers of Aboriginal people come to town to pick up children from boarding schools, visit relatives and shop. At Easter, too, Alice Springs becomes a busy blackfella space when the regional football league starts with a three-day-long carnival. Aboriginal people have a greater presence in Alice Springs all year round, though, compared to most other towns in Australia. The visibly different ways in which some of them are co-present have often been interpreted as reflecting a deep racial and cultural division in town, as well as across the region, between Aboriginal and non-Aboriginal domains, even when many people are, in fact, engaging in the same kind of activities in shared physical space. As we enter the world of the Aboriginal men and musicians in the forthcoming chapters, I will discuss the experienced and imagined dimensions of such a division and the forms of the present-day 'othering', which has a history.

Persistent 'Othering'

An important historical factor in the persistent sociocultural 'othering' in Central Australia has been the systematic and state-funded allocation, or rationing, of food and basics to the Aboriginal population, away from non-indigenous towns. Rowse suggests that the formalized passage of goods from a dominating European to a subordinate Aboriginal party was based on culturally undemanding and unequal relationships in that it requires 'only the most minimal degree of intersubjective accord' and 'no necessary congruity of orientations among the parties' (1998: 5). That is, while rationing brought donors and receivers into daily contact, it did not require the mutual and complex understandings that more equal interactions and acknowledged interdependence between the two parties tend to produce. Instead, each party has been able to foster speculative constructions of the 'other' without much challenge, while preserving its own sets of normative behaviour, values and forms of identification.

The persistent 'othering' that reinforces a binary view of Aboriginal and non-Aboriginal domains ought to make little sense in a setting where members of these categories have long worked together, have gone to the same churches and schools, have been neighbours and have shopped in the same town shops. Marriage and parenting involving both Aboriginal and non-Aboriginal persons continue to be an intrinsic part of regional history, too. However, mixed Aboriginal and non-Aboriginal families are seldom acknowledged or celebrated as 'multiethnic'. Like other parts of the world with a prominent presence of people of mixed ethnic or racial ancestry, the social institutions and public debate instead tend to encourage, even require, that individuals identify with only a single ethnicity (Cornell and Hartmann 1998: 239). It is consistent, too, with Cowlishaw's observations of race relations in the town of Bourke in south-eastern Australia, where she notes how 'a binary system of identification is sustained in the face of ambiguous racial heritage' (2004: 11).

In present-day Alice Springs, the power differences do not map as neatly onto Aboriginal and non-Aboriginal stakeholders as they may have in the past. Forms of authority and recognition have become more complex as national and regional political policy debate and actions have created a more diversified space for forms of legitimate agency. It is still the case, however, that Aboriginal organizations provide a network of a rather separate Aboriginal town space. The Aboriginal recording studio we enter in the forthcoming chapters is part of this space, which also includes the Aboriginal health service, employment and banking service, housing associations (so called 'town camps'), schools and childcare centres, legal aid and more. Aboriginal people can, thus, largely operate and be serviced within an Aboriginal town domain, which is also socially and administratively linked with bush communities.

The Aboriginal musicians' lives are, in these ways, formed in intercultural engagements and also characterized by racial and sociocultural disparity fed by a persistent, mutual 'othering'. This regional dynamic also involves powerful representations of Aboriginal desert people and culture as symbolic types in dominant national 'traditionalist' imagery, which, in turn, is central to the construction of Central Australia as an ideological landscape.

Ideological landscapes

Located in the remote and isolated 'red heart' of the continent, Central Australia and Alice Springs have long been the subject for romantic imaginings represented in explorer tales, bush poetry, music, novels, ethnographic accounts, documentary and fictional film, visual arts, theatre and dance. These representations variably draw on elements of the regions' European and masculinist pioneer history, Aboriginal people who have maintained aspects of ancestral customs, and the dramatic desert scenery with its peculiar wildlife. For instance, Mountford's popular publications on desert people and tourist destinations made an impact with their photos of dusty, near-naked and spear-holding stone-age men (Mountford 1948, 1965). In the 1940s and 1950s, Central Australia became an attractive base for shooting movies such as *The Overlanders* about the last great Australian cattle drivers, *Jedda* about an Aboriginal girl adopted by a non-indigenous family and torn between two cultures, and *A Town Like Alice* from Nevil Shute's war time novel. They all reinforced a romantic outback imagery of a dusty frontier town with rough-cut and resilient non-indigenous Australian characters, and with Aboriginal people cast in traditionalist 'authentic' terms of fundamental spiritual and sociocultural difference.

Such mass-distributed representations have contributed considerably to boosting the region as an 'ideological landscape'; one so charged with affective and symbolic meanings that it helps to induce people's sense of national belonging (Edensor 2002: 37). Imagery of Central Australia has, in this way, underpinned Australian national self-imagery. The white male pioneer figure battling and at least partly taming the remote and harsh natural environment, for instance, has come to stand for more general national virtues of the European Bushman legend and its more modern version of the 'Aussie battler', forged out of adversity and representing progress in general.[27] Homogenized representations of 'authentic' desert Aborigines, and the pristine landscape in which they are firmly imagined, have instead come to stand for fixity: a distant and eternal past, and a primeval naturalness that lends an imagined stability and origin to multicultural visions of Australian nationhood (Lattas 1992).

Continuously recirculated in updated versions of popular, public and political culture that are also exported globally, ideological landscapes frequently become iconic sites for tourism and various forms of spiritual and ideological pilgrimage (Edensor 2002). This is certainly the case with Central Australia, where tourism is the major generator of business and infrastructure, and where the opportunity to experience a 60,000-year-old, still alive Aboriginal culture is an essential part of tourist promotion of the region. It is also a main motivation for a range of neo-missionary pursuits and 'new age' pilgrimage.

Internationally successful books such as Bruce Chatwin's *Songlines* (1987), which 'pulsated with apparently authentic archetypal elaborations' of desert Aborigines as the bearers of ancient wisdom about how to relate holistically to one's environment, have nurtured such pilgrimage (Kondos and Cowlishaw 1995: 8).

The archetypal figure for 'Aboriginal culture' in the ideological landscape of Central Australia is the wizened, 'full-blood' old man portrayed on postcards for sale all over Alice Springs. Unlike many Aboriginal people in Central Australia, these postcard blackfellas are never visibly of mixed Chinese, Afghan or various European ancestries. They are seldom dressed and never pictured in a townscape or run-down desert settlements. Ironically, too, it is the tourists and non-indigenous people who commonly show off bare skin in Central Australia. Many Aboriginal locals instead adopt dress codes of modest Christians and Western rural workers and deem it inappropriate or impractical to expose much skin.

Popular representations of 'traditional Aboriginal desert people' also exist in sonic forms. Just as in Hollywood western movies, where the rhythmic sound of tom-tom drums evokes the North American Indian-on-the-warpath, and melodic flute or strings accompany more romantic, close-to-nature stereotypes of them (Gorbman 2000), Australian Aboriginal people and culture are commonly manifested by the earthy, suggestive sound of the didjeridu (Kibby and Neuenfeldt 1998). The didjeridu was never a traditional instrument in Central Australia but nevertheless reappears in the hands of Aboriginal people in tourist and media representations of the desert region, and in soundtracks to video clips, television images and films picturing Central Australia. It is a generic and popular piece of merchandise in Alice Springs tourist shops, too. Yet, Central Australian Aboriginal musicians seldom include didjeridu in their music making. In fact, they consciously avoid mixing any ancestral features, whether of their own or those of other indigenous peoples, into more recent musical genres, as discussed in Chapter 2.

Upcoming chapters

Having elaborated some privileged understandings that frame Aboriginal men and music making in Central Australia, and having outlined my core conceptual concept of intercultural mediation, the next chapter introduces the social history of the main musical styles of non-ancestral music played in Central Australia, and how these musics mediate aspects of different forms of manhood. This chapter has discussed how the Aboriginal desert musicians do not perform recognized markers of either traditionality or a modern Black rights activist stance. Chapter 2 makes clear why this is the case. It shows how the forces shaping this music scene differ from that of the two indigenous regions that have come to dominate national and global perceptions and expectations of Aboriginal popular music in terms of 'authentic traditional' or 'political resistance': the Top End of the NT and south-eastern Australia.

In the Aboriginal recording studio that I explore in Chapters 3 and 4, I discuss how a 'slack and black' ethos shapes understandings of distinct blackfella male and musical activities in this socio-musical setting. The tension between such valued 'blackfella ways' and professional standards for making and recording music is prominent in the reproduction of the male and blackfella homosociality of this studio. In the process, the men mobilize and articulate aspects of ancestral, Christian, rural industry and music-related models of manhood. An integral part of this mediating dynamic is what the musicians think of as 'healthy competition': their crafting of skills and reputation in competition and alliances with fellow blackfella musicians around the studio. In this, the men draw on local and global masculine norms and musical conventions that further work to exclude non-indigenous persons and women.

Chapter 5 proceeds to explore a prominent theme in the mediating dynamics of music making in remote Aboriginal desert communities: the articulation of regional relatedness and distinctiveness among different Aboriginal communities, kin and language groupings. In these settings, music making and events also become a means for individual men to accumulate respect as men and as musicians. By writing and performing songs about their people, communities and histories in particular ways, the men effectively position themselves in relation to specific groupings, individuals and places, which they can also come to represent when performing outside their community. I show how musicians' experiences of other places and people often become useful in their home communities, where the representative status they gain through their music making may also translate into leadership positions and increased male status in extra-musical realms.

My discussion of blackfella music performances in whitefella-dominated regional towns in Chapter 6 highlights the contradiction between imagined and lived blackfella and whitefella engagement. Bush musicians often talk about gigs in towns as desired occasions for enriching experiences in a non-indigenous mainstream arena. When I investigate what actually takes place around such events, we will see how Aboriginal relatedness, distinctiveness and gendered conventions instead take centre stage. These events, then, often become occasions for demonstrating rather monocultural modes of identifying that reinforce, but also to some extent renegotiate, the historical dominance of whitefella orders and a blackfella insistence on being present on their own, valued 'too much' and 'mongrel' terms.

The Aboriginal musicians often present touring ventures beyond their home region as desired occasions for engaging with 'mainstream' music realms, too, but perhaps more importantly, tours are seen as valued opportunities for participating in a national blackfella musical brotherhood. Both these aspects earn the musicians increased male and Aboriginal status among fellow musicians and people at home. My account of a touring project in Chapter 7 shows how such ventures indeed involve interactions with a range of indigenous and non-indigenous places and people. The desert men do, however, keep their direct engagements with most kinds of 'others' to a minimum. At the same time, they negotiate tensions between different norms for worthy male behaviour among themselves when they, in a sense, 'go abroad' to unknown, but always already imagined, socio-musical territories. A desire to 'play hard' in the field of drinking and sexual adventures is, here, in tension with aspirations to earn increased respect within their home communities' norms for responsible and mature manhood. In this, aspects of already mediated indigenous norms for respected masculinity at home are mediated with global masculine imagery of touring musicians as free of such everyday gendered and behavioural constraints.

A main theme appearing in the desert men's interactions on tours concerns stereotyping of the 'other' and of oneself. In their interactions with urban non-indigenous musicians, which I describe in Chapter 7, I discuss how their mutual typecasting takes on a kind of double-mirrored dynamic. While each party's comments and mimicking address the modus operandi of the other as different from that of one's own kind, these gestures also display a curiosity about the other and demonstrate a capacity for becoming like the other. By exaggerating stereotypes of themselves, I argue, the men moreover depict their own ways of being men and musicians as somewhat ridiculous, while demonstrating the validity as well as limitation of cultural and racial stereotypes.

As I tie together the main themes of music, manhood and indigeneity in the concluding chapter, I expand my argument for music practices as an important and highly rewarding arena for exploring and conceptualizing contemporary 'mongrel' forms of indigeneity and masculinity more generally in Australia and elsewhere.

2

Desert musics

Wherever one goes in the Australian desert region, Aboriginal people play, perform and listen to music on a daily basis. Most desert communities house at least one but often several gospel groups, a couple of country, rock and reggae band formations, and a number of men are skilled in playing the guitar and drums. Passing by Aboriginal housing areas and homes in regional towns, one frequently hears the strumming of guitars, and a variety of music, often by regional Aboriginal musicians, streams out of cassette and CD players. This chapter outlines the social history of the preferred non-ancestral music genres in this highly diverse regional Aboriginal music scene – localized styles and fusions of country, rock and reggae music – in order to show how they have become core expressive forms in Aboriginal life worlds. I discuss how local and global masculine and music-related forms have become historically entangled, and I close the chapter by comparing Aboriginal music making in the desert region with that of the NT 'Top End' and the south-east of Australia. Music from the latter two regions have come to represent the traditionalist and the political resistance models by which Australian Aboriginal popular music is commonly perceived, represented and evaluated, as I had discussed in Chapter 1. My argument for broader conceptual approaches to better capture contemporary indigenous lives relies on an understanding of how the desert men have other grounds for making music than those two models suggest.

A few general features should be kept in mind regarding all the genres and styles of music discussed. First, few of the Central Australian musicians have received formal music training or can read music. They have learnt how to play by watching and imitating older male Aboriginal musicians, and occasionally by watching non-Aboriginal artists. Most of them develop instrumental skills and styles of playing, together with Aboriginal male relatives and friends. Playable instruments and functioning musical equipment are scarce in many Aboriginal settings, and many musicians recount how they, as boys, practised on air guitars and drums or on instruments and loudspeakers made from cardboard boxes, tins and strings while they made all the sounds with their voices. These ways of learning means that the men are highly skilled in picking up and applying new sounds and techniques by ear and eyes in the process of playing with others. Most musicians in the desert region are also multiskilled instrumentalists and can easily swap between drums, bass, rhythm and lead guitars, and some play the keyboard, banjo and pedal-steel guitar.

Similar to descriptions of local music scenes in colonized settings elsewhere in Australia and the world, Aboriginal popular music making in Central Australia is also characterized by a fusion and mix of musical genres and styles both in the one song and in the broader repertoire of any one musician or band (Bilby 1999; Collins and Richards 1989; Neuenfeldt 2001; Samuels 2004). Barber and Waterman describe how Yorùbá music in West Africa involves a process of 'incorporating fragments from a multiplicity of sources into local stylistic configurations and social strategies', a process in which personalities are created and consolidated 'out of diverse, multifarious, overlapping materials ... often borrowed from other people' (1995: 243). It applies also to non-ancestral music in Aboriginal Central Australia, where the musicians' recordings are usually fairly eclectic affairs.

Many Aboriginal kids and teenagers are keen rap dancers and listen to American hip-hop. However, I came across only a few younger persons in Central Australia who practised or wrote hip-hop regularly, and these acts ceased when the members gradually took on adult responsibilities. Hip-hop styles of music are, therefore, not part of this book. Also, only one regional artist, Pitjantjatjara man Frank Yamma, is marketed as a 'world music' artist, and mainly outside Central Australia. 'World music' is not a category that Aboriginal musicians or audiences in Central Australia relate much to, and the ideas and conventions that surround the world music industry have not influenced the regional music scene or practices to any noticeable degree. I, therefore, leave discussions regarding 'world music' aside and focus on the dominant music styles of country, rock and reggae. These styles were preceded and partly influenced by gospel music.

Gospel influences

Aboriginal people's adoptions of introduced European music forms in Central Australia began with Christian hymns, first introduced by Lutheran missionaries. For the missionaries, as in colonial missionary and evangelical movements in other parts of the world, 'music served as a crucial vehicle for conversion' (Radano and Bohlman 2000: 20) and ancestral music was condemned as 'either primitive, or sinful, or both' (Kaemmer 1993: 197). Over time, the music of the missionaries has been reinterpreted and reworked, and new songs composed through Aboriginal people's day-to-day experiences, languages and singing styles in a genre called 'desert gospel'. The style is not related to the gospel music that usually comes to mind: the African American or colonial-African funky, exuberant, call-and-response singing, accompanied by exalted body movement, a music which is, in turn, associated with work song, soul and blues traditions (Hunter 2000). Mediating European Christian and regional Aboriginal norms for appropriate musical and bodily expressions, desert gospel is instead characterized by emotionally fairly sparse singing styles and highly composed bodily expression.[1] It is often sung in a high-pitched, non-melodic style that borrows from regional ancestral Aboriginal singing styles, and it further differs from European hymn traditions by a frequent shortening or extension of bars to produce a distinct rhythmic pattern (common also in regional country playing).

Desert gospel groups may consist of women only, men only, or of mixed-gender. In this respect, gospel becomes the one important exception from the otherwise prevailing male dominance of non-ancestral musics in Aboriginal Central Australia. Embedded in local church socialities and activities, and shaped by a religious focus and motivations, gospel further differs from the forces that shape other non-ancestral music practices. Gospel still influences other musical practices and styles, as well as the ways in which the musicians identify themselves as Aboriginal and as men. For instance, while instrumental skills are highly valued among men in this music scene, vocals are not, and there is little incentive for boys to develop singing skills. Local church choirs are a rare site where they are able to develop a sense for harmonies and vocal techniques, and versatile Aboriginal male singers have usually sung in boy choirs.

The historical association between gospel and country music is, of course, well established, most famously through the widely popular Carter family that performed from the 1920s in the United States. In Central Australia, country-gospel bands have been a mainstay of Aboriginal community life since the 1950s, albeit not readily accepted by the missionaries.[2] When country music was introduced in the Hermannsburg mission during the late 1940s and 1950s, for instance, the Lutherans perceived it as the work of the devil and banned it in the mission.[3] Local Aboriginal country devotees still practised their music in secret and found more appreciative audiences in nearby Palm Valley, an early tourist destination. By the early 1960s, the Lutherans had come to accept that country music was here to stay and it became an integrated feature of gospel music in the mission.

Another connection between gospel and country concerns the ways in which musicians who identify strongly with country music genres may draw on Christian rhetoric and ideals of a morally responsible and mature manhood in order to assert a distinct and morally elevated attitude to music making and life in general, which I discuss in Chapter 4. Also, as rock, reggae and country musicians grow older, it is not unusual that they gradually turn to playing gospel. This coincides with their increased male social and ritual responsibilities and status that comes with maturing age in local Aboriginal regimes, which, in turn, resonate with aspects of ideal Christian models of adult masculinity that emphasize male responsibility for the protection and leadership of families and communities. An increased commitment to gospel music may, in other words, be seen as a private and public affirmation of a model of mature manhood in which customary and Christian values are co-implicated.

There are more pragmatic connections between gospel and other music practices. Members of rock and reggae bands are frequently scattered when doing time in prison, playing football, visiting relatives, drinking in towns, and so forth. As Warlpiri rock guitarist Clifford Brown explained to me, to play with the 'gospel mob' is a good way to keep one's fingers in practice while one's fellow band members get their act together. Importantly, too, churches are often able to keep a decent set of instruments and sound equipment because of their somewhat elevated moral standing. Other musical gear normally circulates in networks of kin and friends and is heavily used and soon deteriorates. Many rock, reggae and country musicians are also nostalgically attached to the sound and familiarity of the gospel tunes that they grew up with, and they tell me that they simply like playing the 'nice sound' of gospel.

In contrast to local Aboriginal women, then, men move in and out of the gospel music realm with relative ease, with country music being the most closely related in terms of musical styles and sets of values.

Country rules

One cannot overestimate the social, emotional and musical importance of country music in indigenous Australian settings. More or less every adult indigenous person I meet in Australia can recount childhoods with uncles strumming away on beat-up acoustic guitars, singing tunes of old American country greats such as Hank Williams, Jimmie Rodgers and Charlie Pride, as well as Australian country legends such as Tex Morton, Buddy Williams and Slim Dusty. Mothers, aunties and sisters know their Loretta Lynn, Patsy Cline and Peggy Lee songs.

The immense private and public importance country music plays in indigenous Australia has also been noted by an increasing number of music scholars and writers (Breen 1989; Brunton 1987; Dunbar-Hall and Gibson 2004; Ellis 1994; Ryan 2003; Smith 2005; Walker 2000). Country music has been similarly adopted and embedded as meaningful among indigenous peoples elsewhere in the world (Diamond 2001; Keillor 1995; Whidden 1984). In Central Australia, Aboriginal musicians take country music so much for granted as a constant in their lives that they often forget to mention it when I ask what types of non-traditional or non-indigenous music they heard when growing up. As they always have had men playing this music around them, many do not think of country as introduced or whitefella music either, but as a diverse, blackfella everyday practice and musical tradition.

As mentioned, one common country style in Aboriginal Central Australia is a rustic country-gospel. Another persistent regional country style and related male imagery derives from the early non-secular American hillbilly, cowboy-style singing and Australian bush balladry. These styles arrived in Central Australia in the 1930s with travelling non-indigenous showmen such as the legendary, New Zealand-born Tex Morton and Australians Buddy Williams and Slim Dusty. This music was also a mainstay of touring country variety shows that became highly popular in rural and remote Australia from the 1940s (Latta 1991; Whiteoak 2003). The shows' talent quests played an important role for shaping generations of local indigenous country styles and careers. Indigenous men would enter these quests and a few shows, most notably the Brian Young show in the 1970s and 1980s, would offer the most skilled musicians a place in the touring show band for a period. A few of these indigenous men, and a few indigenous women, went on to successful solo careers as musicians in both county music and other musical genres.

Hollywood western movies featuring singing cowboys were screened in Alice Springs and in remote Aboriginal settlements from the 1950s, contributing further to the hillbilly repertoire and related male imagery. Western films also introduced instrumental country guitar music, which remains prevalent throughout the desert region, mainly in the style of The Shadows and in the finger-picking Mexican/Spanish guitar styles. Another prominent desert country style is in the tradition of American 1950s and 1960s' honky-tonk-style country, embodied by American artists such as Hank Williams, Merle Haggard and George Jones. These styles arrived through recordings, films and radio and later through television and video. In the 1960s, rock versions of honky-tonk music were adopted and developed by younger Aboriginal men, and forms of bluegrass can also be heard. While emerging in intercultural processes, the social history of the dominating styles of Aboriginal country music is closely linked to a few 'oldfella' Aboriginal musicians.

'Oldfella' country men

The man who firmly established hillbilly country and bush balladry in Aboriginal Central Australia during the 1940s was Herbie Laughton, acknowledged as

PHOTO 1 *Herbie Laughton.*

'the grandfather of country music in the Northern Territory' (Walker 2000: 70). Herbie passed away in 2012, but when I first met him, he was a fit-looking man in his eighties who peered curiously through his glasses and always appeared in a light brown Akubra hat. Fair skinned enough to pass for a white man, he was fathered by a Russian miner and his mother was of mixed Arrernte and European ancestry. Under the 'breeding out the colour' policy at the time, Herbie was taken from his mother (who, in turn, had been taken from her mother) at the age of two and kept in the Bungalow, the 'half-caste' institution in Alice Springs, until he was twelve. It was here that Herbie first heard country music when the yodelling hillbilly showman Tex Morton came through and performed. 'First time I've seen anyone playing the guitar and playing the mouth organ, you see. I would've been seven, eight, and I thought, jeez, I would love to play like that, get into music like that,' Herbie told me.

Leaving the abuse and constant hunger at the Bungalow in 1939, Herbie spent the war and the post-war years moving around the NT and South Australia looking for his mother. He survived on work on cattle and sheep stations, in mining camps, in the civil corps and in other odd jobs. He bought his first guitar at the age of fifteen and taught himself to play, and after the war he formed the first country band in Central Australia, playing for Aboriginal audiences at the 'old Gap cottages': the early, basic and overcrowded housing for 'half-castes' in Alice Springs.

Herbie taught himself to read and write after leaving the Bungalow and penned his first song in 1947, the regional classic 'Old MacDonnell Ranges' (a significant feature of the Alice Springs landscape). It took another eighteen years before he wrote down his next tune. From the dust and grit of working with sheep and cattle, he came down with a throat condition that damaged his vocal cords and he gave up singing for years. He married in the early 1950s, had six children and had worked in a government job constructing roads all over the Territory for thirty-eight years until he retired. He kept playing his country guitar at the road camps, which also attracted Aboriginal locals, and he gradually reclaimed his singing voice, although not his ability to yodel.

In the mid-1960s, Herbie was urged to return as a stage performer by Western Arrernte-Warumungu man Gus Williams, who also remained a formidable force in the Central Australian country music scene until he passed away in 2011. As a boy, Gus saw Herbie perform at the Gap cottages, an experience that shaped Gus's life-long devotion to country music. Encouraged by Gus, Herbie started writing music again and had produced by the mid-1970s a large repertoire of now classic regional bush ballads. His lyrics are firmly rooted in the Central Australian landscape and tell somewhat nostalgic stories of his own and other Aboriginal people's life experiences through radically changing times (Laughton 1983, 1999). At his kitchen table one afternoon, Herbie told me it was through playing, singing and writing country music that he could deal with his deep feelings of alienation as a 'half-caste' man estranged from his Aboriginal kin and never feeling accepted among whitefellas:

> The only thing that kept me going was my music, you know. It was me' wife, it was my friend, it was my everything! … In my music, I wasn't trying to put in the bad things that were hurting me. I didn't like to put that in songs to hurt other people. I wanted to put a little bit in there, just to show that sadness I went through.

While causing such grief, Herbie's mixed ancestry and fair skin also gave him greater freedom to move around than most Aboriginal people in Central Australia at the time. He could, therefore, inspire and teach people in a variety of indigenous settings, including Isaac Yamma, another influential 'oldfella' country musician in the region. Herbie taught young Isaac how to play the guitar and, mostly as a joke, urged him to go to Alice Springs town and play in the streets. Yamma took the advice seriously and his showy busking performances in Alice Springs main street became part of the now legendary Yamma musical and personal character.

Isaac Yamma was born in the mid-1940s in the remote Western desert to Pitjantjatjara parents who had not yet seen a white man. From an early age, he was hooked on American Jimmy Reeves' early hillbilly style music (before his crooning career), and he started performing and writing songs in Pitjantjatjara language in the late 1960s. He drilled his four sons in playing the guitar and drums in his Pitjantjatjara Country Band that toured Aboriginal desert communities for years. That Yamma was never shy to promote himself and his music on air was borne by the fact that his regional fame took on a mass-mediated dimension when he became one of the first broadcasters with the Aboriginal CAAMA Radio in the early 1980s.[4] Many remarkable stories circulate about Yamma's unorthodox kind of hillbilly music that was interceded with yells, rap-style talking and hollers, his showy performance style in flash satin shirts and Santa Fe boots, his charismatic personality and ringing laugh. Other accounts evoke a man with an oversized ego who demanded to be treated as a star and a genius, and a stern father and husband who did not hesitate to use violence to resolve domestic and other matters. Part of the Yamma legend was made at one of the biggest Aboriginal music festivals in NT history, 'Sing Loud Play Strong', held in Darwin in 1989 (Various 1990). Non-indigenous Bill Davis, festival organizer and a good friend of Yamma, recalls the difficulties with bringing together a large number of Aboriginal musicians from different regions. Many camped at the Bagot Aboriginal Reserve, where the drinking went somewhat overboard and fights erupted. Bill describes how Yamma yelled at the fighters to stop 'or he was gonna knock them all out. Somebody cheesed him and he took off his belt and he wrapped it around his hand, and according to legend he laid out fourteen of them. And the big point is that he knocked out two of his sons as well. So it was non-discriminatory!' Isaac Yamma passed away in 1990.

As mentioned, Gus Williams was a third, widely influential 'oldfella' country music man. He did not write his own material but was a formidable force as

PHOTO 2 *Gus Williams.*

an organizer and promoter for Aboriginal country music in the desert region, and he encouraged numerous young men to pursue country music careers.

Born in Alice Springs in the late 1930s, Gus was taken to his grandfather in Hermannsburg mission when his parents passed away in the 1950s. He sang in the church choir and took to playing the country he heard in Alice Springs and on vinyl recordings brought to the mission by his uncles. Gus trained his sons to play the guitar from a very young age and included them in his band that played in Aboriginal settings from the mid-1960s. By the 1970s he had moved the family to his mother's country some 500 km north of Alice Springs where he was the elected president of Warrabri council (now Ali Curung, see Map 2). Here he formed the first electric country band in the NT, the Warrabri Country Bluegrass Band. After performing at a national Aboriginal country music festival in 1978, Gus organized the first NT Aboriginal Country Music Festival. It became an annual showcase for regional Aboriginal country music for a few years and attracted thousands of people. In the late 1980s, Gus moved the family back to Hermannsburg, where he was the council chairman for many years. He recorded on his own label (Williams 1993; Williams and Country Ebony 1989, 1991, 1992, 1993, 1994), and his commitment as a well-respected leader and advocate for his people earned him the Order of Australia in 1983.[5]

Gus' oldest son, Warren H. Williams, is currently the most well-known Aboriginal country artist from Central Australia. Valuing both Aboriginal and Western education, Gus sent Warren to interstate boarding schools after he had been initiated in traditional ways. 'I didn't appreciate what he was doing at the time,' Warren says, shaking his head over the strict discipline and alien worlds he experienced in those faraway and non-indigenous places. 'But looking from where I am at now,' he continues, 'I'm one of the fortunate ones. I have always lived in both sides, I can talk to everyone.' Now in his early fifties, Warren was thoroughly schooled in oldfella desert country by performing with his father and Herbie. He also took up all the bad habits he thought came with being a true musician. He became a heavy drinker, took drugs, sniffed petrol and got into fights and all kinds of related trouble. The lifestyle directly impacted on his musical styles. For instance, he damaged a hand in a car accident which changed the way he plays the guitar, and he credits his husky singing voice to having his nose broken more than once in fights. After a heart scare in the early 1990s, Warren stopped drinking, smoking, taking drugs and even drinking coffee. He has since written a string of country songs with a swinging folk-rock groove to them, while other songs are firmly in the honky-tonk tradition (Williams 1995, 1998, 2000, 2002, 2005, 2009). He has collaborated with ancestral singers (Williams and the Warumungu Songmen 2012) and has formed a musical partnership with non-indigenous John Williamson, Australia's foremost folk-country musician.[6] Warren's work as a CAAMA Radio broadcaster has bolstered his local profile, and he is also frequently invited to perform at high-profile national events and he has won national music awards.

'Real' country men

As in any musical culture, the Central Australian Aboriginal country music scene is highly diverse and continuously changing. Regardless of this diversity, the desert musicians usually distinguish their country music as 'real' country, which they commonly substantiate by contrasting it with what they perceive it is not: 'American' or 'Nashville' country, denoting a commercially standardized pop quality and attitude. Committed local country musicians occasionally lament that mainstream Australian country music seems to develop in precisely that American direction, and they tend to perceive their own music making as part of a last stronghold for 'real' country.

I discuss in more detail elsewhere (Ottosson 2012, 2015) how the local meanings the Aboriginal musicians attach to 'real' versus 'American' country largely coincide with the opposing concepts of 'hard-core' and 'soft-shell', which have long been part of understanding, identifying with, and marketing different styles of country music worldwide (Akenson 2003; Beal and Peterson 2001; Peterson 1997). The music and performance styles, dress codes, lyrical themes and artistic imagery of 'hard-core' country in general involve looking, talking and acting like one of the audience and not looking like a professional entertainer with a fine singing voice, fashionable clothes, and like the professional stage manner of a soft-shell entertainer' (Beal and Peterson 2001: 236). In contrast to notions of 'soft-shell' country as commercial, inauthentic, insincere, slick and formulaic, the 'hard-core' end of country is also generally associated with notions of 'home made, traditional, authentic, sincere, honest, from the heart' (Akenson 2003: 191).

All the mentioned 'hard-core' features reappear in the desert musicians' understandings of 'real' country. These features are also historically intertwined with some highly valued adult male characteristics and ways of sustaining relatedness in Aboriginal desert societies. As described in the literature, generosity and unselfishness are the primary virtues in gaining respect as an autonomous, mature man in these societies, which is associated with a show of 'general restraint and unassertiveness of individuals over their comrades' (Myers 1986: 103) and not appearing self-important (e.g. Meggitt 1962; Tonkinson 1974). Such respected male demeanour corresponds with the low-key, unassuming artistic imagery in 'real' or 'hard-core' country (Beal and Peterson 2001: 234). The interculturally produced modest, self-made and sincere male styles of the regional rural industry and Christianity mentioned in Chapter 1 resonate with these masculine and musical forms, too. Local notions of a 'real' quality of Aboriginal country music, in these ways, involve the merging of partly resonating male and musical models from which coherent, always 'mongrel' senses of contemporary male and Aboriginal selves and musics emerge.

Some lyrical themes of Aboriginal desert country songs correspond with those of 'hard-core' global country conventions, too: male loners expressing nostalgic and heartfelt longings for one's home country, being down and out in a bar, in jail or on the road, and striving to become a better person. The theme of heartbreak and love is likewise common, although female subjects may be both human and mythical beings. None of these themes are exclusive to country songs, though; they are also common in Aboriginal desert rock and reggae music.

Desert rock and reggae

Various styles of Anglo-American rockabilly, rock'n'roll and pop music arrived in Aboriginal settings in Central Australia from the 1950s in the form of vinyl recordings, cassette tapes and via radio. Movies, and later, television and video-film are other avenues for new sounds to reach remote communities and townships, and for introducing faraway life worlds and masculine styles associated with these musics. The earliest regional Aboriginal rock bands and musicians appeared in the 1970s and mainly played straight country-rock covers. Surf-rock styles and instrumental country-rock guitar music from the 1960s have also been persistently popular all over the region. The Surfaris' surf-rock tune 'Wipe Out', for instance, is frequently requested at any local Aboriginal music event.

Early country-rock bands like the Poor Boys in Yuendumu, Ilkari Maru from Docker River and the Warumpi Band from Papunya started out performing for Aboriginal audiences in their own and neighbouring desert settlements. When CAAMA began broadcasting locally made Aboriginal music in the early 1980s, musicians all over the region were inspired to form bands and write new music in their own languages about their own experiences, people and country. They took their songs to CAAMA to be broadcast and recorded. CAAMA thus became a catalyst for the expansion of the regional Aboriginal music scene. The 1970s and early 1980s was the golden age for edgy, loud, male pub rock and hard rock more generally in Australia (Creswell and Fabinyi 1999; Hayward 1992). It was reflected in the musical direction taken by the staff and musicians around CAAMA: black rock with a certain male attitude.

Ross Muir, an early, non-indigenous studio officer captures some of this stance when describing the Wedgetail Eagles, a band from Fregon (Kaltjiti) community. In Ross' words, they turned up at the studio and declared '"Yeah, we've got these songs", and we'd say "OK! Cool!" ... Oh, I love them, just the black boys from the bush! They got no suit, they got no shoes, and (it was) like, "all you white boys better watch out, us black boys are in town!"' It was also rock music that associated with hard drinking, drug taking and sexually potent male musicians, an image Ross saw many of the musicians adopt:

> All of a sudden them boys who were innocent and came in with the best desire to play music, suddenly they became famous in their own sort of lunch-time when played on the radio. And they got into all the sort of accoutrements of fame. They got drinking, women ... not necessarily bad things, but if you don't know how to do it in moderation, you're going to go for a fall. And a lot of these people have, well, died. If they haven't died, they've been in jail, they've hurt themselves. ... So it was amazing transformation, and it was very hard for some to take.

Variations of reggae music became increasingly prominent in the repertoire of Aboriginal bush musicians from the late 1980s. Part of a worldwide musical and political movement, reggae music had a huge impact on indigenous popular music all over Australia from the late 1970s, when Bob Marley toured the country.[7] The particular styles of reggae that have emerged in the Aboriginal desert region contain the trademarks of its globally highly diffused meta-genre, such as a continuous, repetitive riff and accented off-beats on all four beats on the rhythm guitar. However, in the desert, these features are commonly reworked into a quicker tempo, rock-drum patterns, country-style guitars and gospel-tinged keyboards. Both desert reggae and rock styles are also typically 'guitarocentric', with guitarists being the primary composers and soloists.

The lyrics and titles of desert reggae and rock songs, as well as country tunes, are usually literal and free of decorative metaphors, such as 'Woman Wants Me to Come Home', 'Worried about My Horse'[8] and 'Soakage Water Hole'.[9] Also typically free of musical elaborations or nuances, desert rock and reggae take on a distinctive 'no-frills', urgent and somewhat rustic sound. Part of this sound can be attributed to the fact that musicians are more likely to add features in order to create a certain feel or sound than to vary or nuance their playing, which results in a busy or dense tendency. Also, vocals are usually secondary to instrumental skills, in contrast to global rock and reggae conventions, where the singing voice is often used to emphasize melodic qualities or for expressing a range of evocative sounds and states of mind. In Aboriginal Central Australia, few singers develop a great range of vocal depths or nuances, and vocals are commonly delivered in an urgent and spontaneous manner, frequently lacking vibrato or emotional elaborations. The intensity and yearning quality of a voice, the singer's social affiliations or the local language that is sung typically produce more passionate responses in regional Aboriginal audiences, too, than the delivery of melodic and perfect tonal harmonies according to Western musical traditions. Aboriginal musicians and audiences in the region, in these ways, recognize and evaluate localized styles not only through musical detail, but also through associations with individual men and the particular Aboriginal socialities in which particular styles of music and sounds operate. Papunya Rock and Warlpiri Reggae can illustrate how such socio-musical conceptions work to produce a complex of regional Aboriginal distinctions.

Papunya Rock and Warlpiri Reggae

'Papunya Rock' is a rock style that is widely recognized by Aboriginal musicians in the region. It alludes to the kind of basic, straight and urgent rock beat that the Warumpi Band from Papunya community developed during the 1970s and early 1980s and that relied heavily on the characteristic guitar-playing style of Sammy Butcher. I often heard Aboriginal musicians dropping comments like 'ah, now that's a real Sammy Butcher!' about a guitar riff or a shift of pace in a song during recordings or rehearsals, or they could refer to 'a Sammy Butcher' when explaining to fellow musicians how to play a particular guitar or drum pattern in the Papunya style.

Sammy is a Luritja-speaking man, now in his mid-fifties, who grew up in Papunya (Map 2). He learnt to play the guitar in primary school-age by sneaking in to the non-indigenous schoolteacher's house where one of the few playable guitars in Papunya was kept. He mentions the Beatles and Spanish-Mexican guitar music of Hollywood western movies as important early musical influences. Later on, the style of Dire Straits guitarist Mark Knopfler clearly impacted on his guitar playing. When Sammy returned to Papunya after boarding college in Alice Springs he and a few male relatives formed the country-rock band that was to become the Warumpi Band. Neil Murray, a young, non-indigenous schoolteacher from Victoria came to work in Papunya and soon joined the band, and he and Sammy began to write songs in English and Luritja together. George Rurrambu, a young, extrovert Gumatj man from Elcho Island off the northern coast came to the desert to learn languages, and he joined the band as lead singer and co-songwriter.

The band performed for Aboriginal audiences across the desert region, where their thumping, rustic guitar-rock became immensely popular. In 1983,

PHOTO 3 *Sammy Butcher.*

they became the first Australian band to record a rock song in an indigenous language, 'Jailanguru Pakarnu' (Luritja for 'Out from Jail'). It attracted national attention, and in the years that followed, the band was invited to perform at many high-profile music events and as supporting acts for famous non-indigenous rock bands. It then became increasingly clear that the members had different priorities and aspirations. Neil worked hard to launch Warumpi on a professional national and international circuit, and George was set on becoming a famous black rock star, not unlike his role model Little Richard. The remaining Papunya-based members, Sammy and his brother Gordon, were less concerned with becoming stars in a mainstream music industry. At times, they did not turn up for tours or concerts because they prioritized commitments at home. They could not always find a lift to Alice to catch a flight either. Their spots were, therefore, frequently filled with mainly non-indigenous musicians from the south-east. When his parents passed away and one of his brothers lost himself in drinking, Sammy effectively retired from the band in order to focus on family and responsibilities in Papunya.

During Warumpi's comeback in the 1990s, Neil and George continued to carry the band's profile as an Aboriginal band from the desert, and Sammy appeared for occasional performances. By now, their music had inevitably changed towards a more refined rock sound, which is evident in their recordings (Warumpi Band 1985, 1987, 1996).[10] As discussed in Chapter 7, the later Warumpi sound has been embraced and has taken on diverse political and emotional meanings among indigenous and non-indigenous followers all over Australia. For Central Australian Aboriginal musicians and audiences, though, Sammy Butcher still embodies the Papunya Rock style of the original Warumpi. He has taught this style to younger men at home and it can be recognized in most music coming out of Papunya, as well as influencing Aboriginal musicians across the region.

'Desert reggae' is not very closely associated with a particular musician or band. The term is, in fact, seldom used in conversations between local musicians, who instead usually describe the distinct style by mouthing the basic beat, or strumming the characteristic rhythm guitar-playing style on real or imagined guitars. They may also mimic a bodily pose that is common when desert guitarists play reggae: a rather disinterested attitude with one hand working overtime in a constant, upward strumming. When I heard 'desert reggae' used or shown, it often referred to music from the Tanami Desert region north-west of Alice Springs. The area is largely populated by Warlpiri people and for many Aboriginal people in the region, desert reggae in particular, denotes a Warlpiri musicality and sociality.

One likely reason for the strong Warlpiri connotations of desert reggae is the work of the Warlpiri Media Association (WMA) in Yuendumu, the largest Warlpiri settlement (Map 2). WMA was established in 1983 out of local concerns that Warlpiri communities would be bombarded by foreign television when the AUSSAT broadcasting satellite was launched (Michaels 1986). As part of broader government policy efforts to establish forms for indigenous self-determination, WMA became a means for the Warlpiri also to control the production and circulation of self-representations. Initially focusing on video production, WMA turned its attention to radio activities, which later became a central part of its operations. As in most indigenous radio stations, music is a major feature in WMA's broadcasts, and it tends to prioritize locally produced music, with its indigenous audiences also frequently requesting it to air such music (Hinkson 2004). By continuously recording and broadcasting music from the WMA studio, Warlpiri musicians have, thus, made their particular form of desert reggae (and other musical styles) known all over the region and beyond.

As this outline of music making in the desert region shows, Central Australian Aboriginal music making incorporates a diversity of indigenous and other music styles, sounds, practices, ideas and technologies, which are co-implicated in the ongoing production of distinct 'mongrel' Aboriginal musical and male styles, practices and experiences. This music scene does not fit the prevailing two-sided conceptual model of Australian indigenous popular music that draws on music and people from elsewhere in Australia: certain music from the Aboriginal Top End of the NT has become a powerful global and national standard for traditionalist imagery, while that of the south-east has shaped perceptions of Aboriginal music as a political tool of resistance. It is beyond the scope of my research to analyse these two socio-musical regions in detail, but it is important to understand how indigenous music making and life in Central Australia diverts from the privileged conceptualizations of indigenous people and popular music discussed in Chapter 1.

Central Australian and Top End music

The Australian Top End is the northernmost region of the NT. Besides Darwin (pop. 131,700) and Nhulunbuy (pop. 3,933), where Aboriginal people make up less than 10 per cent of the population, the rest of the Top End has a high proportion of Aboriginal people (Map 2).[11] As in Central Australia, Aboriginal language and kinship groups in these areas maintain an active ceremonial life, while battling with persistent social problems. Again, as in Central Australia, a large number of rock, country, reggae and also blues bands have emerged in Aboriginal Top End communities over several decades (Corn 1999).

The most striking difference between Central Australian and Top End non-ancestral music making is that Top End artists include the most powerful national and international markers of 'traditional' Aboriginal Australia: their traditional instrument *yidaki* (didjeridu) and dancers with traditionally decorated bodies. Top End musicians also mix ancestral song styles into popular songs, may add ancestral songs on separate tracks on their albums, and often integrate detailed ancestral narratives into rock, country, pop and reggae lyrics. On stage and on CD sleeves, Top End bands frequently explain such stories and their importance for the beliefs and customs of their people. Many Top End musicians also state that one of their main aims is to make their ancestral stories, musical elements and values more accessible through non-ancestral music forms, as a means to, on the one hand, encourage younger generations to maintain their distinctive cultural life, and, on the other hand, achieve greater recognition and respect among non-indigenous audiences. The front man of the most famous Top End band, Yothu Yindi, the late Yolngu man and school teacher Mandawuy Yunupingu, was perhaps the most influential promoter of this 'both-ways' approach (Neuenfeldt 1993b, 1998b).

In Central Australia, musicians do not mix many ancestral/traditional features with more recent music genres. At times, they may perform with the red headband that marks them as initiated men, but this may be frowned upon as inappropriate by locals. On one such occasion, for instance, a musician took off his headband backstage and let children play with it. Other musicians commented disapprovingly, basically seeing it as defilement. On another occasion a musician appeared at the recording studio without having washed off the body paint from a ceremonial event. This offended another musician to the extent that he walked off, stating curtly that only men who do not know their Law have to show it off. The mere presence of ancestral features at sites of non-ancestral music making can thus be seen as inappropriate.

Also unlike the Top Enders, the desert musicians rarely put ancestral song themes into context for audiences or on CD jackets. When they do write songs on ancestral themes they mainly refer to the broader categories of natural and mythical phenomena, as in 'Yukurrpa Dreaming' (North Tanami Band 1999). *Jukurrpa* (misspelt on the CD cover) is the Warlpiri term for the fundamental ideological doctrine that was laid down when the world was created. In English, this cosmological order is usually called the Dreaming/Law. The song is a general statement about the band members' mythical ancestral past and affiliations, without referring to specific events, places or beings. The song may still have specific and powerful meanings for Warlpiri listeners. As Bell notes with regard to the politics of knowledge in Australian indigenous (and other) oral cultures that are characterized by restrictions on access to certain knowledge, 'one may believe in the power of a story, yet not know the details' (Bell 1998: 370).

The desert musicians take the separation of ancestral and non-ancestral music forms for granted and do not reflect much on the matter. If prompted, most of them simply state that 'the Law is too strong, too secret' or words to similar effect. 'The Law' in some more specific meaning relates to 'going through Law', which is the ritual initiation of young Aboriginal men.[12] The term is also used more generally for the bodies of localized knowledge and norms that guide place- and gender-specific interpersonal and intergroup relations and practices. The Law is perceived to come from the mythological past of the Dreaming, when ancestral beings (Dreamings) gave the world its shape and moral order through their travels and associated events. The Dreamings importantly remain as life-giving forces in the landscape, embodied in rocks, waterholes, trees, animals and other natural features.

The knowledge of specific Dreamings has been held, transferred and re-enacted over generations through narrative song and dance cycles that are performed in rituals and ceremonies circumscribed by degrees of sacred, secret or open status. The right to perform and the right to access different levels of knowledge of any one song cycle or performance is also restricted according to a person's or group's gender, age, totem and kin category.[13] Adherence to the restrictions is crucial if the life-giving forces inherent in the performed knowledge are to be recreated. The harsh consequences of breaking such restrictions are very real to the musicians. As an Arrernte musician explained: 'I *could* sing about my Dreaming and stuff. Who can stop me? But I'll probably end up with a spear in my leg.'

Most desert musicians also state that they do not see any reason to mix ancestral and non-ancestral musical traditions. 'This is this music, and that is a different one,' as one Warlpiri musician said matter-of-factly, holding his hands together to the right and then to the left. 'See? Different. Side by side!' he concluded. This compartmentalization of musical experiences and the separation of musical idioms and expressions are common also in other indigenous settings. Kaemmer (1993) notes, for instance, how Native Americans and Inuit people of Greenland and Alaska use both ancestral and non-ancestral musical expression but do not mix them. He interprets this as a social, psychological and political phenomenon and suggests that Native Americans compartmentalize occidental and traditional music 'so they can enjoy modern idioms but still use traditional music as a means to lay claim to Indian status for the purpose of obtaining land' (190).

Magowan (1994) proposes that internal Yolngu ideological principles serve as a model for the common 'two-ways' attitudes in Top End music making. It may also be a result of the particular combination of missionary influences and political developments in Yolngu settlements, which have shaped more open attitudes to non-Yolngu worlds, including strategic revelation of sacred aspects to non-indigenous people and state powers (e.g. Berndt 1962; Morphy 1991). Apart from tightly controlled legal proceedings in relation to land claims, there is scant evidence of Central Australian people adopting similar strategies of sharing ancestral knowledge to achieve political goals or a greater understanding of their life worlds in non-indigenous realms. Non-indigenous scholars have suggested to me that a reason for this may be that there are fewer 'open' ancestral song genres in the desert than in the Top End societies. Another explanation they offer in conversations is that desert people were colonized earlier when settlers and missionaries had little regard for indigenous knowledge systems, and accounts and photos of secret desert rituals were published all over the world, which would render them less meaningful in local hierarchies of knowledge-control. Desert peoples would, therefore, have more reason to protect their ancestral knowledge, and not share it.

However, several senior Aboriginal men have explained to me that their concerns about protecting secret and restricted knowledge are mainly intra-Aboriginal affairs. It is when particular Aboriginal 'others' are exposed to the knowledge that is restricted to them that the authority and integrity of local knowledge systems may be threatened. This view is supported in the literature (Bell 1998; Michaels 1985; Myers 2002). A more likely reason for keeping musical idioms separate may, therefore, be that people do not wish to display certain ancestral knowledge to particular other Aboriginal individuals and groups. As described in forthcoming chapters, most desert musicians also direct their music mainly to regional Aboriginal people, not non-indigenous audiences, which further supports this partial explanation.

The different motivations and approaches in music making in the desert and the Top End have, in these ways, emerged in particular intercultural constellations and localized historical processes, which are better analysed elsewhere. My main point here is that the fusion of ancestral and non-ancestral elements in Top End music has become an important standard for expectations of Aboriginal Australian popular music in general. The ways in which Yothu Yindi, and more recently one of its members, Gurrumul Yunupingu, has achieved global success prove the point made in Chapter 1 about the privileging of traditional features in the evaluation of indigenous artistic expression. For musicians in Central Australia, however, the two spheres of ancestral and non-ancestral music and knowledge are ideally kept separate. In the desert, then, the compartmentalization of musical expressions tends to be part of wider strategies to maintain the strength of ancestral traditions. In the Top End, the very linking of ancestral and non-ancestral expressive forms seems to achieve similar results.

Turning to differences between Central Australia and the south-east, one will find that matters of rights politics and resistance become more prominent in music and identity work.

Central Australia and the South-east

The south-eastern states of New South Wales, Victoria and South Australia (Map 1) make up the most populated regions of Australia, including the country's two largest metropolitan areas, Sydney (pop. 4.76 million, 1.2 per cent indigenous people) and Melbourne (pop. 4.35 million, 0.5 per cent indigenous).[14] The national capital, Canberra (pop. 381,500, 1.7 per cent indigenous), is situated between these two cities. The population of South Australia is concentrated on the southern coast, where the state capital Adelaide (pop. 1.3 million, 1.3 per cent indigenous) is located. Today, most indigenous people in the south-east come from several generations of mixed descent and speak English as their first or only language. Scholars have argued at length that south-eastern Aboriginal people sustain unique cultural forms and ways of life as a 'distinct, though heterogeneous and loosely bounded ethnic category' (Keen 1988: 3; also see Beckett 1988a; Cowlishaw 2004; Gale 1973; Morris 1989).

Many of the most vocal, radical and accessible Aboriginal rights advocates have been urban, south-eastern Aboriginal groups and individuals. As Beckett notes, 'If the Gurindji and their friends brought land rights before the Australian public, it was the urban Aborigines who made it a national issue' (Beckett 1988b: 208) (the Gurindji being a northern desert group). The south-eastern cities have also been the primary arena for Aboriginal activist campaigns and protest actions, such as the 1972 Aboriginal Tent Embassy in Canberra and during the 1988 bicentennial celebration of British settlement (Attwood and Markus 1999: 256; Beckett 1988c; Bennett 1992). It is, therefore, rather self-explanatory that the genre of indigenous protest music has a continued strong presence in the south-east as a means to express the main themes of the Aboriginal rights movement: resistance, survival and cultural revival. I do also find that Koori musician friends and acquaintances tend to be motivated by experiences of racial injustice and discrimination to a greater extent than people in Central Australia do.[15] The shaping of a Koori musician's career can illustrate the difference.

Now in his early fifties, Andy is of the Gunditjmara people and grew up on an Aboriginal mission outside Warrnambool in Western Victoria. He describes a carefree childhood, roaming around the forest and male relatives playing country songs by the fire every night. His parents were drinkers and when Andy was ten years old the welfare office moved the family into state housing in Warrnambool. Andy describes the 'deep culture shock' he experienced. In school 'I took a lot of flak, racism, a lot of the kids were calling me names ... I just bottled it up ... every day was a struggle'. Leaving school he started drinking and 'ended up in a lot of strife, because of all that racism'. He went to jail several times and describes a young black man struggling with his place in a racially structured environment.

In the early 1980s, the Gunditjmara people fought and lost one of the first land rights cases through the Australian court system (Rutherford 1980), and there was a blockade against logging of the forest at the mission where Andy grew up (Clarke 2003). At this time, the local, non-indigenous band Goanna released the song 'Solid Rock' about belonging to land and the necessity of recognizing indigenous ownership of this country. It became a national hit, and similar to many Koori people I talk with in Victoria, Andy refers to the song as a major musical and political influence: 'That's what it took for me to notice indigenous issues myself. They paved the way, showing you could sing about Koori issues!'

'Solid Rock' inspired Andy to start writing songs about his own experiences, which took him back to the mission to talk to senior Gunditjmara men about 'the old stories' that he subsequently wrote into songs. 'My indigenous identity, it was always there, never questioned, but it became much stronger when I got angry about racism, when I see the old disappear,' he explains. After a serious health scare, Andy quit drinking and smoking. He has since become a successful musician and respected Gunditjmara man.

Like numerous Koori musicians, Andy continues to musically explore and assert his sense of being indigenous in and against a non-indigenous majority and identifying himself as a member of a Koori community as well as with a pan-Aboriginal commonality (Alberts 1998, 2001). When I ask what they define as 'Aboriginal' in their music making, many Koori musicians talk about a 'natural instinct' that connects them with a fundamental indigenous oneness with the land, and that non-indigenous people lack. In this, they often incorporate ancestral elements from the desert and other remote indigenous regions. Traditionalist, mass-mediated imagery of the 'ideological landscape' discussed in Chapter 1, in this way, provides a kind of sociocultural palette from which Koori musicians can incorporate historical and spiritual depth into their own sincerely experienced music and self-knowledge, similar to how other peoples refer to a common culture of indigenes who can claim a distinctive status as original occupants (Dyck 1985; Jackson 1989; Levin 1993).

Gilroy (1993) discusses how a trans-Atlantic black vernacular musical culture is reinforced by particularistic and narrow conceptions of cultural difference and unifying notions of blackness: 'Indeed, the aura of authentic ethnicity supplies a special form of comfort in a situation where the very historicity of black experience is constantly undermined' (86). He suggests that 'this new ethnicity is all the more powerful because it corresponds to no actually existing black communities' (87). Similarly in Australia, the mobilization of universal, unifying notions of an authentic Aboriginal self-identity is often anchored in a mythologized past that, in fact, originates in contemporary urban pan-Aboriginal identity politics and articulates experiences of racism, negative stereotyping and marginalizing state policies (e.g. Beckett 1988b; Lattas 1993; Tonkinson 1998).

Back in Central Australia, such oppositional 'talking back' to non-indigenous realms and powers are not a prominent feature of music making. Few of the desert musicians perceive their music or themselves as part of a national, pan-Aboriginal rights movement, neither back in the 1980s nor today. Many of them did not even think of themselves as 'Aboriginal' when growing up. For instance, and as compared with Andy in Warrnambool, Stanley is of the same age as Andy, has mixed Aboriginal and Afghan ancestry, and grew up around Alice Springs. Describing his life history, Stanley never mentions his Aboriginal status as a factor in his musical development or life circumstances. When I ask if he ever experienced his Aboriginal identity as an issue, he thinks for a while and then says: 'I never really had one (Aboriginal identity) until I came of some sort of age ... Growing up in Alice, it was never "that way"', he says, making quotation marks in the air. 'Basically all that shit started coming in the 70s, you know, racial hatred, hating whites, the Aboriginal flag, and everybody found out that they were Aboriginal! Half of us didn't even know what it was, including myself.' On one level, this account is about a boy growing up and becoming increasingly aware of himself as a coloured man in Alice Springs in a particular era, when Aboriginal rights activism became increasingly important. It also reflects how, in contrast to Andy, Stanley and many of the musicians in Central Australia tend to talk of racism and Black activism as something external to themselves and their everyday experiences. It was not until 'all that shit started coming', meaning southern, urban people and musicians shaped by Black rights activism, that they discovered that they were 'Aboriginal', that they should hate whites and that they should stick Aboriginal flags on the wall.

Aboriginal music activities and organizations in Central Australia have unquestionably been influenced and stimulated by national Aboriginal activism. However, no Central Australian musician I have talked to has mentioned experiences of racism or activist forms of resistance as an impetus for their music making. As the forthcoming chapters will show, their music is seldom directed at a non-indigenous political realm either, even if this is how their lyrics have occasionally been interpreted (e.g. Dunbar-Hall 1997; Dunbar-Hall and Gibson 2004; Mitchell 1996: 173ff). At times, the Central Australian musicians speak disapprovingly of southern indigenous music as somewhat 'angry', which refers to the confrontational words of black activism and protest songs. I discuss in later chapters how the desert men tend to be uncomfortable with 'in-your-face' confrontational manners in general, because it appears as inappropriate in their regional Aboriginal interactional conventions. Desert musicians do not talk about coming to terms with a 'lost' Aboriginal identity either. They basically know their relatedness to Aboriginal kin and country, and many express pity for blackfellas down south who do not. They are also aware of how people down south borrow elements from the desert men's societies and typecast them in romantic and homogenous ways. They variously find this entertaining, dismiss it and use it to their advantage.

To sum up the comparison of indigenous music scenes, the desert musicians often relate to both the 'Top End mob' and 'southerners' simultaneously with sympathy and a somewhat self-assertive complacency. They tend to express a view of themselves as men grounded within specific Aboriginal kin and language groupings, and in relation to certain ancestral lands. Therefore, they do not have to 'flog their traditional gear' like the Top Enders, or chase a lost identity like the 'angry' southerners. At the same time, they recognize nationwide bonds and shared experience with other indigenous peoples, especially in the two regions discussed, but also in other places and occasionally worldwide. Indeed, their very preoccupation with marking out their distinctiveness in relation to blackfella musicians and people from the Top End and the south-east indicates how such bonds are reinforced.

Glowczewski suggests that 'to claim their Aboriginality, rather than opposing themselves as a political entity versus non-Aborigines, Aboriginal people affirm themselves first as different from and eventually opposed to their other Aboriginal neighbours' (1998: 335). She here associates Aboriginal diversity with perceptions of difference. As Harrison argues, though, one should also recognize how 'cultural similarity, or rather perceptions or attributions of similarity, can contribute to creating and maintaining ethnic oppositions and boundaries' (2002: 213). The very fact that people occupy similar regions of 'identity space' with closely shared histories and (diverse) sources of identification, he suggests, tends to engender a situation where individuals and groups struggle to differentiate themselves from others in this space. In this view, people form a sense of selves and others in ambivalent relations of interdependence and bonding as well as rivalry and competition, or 'by their felt resemblances, perhaps just as much as by felt differences' (229). Both these dynamics are involved in the evolving Central Australian music scene I have outlined in this chapter, and they are put into play in the recording studio investigated in the next chapter.

3

Music and men in the Aboriginal studio

The only southward road in and out of Alice Springs is through the Heavitree Gap, a narrow pass between steep, rugged, deep-red mountain walls through the MacDonnell Ranges. Just south of the Gap, a cluster of plain-looking houses makes up the Little Sisters Aboriginal town camp, named after the Uniting Church sisters who used to run it.[1] At the edge of the camp, right at the foot of the ranges, the first recording studio of the CAAMA, started operating in the mid-1980s.

Incorporated in 1980, CAAMA became the first indigenous media organization in Australia to be awarded a public radio licence in 1984 (Batty 2003). The CAAMA Music department emerged in response to the radio station's need for music for jingles, advertisements, educational programmes and community campaigns, for which they brought in local Aboriginal musicians. As mentioned in Chapter 2, when their music were put on air, musicians from all over the region soon turned up and wanted to be recorded and broadcast, too, in order to make their languages and communities heard. To meet these demands, the original idea for CAAMA Music was to drive out to desert communities and record musicians with a mobile recording unit, but this attempt failed. Non-indigenous Bill Davis was subsequently employed as the first Music manager with the task of setting up a recording studio in Alice Springs. When he left six years later, CAAMA Music had released seventy recordings and ran a record label and music publishing company.

In the 1990s, CAAMA expanded into a media group with four subsidiary entities: CAAMA Radio, CAAMA Music, CAAMA Productions (film and video) and CAAMA Shops. It also became a major shareholder of Imparja, the first Aboriginal-owned commercial television service in Australia in 1987. After the expansion, the CAAMA Group and Imparja employed about 100 people, with approximately 70 per cent of the CAAMA staff being indigenous. In 2001, the number of CAAMA employees had been halved, partly as a result of increased competition for funding from a growing number of indigenous media associations around the country, and partly as a result of increased demands for budgetary prudence from funding institutions.

From its beginnings in a shared house in an Aboriginal town camp, the music studio moved uptown to purpose-built premises in 1995: a pale-red, two-storey building facing Alice Springs' main street. The music studio is located at the downstairs back of the building, and at the time of my work here, CAAMA Music had four employees. In the downstairs studio, Stan was the studio manager and senior sound engineer, and Steve the assistant engineer. The music manager and the administrator sat upstairs. Stan is in his early forties, of Aboriginal Jingili and Afghan ancestry, and besides his qualifications in sound-engineering, media production and music theory, he has played bass guitar in numerous more or less famous Aboriginal bands all over the country and at times overseas since the mid-1980s. Ten years younger, Steve is of mixed Aboriginal Alyawarre, British and Belgian ancestry and began as a CAAMA trainee at the age of sixteen to seventeen. These two long-time employees have been involved in most recordings and events the studio has been involved with since the late 1980s, and for most musicians who have worked here, it is these two Aboriginal men who embody the studio, not the upstairs managers who have come and gone. A new manager arrived just as my work began: a non-indigenous woman in her fifties. Several younger indigenous women held the administrator position during my eight months at the studio.[2]

The studio area consists of a glass-walled studio office and, behind double, soundproof doors, the control room and the studio stage. The studio stage is a two-storey-high performance room with an open floor space big enough to fit an orchestra. The control room sits behind a triple-glassed acoustic window that offers a full view of the studio stage. Equipped with an automated 24-track recording unit, analogue as well as digital recording technology for recording, mixing and mastering, the control room is the technological nerve centre of the studio operations. At the time of my work here, this room was also a kind of inner sanctum for the male socio-musical life of the studio; this is where Aboriginal men gathered, often behind closed doors, sharing, comparing and evaluating their diverse experiences and skills, and their different ways of being men.

Waterman (2000) notes how the musical taste and repertoires of southern African American blues men in the 1920s and 1930s were strongly shaped by the availability of certain styles and performers on gramophone records, and by advertising directed at black communities. These factors were, in turn, shaped by racialized imagery and sociopolitical ideologies at the time, which were also reflected in the commercial profiling of black record labels, studios and music (Garofalo 1993). In contrast to Waterman's observations, the mainstream music industry has shown little interest in marketing music specifically to indigenous Australian consumers, and has only been marginal in codifying particular images of Australian indigeneity for Central Australian musicians. Regional Aboriginal music and media production sites such as CAAMA – established as part of local efforts to maintain cultural practices and values, and the broader sociopolitical aspirations for Aboriginal self-determination – have been much more important for the shaping of music styles and associated male forms in Aboriginal Central Australia.

This chapter describes and discusses how various forms of masculinity and indigeneity are negotiated in the day-to-day music work and social life of the CAAMA Music studio. I explore the particular ethos – sets of ideas, values and practices – that underpins activities and relationships in this studio, and that involves tensions between notions of 'professional' and 'blackfella way' practices and approaches to music making and life in general. As musicians and the studio employees negotiate such tensions, differently valued blackfella, whitefella, musical and masculine idioms are accentuated and articulated. In the process, a male and blackfella 'ownership' of this musical and technological space is reproduced. An account of a day at the studio can introduce the diverse lot of musicians and men who actively participate in recreating its particular ethos and ownership.

A day at the studio

It is 8.45 on a Monday morning, and a tall black man in jeans and a dirty football jersey walks in to the studio area. He is a member of the Blackshadow Band from Mt Liebig Aboriginal community, a couple of hours west of Alice Springs (Map 2). The band recently recorded an album that still has to be mixed, mastered and released, but the songs are already played on CAAMA radio, requested by regional Aboriginal listeners. This band member has come in more or less every day lately, usually first thing in the morning and looking a bit wasted. The purpose of his visits is not always clear. Some days he asks for cassette copies of the band's recordings, other times he asks for royalty money despite the album not being released yet. This morning, he wants to talk about new recordings. When it seems he will not leave until he gets a response, Steve gets Stan and the men sit down in the office.

Stan makes it clear that before they will even think of investing any studio time in the band, they have to present a set of solid, well-rehearsed songs. This is not always the case with bush musicians, who largely make music and constantly adapt their playing in everyday activities and relations in their home communities. A great deal of basic pre-production work on musical arrangements, therefore, eats up costly studio time, which should ideally be used for refining songs and musical expressions. Stan and Steve also have to spend more time 'fixing up' those recordings in the mixing process, including bringing in other musicians for overdubs.

As in most cases, when approached about recordings by bush bands, Stan tries to keep a balance in being a 'professionally' firm by emphasizing the necessity of hard, committed work to reach a standard worth recording, while not discouraging the musicians' aspirations and enthusiasm. Stan and Steve are well aware that any encouraging words from them may be taken as a confirmed recording deal with CAAMA, which can cause unwanted problems. Other musicians who want to record can, for instance, accuse the studio of bypassing them. In the rather volatile environment of regional Aboriginal community and family politics, such critique implies that the studio favours particular groupings and ignores others. Stan finishes the conversation with a non-committed 'Keep it up bros'!' and walks into the control room, closing the door behind him.

Soon thereafter, three other Aboriginal men wander in, obviously from out bush in their dusty jeans and boots. Steve again gets Stan and they all go down to the coffee shop 'for half an hour'. They return almost two hours later. The men are members of the Pukatja Band from Pitjantjatjara territory, a day's journey to the south. Stan recorded them in the early 1990s when their tight rock beat and edgy lyrics made quite an impact on the regional Aboriginal music scene (Pukatja Band 1992). The band has not been seen much in recent years and their return to the studio to discuss recordings is welcomed by the studio men.

There are no recordings booked in for the day. The days or weeks when recording session are in progress, the feel of the studio space is obviously different. Bush musicians usually bring, or attract, a whole entourage of Aboriginal people who continually move in and out of the building, and in and out of the control room and the studio stage, causing the sound of loud drums and wailing guitars to spill out and affecting the sound recorded. There are Aboriginal languages spoken, laughter and shouting, and kids picking pieces of equipment apart and climbing over people and instruments. All the while, the phones keep ringing and voices keep trying to make themselves heard over the intercom system. Community people also bring with them the distinct bush aromas of smoky fire wood, dusty sweat and the strong smell of kangaroo meat and blood. Recording sessions with musicians from town or elsewhere in the country are usually less chaotic happenings, but friends and fellow musicians, predominantly men, frequently drop in on such recordings, too, to follow and comment on the work from the control room, and at times stepping in for instrumental or vocal work.

When the studio men are gone this morning, I am interrupted only by the normal stream of phone calls from people all over Australia who want to talk recordings, sound equipment and music projects. A non-indigenous musician in Adelaide, for instance, is looking for an Aboriginal musician for a self-produced album. What he has in mind, and why he calls CAAMA in Central Australia, is a 'real Aboriginal' who plays the didjeridu and sing traditional songs. This would 'ground' his 'modern' Australian compositions, he tells me.[3]

Several Aboriginal men also come by in person. Rod, a cousin of Steve, and the lead singer in their rock band, Jagit, wants to know if they are rehearsing tonight. Warren, a well-known Aboriginal country musician and CAAMA radio broadcaster, comes by a few times, keen to see Stan. Country-bluegrass musician Lyndon turns up briefly, as he does more or less daily. He is eager to record his first solo album but gets a let's-see-what-happens response from Stan and the music manager because he lacks project funding. A non-indigenous woman working for CAAMA Shops comes looking for Stan a couple of times, increasingly looking irritated when he is not back. An event organizer wants a particular song for the opening of an Aboriginal exhibition and Stan was going to copy it to a CD. In the end, the shop woman sticks a note on the office door, urging him to get the CD for her. When the men are back, Stan looks at the note, leaves it on the door, and he and Steve take off to their respective homes for lunch.

After lunch, Stan walks straight into the control room and closes the doors, making a new attempt to finish the mixing of the Blackshadow recordings. Steve is fixing an amplifier in the studio. The shop woman returns, agitated. I point at the control room door and she hesitates, then knocks and opens the doors and in a friendly voice asks Stan for the song. He does not answer or look at her. He does not turn down the volume of the track playing and keeps adjusting levels on the sound-desk. She repeats the question. In the end, Stan makes a kind of hum and she leaves, frustrated. A moment later, Stan barges into the office, rummaging for the CD on desks, in filing cabinets and cardboard boxes. He takes off upstairs, thinking that he put the CD on the manager's desk. He soon returns with a spring in his step and a CD in his hand, closes the office door and connects the CD-player to a couple of loudspeakers. 'You've got to hear this!' he says and turns up the volume. Loud, thumping rock music hits the glass walls of the office, which attracts Steve to join us. It is a live recording of a Warumpi Band performance where Stan played bass. He has told me that this gig was special and he now embroiders the music with one-liners about off- and on-stage events at the time. Steve chuckles and says that he cannot wait to be part of it all when their band gets its act together.

The men return to their tasks, and Frank, a solidly built and dark-skinned Pitjantjatjara musician, turns up. He puts a hand on my back as a greeting

PHOTO 4 *Stan and Frank jamming.*

and asks for 'the old man', meaning Stan. I nod towards the control room but Frank proceeds to flick about things on the office desk, asking if there is any mail for him. He looks somehow 'cleaned up' to me, and I assume that he is on his way to Melbourne, where he is mostly performing at inner-city clubs nowadays. When he is in Alice Springs, he is usually drawn into drinking and family conflicts and can look rather worn out. I comment on his good looks and ask if he wants a lift to the airport. 'Ha. Ha. *Very* funny!' he retorts, as if I was mocking him. He then picks up the phone, sits himself down with his feet on a desk and calls his manager in Melbourne.

The music studio is named after Frank's late father, the eminent regional, country music star Isaac Yamma, introduced in Chapter 2. Frank has been around CAAMA since its early days and has recorded four albums here (Ulpanyali Band 1991; Yamma 1997, 1999, 2006). When in Alice Springs, Frank has no fixed address and the studio seems to be one of his few permanent points, and he tends to treat it as his personal 'office'. When he is elsewhere in Australia and at times overseas, he frequently calls the studio, for no particular reason. It is, thus, a reference point also in his wider geographical and musical movements. His chatty calls about nothing can at times wear all of us out, while we recognize that he just wants to connect with 'home': the musical and blackfella place where he belongs and started out, and where he, therefore, seeks affirmation. It is also the source for the making of his unique Aboriginal 'desert song man' world music profile when out of Central Australia.

Frank hangs up on his manager when Stan comes out for a cigarette break. They exchange a few words and Stan takes off to pick up some papers for Frank. Meanwhile, Frank takes over the control room and puts on a CD from one of his live performances. Even with the soundproof doors closed we can hear him listening to himself on top volume. When Stan is back, Frank leaves with a wide grin and a 'see ya' later', adding 'in a couple of months!' from down the corridor. I now remember that he is going into prison today, which explains his smart looks and response to my offer to take him to the airport.

Warren returns, finally able to catch Stan. His latest recordings, which Stan sound-engineered and mixed, have come back from mastering in Melbourne. We gather in the control room and put it on. The sound is much clearer than Warren expected and he is rapt, grinning widely. Stan nods with a pleased smile over Warren's excitement. The high quality of the mastered sound is no doubt also recognition of the quality of Stan's sound recording.

Afterward, we walk out for a smoke and talk at the back door, and two Aboriginal men turn up from the backyard. One is Clifford Brown, a dark-skinned Warlpiri man in his early thirties and a lead guitarist of the Rising Wind Band from Yuendumu community (Map 2). The other man is older and his steps are somewhat unsteady, but he does not seem to be drunk, more like recovering. I realize later who he is: an influential Yuendumu musician back in the 1970s who has ended up 'living on the grog' in town. Clifford's wife has just given birth to their third child at the hospital and he came by last week to see if he could record while in town. In a few words and hand gestures he tells Stan that he has three songs with him now. Stan looks at them as if judging if they are up to it. If he thought they were drunk, he would refuse point-blank. 'Play it to me bros'!' he says and Clifford sits down with an acoustic guitar in the studio. The first song is a sweet-sounding ballad in Warlpiri language about the 1928 Coniston killings, when a large number of Aboriginal people were shot, a traumatic event that still evokes strong emotions in Central Australian Aboriginal communities. The second song is faster, rockier and in English about missing family and having to get away from a troubled situation. The third tune, co-written with the older man, is called 'Motorcycle Mama' and reminiscent of rocked-up blues songs of the 1960s, paying homage to musicians such as John Lee Hooker and Muddy Waters.[4]

With an hour left of the working day, Stan connects microphones at the drums and plugs in guitars and amplifiers. He sees potential in Clifford's two songs. Ten minutes later they start recording with Clifford on acoustic guitar, the old man on drums and Warren on bass. After a few takes of the 'Getaway' song, Stan stops the session, suggests that they pick up the tempo, gently asks the shaky old man to hand over the drum sticks to Warren, and Stan takes over the bass himself. They work the song in a quicker pace and tighter beat but Stan is still not happy with the drums, where Warren keeps slipping back into a kind of country beat.

The back door is open, and Damien, one of two Aboriginal members of the heavy metal rock band NoKTuRNL, walks in. This Alice Springs act has 'stayed clear of CAAMA', as their non-indigenous manager has put it to me, and they have instead signed up with a subsidiary of a music industry multinational (NoKTuRNL 2003). Damien works in a music shop and is here to pick up equipment from a gig on Friday night that Stan sound-engineered. Soon thereafter, local non-indigenous musician Leon who played at that gig turns up through the back door. He is mostly known for his modern troubadour-style albums, but over the years he has also recorded heavy rock with Stan in this studio for a self-financed album. He wants to check if they can work tonight. Stan replies by asking if Leon can play the bass and hands it over, then points Damien to the drums. They start Clifford's songs from the top, with Stan clapping the quicker tempo. He then returns to the control room and they record the two songs in one take. They now have a basic structure to work from. 'Let's do them on Thursday,' Stan tells Clifford before the men lock up and leave. In a few hours, Stan is back, recording with Leon and an Aboriginal drummer in a high-spirited session that lasts till midnight.

The studio blackfella sociality

As this account shows, most of the people who frequent the studio on any one day are male and indigenous from different backgrounds, and they come here for many different musical and social reasons. In her ethnography of Downtown Studios in Johannesburg, South Africa, Meintjes talks of how the quality of that studio space 'can come to be constructed and experienced as magical and as a fetish by music-makers who work within it' (2003: 73). By 'magical', she means remote from the ordinary, and by understanding it as 'a fetish', she thinks of the studio as having a creative force or 'spirit' lodged within it that those who earn access to it can tap into to produce 'compelling art' (73). Many Aboriginal men and musicians that come by the CAAMA studio probably experience this studio less as a space where compelling art is produced and more as a well-equipped site for recording music. This indeed makes it remote from their ordinary circumstances, where well-maintained instruments and equipment are rare. For community musicians who spend time in Alice Springs and for town musicians without a day job, any reason to come into this studio is, however, good enough. The visits are in themselves the purpose, giving workless days a sense of direction. For men such as Frank and Warren, the studio has, furthermore, become a kind of extended home over many years.

Taking a closer look at the people who co-create the studio sociality, they can be categorized in three distinct, albeit internally heterogeneous and overlapping groupings based on where they live and their life orientations, which informs (but does not determine) different approaches to music making and valued forms of manhood: bush or community musicians, town musicians and out-of-town musicians. The terms of categorizing are mine, but they largely concur with the distinctions made by the studio men and regional musicians.

The Blackshadow guitarist, the Pukatja Band and Clifford Brown belong to the bush or community musician grouping. They have been brought up and continue to practice and perform their music in remote Aboriginal community settings, where many aspects of day-to-day life are shaped by modified ancestral and kin-based norms and values. Chapter 5 discusses how their music making is intimately connected to crafting their sense of manhood in such localized normative settings. Bush musicians often speak several Aboriginal languages while their skills in Standard English vary, and most of them have been 'through Law', which means they are traditionally initiated. The degree to which they continue to participate in ceremonial activities varies. Many bush musicians play occasional gigs in regional non-indigenous towns and perform at regional Aboriginal festivals, and a few have performed in other Australian states.

Town musicians include men who live around Alice Springs, and who have lived in urban settings for most of their lives. They may turn up at the studio more often but are fewer in number than the bush musicians. Lyndon, Rod, Steve, Stan and the member of NoKTuRNL are in this grouping. They speak mainly or only English, not all of them have been through Law, and their knowledge of, and interest in, traditional Aboriginal matters varies widely. Most of them are, however, aware of their position and associated rights and responsibilities as men of particular Aboriginal kin networks and are acquainted with their ancestral lands. Town musicians perform mainly in Alice Springs, at times in other regional townships, and occasionally in desert communities. Some of them have performed extensively interstate and occasionally overseas, and they tend to aspire to musical and male recognition in a professional realm to a higher degree than bush musicians.

Frank and Warren are simultaneously town and community musicians and can illustrate what regional Aboriginal musicians have to negotiate in order to achieve national recognition and a professional career, Frank as a world music artist and Warren as a country musician. They grew up and are still firmly connected to their desert community socialities, traditions and commitments, and both are initiated men and speak local languages. They also live in Alice Springs, and Frank interstate, for extended periods. Both have non-indigenous managers, they frequently perform out of Central Australia and both have performed overseas. Warren still plays at venues around Alice Springs while Frank's fan base mainly expands in the south-east (Yamma 2010, 2014).

Around the studio, Frank and Warren tend to downplay their increasing national fame in accordance with regional Aboriginal norms of not appearing self-important (as I return to later). Other local musicians and the studio men no doubt recognize that the two men have moved into a higher league of music making, but in public, local men continue to treat them as fellow local music makers. For instance, they expect them to fill in as instrumentalists or back-up singers if needed on any recording they walk in on, and they usually do. Hence, by appearing both generous and not self-important, they earn continued respect around the studio. Both of them also know that because of their increased fame, people will be looking for any sign of big-headedness on their part. If they 'slip', it would soon be amplified, which would damage their relationships and male standing in regional Aboriginal realms.

Out-of-town musicians are basically all other musicians, who come from outside the Central Australian region to record at the studio and then leave again. They may come from urban settings in the south-east or bush communities in the Top End, the Torres Strait Islands, and elsewhere. Some have relatives in Central Australia, a few have long-time work relations with CAAMA, and most of them are, to some extent, professionally established. In contrast to the often impromptu and loosely organized recordings of town and bush musicians, projects with out-of-town musicians tend to be more formalized sessions, as in following a time-plan based on a funded budget.

As musicians and men of these different musical, professional and indigenous backgrounds and aspirations work in the studio, they co-create its particular male and indigenous character. To see this studio in Meintjes' terms as a 'fetish' may be to exoticize the Aboriginal musicians' intentions and practices. It is nevertheless characterized by a particular 'spirit', a dynamic ethos, as in distinctive sets of values and ideas that guide the organization of work and relations. A key tension in the reproduction of this studio ethos is that between 'professional ways' and certain valued male 'blackfella ways' of doing things, which illuminates the process in which men are making and remaking themselves in the studio setting.

The studio ethos – 'Slack and Black'

As indicated on the day revisited, the organization of practices around the music studio is guided by fairly informal and non-conformist attitudes to formal work structures and authority. Studio manager Stan does not prioritize workplace rules or related paperwork and he adopts a relaxed attitude to instructions from management on points of order for employees. He considers many such matters obstacles to getting on with what he thinks the studio is fundamentally here for: producing good music and developing Aboriginal musical skills and careers. Steve may accommodate the management's wishes to a greater extent, but he, too, assumes a relatively relaxed approach to structures of authority within the building.

Both men are usually found in the building during formal work hours, but depending on the work at hand, Stan may work until midnight seven days a week during recording projects. When mixing recordings he may come and go during the day and instead work late at night when nobody disturbs him. He is, therefore, not always around when people come looking for him, which reinforces a perception of the studio as a somewhat inefficient and undisciplined work site among people within and from outside CAAMA. Stan and Steve also tend to treat booked-in recordings or plans for upcoming studio work more as possibilities than realities and are often reluctant to provide details on times and the order of proceedings when asked. This causes further frustration among people in and from outside CAAMA who are involved in particular projects, or want to be, and adds force to views of the studio as poorly organized. Stan, moreover, thrives on jobs that just happen. When the right combination of musicians turn up without notice and keen to record, he is likely to say 'let's do it!' and can soon be seen setting up the studio, as he did with Clifford. Other tasks are then abandoned, which can annoy people who expect these jobs to be finished at a certain time.

Many aspects of this 'slack' approach and unpredictable organization of activities has a legacy in the history of the studio. Most of the stories that the men around the studio share and enjoy about past happenings reinforce a laid-back and non-conforming approach to management directives or outside expectations. Daily notes in the decade worth of studio diaries that I combed through for details of archived recordings confirm this attitude, too. Non-conformity to formal work structures and wider social expectations is recognized in popular music culture worldwide, and is an aspect of studio practices and ideologies elsewhere.[5] In this particular studio, however, such features are frequently understood, explained and valued as specifically blackfella, male-to-male characteristics, as opposed to how whitefellas do things and how men are expected to behave when women are present. That is, in contrast to whitefellas, blackfellas in general are perceived to operate in loose, flexible and negotiable ways, adapting to situations and individuals rather than complying with formal workplace rules. The latter is essentially seen by the men as negatively valued whitefella innovations. As discussed in the next chapter, men around the studio also value an absence of restrictions associated with appropriate behaviour between men and women.

The particular blackfella meanings assigned to the 'slack' quality of the studio ethos are reinforced by the circumstances of the musicians around this studio. Only a few of these men have a history of being full-time employees who organize their time or movements around standard working weeks or hours. Money and material things like instruments and vehicles also tend to circulate within indigenous socialities according to mutual rights and obligations, and the musicians commonly adjust their musical activities to the resources they can access at the moment. The men tend to move around, too, and the timing and directions for their mobility are often unpredictable because it is decided by opportunities in the form of transport, money and other people's actions.

All of this means that intentions and actual outcomes can diverge greatly in the socio-musical setting of the studio. How and when planned events like recordings take place, and which people end up being involved, are often uncertain until in progress. Extra-musical circumstances frequently change during recording projects, too, causing musicians to leave or not return after a break in the work. Recordings in themselves, in this way, become fairly unpredictable processes and require a capacity for improvisation and flexibility from everyone involved. It is a widespread, taken-for-granted view among the men that blackfellas possess such a capacity to a higher degree than most whitefellas, because of the different ways their respective life worlds operate. Such perceptions are also frequently confirmed around the studio; just like the described shop woman, it is, in the main, non-indigenous people who become tense about the unpredictability and 'slackness' around the studio, while Aboriginal people tend to go with whatever happens.

As on the day described, the studio is constantly contacted by people who push a range of ideas about musical projects. At any one time, Stan and Steve, thus, juggle a number of eventualities and possibilities. Only a few will ever be realized, and usually in forms other than the original idea. In productivity terms, it may look reassuring to present such eventualities as firm plans to funding agencies, the CAAMA board and stakeholders in the media industry. At the same time, formalized plans create expectations, questions and demands. When things do not happen as planned on paper, or not at all, people end up disappointed or frustrated and may want somebody to blame, which partly explains the studio men's reluctance to take responsibility for such 'plans' by supplying details for events.

The impromptu approach to studio activities is also linked to the musicians' and studio men's conceptions of artistic creativity, ways of making music and living in general.

Blackfella creativity and skills

The primary creative motivation for most Aboriginal music makers I have met in Central Australia is the social rewards. However, some of the more committed musicians, such as Warren, Clifford, Frank and Stan, tend to put personal aspects first. They express ideas about their creativity as a special force that drives their passion for the crafting of musical expressions. They talk of the personal satisfaction they achieve from developing instrumental skills that can carry and expand those expressions. A town musician who has toured the interstate told me that one of the attractions for him to pursue a musical career was the creative 'attitudes and feelings' he encountered in many musical scenes (and that he also associated with a liberal attitude to drugs). 'They're a bit up-mind of the average person in the street, so to say, because there are a lot of closed minds out there,' he explained. When I asked what he meant by 'closed minds', he made it clear that he associated it with formalized and highly structured work regimes, which he thought stifle creativity and inspiration.

Similar ideas about creative powers are common in various intellectual traditions in the world (Negus and Pickering 2002), and in Aboriginal music realms they are often invested with particular blackfella values and meanings. While many indigenous musicians in the more urbanized south-east insist that their creativity is sourced from a particular Aboriginal natural talent ('it's in our genes') or spiritual instinct for music, the desert musicians are more likely to describe creativity in pragmatic and experiential terms. They typically explain their own talents by describing how they grew up surrounded by people who sing and dance as part of their social and ceremonial life. They similarly understand their particular kind of laid-back attitude to music practices to derive from a familiarity with music as part of their daily activities and soundscape, instead of learning and listening to music as a distinct and formalized activity.

At times, the men perceive their blackfella musicality as part of a wider, even global black musical expressive culture. For instance, when asked to compare his experience of playing with blackfellas and whitefellas, one town musician found that 'most Aboriginal artists, or any black artist, have a way of pushing the time out a little bit further, so that you become a little bit more relaxed, a little bit more, you know, hands on your hip within the same time frame'. He contrasted this with a non-indigenous guitarist we both knew:

'He plays like he's got really tight pants on ... tightening up in a way that it becomes quirky ... like tight, pink trousers, you know, that tight it's pulling your knees together.'

Wong quotes an African American jazz musician talking in similar terms when observing how non-African American musicians are 'technically good but "stiff"' (2000: 71). The musician goes on to demonstrate, by playing an instrument, how an African American musician can play a musical phrase 'with a looser, more fluid sense of rhythm and even timbre' (71). Wade similarly quotes black musicians in Colombia describing white musicians as 'very lifeless' and 'like sticks' (Wade 2002: 101). Akin to many Aboriginal musicians in Central Australia, these black musicians do not so much criticize white musicians, or define themselves in relation to those musicians, as they are able to recognize the absence and presence of black features of music-making. When trying to pin down exactly what those blackfella features are, the Aboriginal musicians usually describe or mimic the no-frills, direct and live quality of desert music-making that I called 'rustic' in Chapter 2. They contrast this to the more regimented and 'square' ways in which whitefellas tend to play. As one musician said, 'Whitefellas can do it, too, but most don't. And there are square blackfellas around, too.' To him, this has to do with the way in which most whitefellas, and some more 'educated' blackfellas, learn music and other things 'from paper'; they play according to notation and formal musical structures, while most blackfellas he knows learn music through listening, looking and picking it up in the process of playing with others.

As the reference to 'tight pink pants' indicates, the Aboriginal musicians also tend to associate whitefella and blackfella ways of playing music with different masculine styles. Another Aboriginal musician was more straightforward when arguing against keeping a highly experienced non-indigenous drummer in their band: 'He doesn't play black enough! He's got no fucking balls!' When I asked what he meant, he described the drummer's habit of wanting to discuss and agree on their playing in their band, and how he tried to engage the Aboriginal band members in friendly small talk and get to know them. The Aboriginal men tend to view this kind of continuous verbal commentary and the need for confirmation as female characteristics. In men's conduct, they tend to interpret such talk as insecurity, which is seen as somewhat annoying or 'uptight', and they usually respond to it with silence.

Among themselves, the Aboriginal musicians seldom discuss or decide verbally how to play a tune. They reach consensus in the flow of playing and through reading each other's hand, body and facial gestures. Occasional suggestions or questions are put in a couple of rather crude words. The laid-back go-with-the-flow approach to music making is, in this way, associated with a more powerful and desirable black masculine attitude among the Aboriginal musicians. For the 'no-balls' non-indigenous drummer, as he told me later, the Aboriginal musicians' 'unfocused' and unpredictable ways of playing and doing things, their lack of 'social skills' (i.e. small talk) and nobody seemingly willing to make decisions, were just 'too loose to work, too frustrating'.

The valued laid-back and loose 'blackfella way' of making music does not go unchallenged, however. It has to be negotiated in relation to another dominant aspect of the studio ethos: demands for a more professional attitude and effort that is required to produce recordings that meet the standards by which the CAAMA Music as a producer of 'Aboriginal Music for the World' is judged in a larger music industry and market.[6] Although the practice of professional standards may not be the main priority for all musicians in the Aboriginal studio, its 'spirit' of professionalism is nonetheless an important reason for their studio visits. Like for the Blackshadow and Pukatja Band members, this is a place where they can connect with a professional music industry by producing technologically more sophisticated and commercially released recordings. In the studio, they may become part of other people's recordings, meet other music people, be updated on upcoming musical events, and keep up with what fellow musicians are doing. All this strengthens their position in their everyday music scene of backyards, town camps or remote communities.

Also, to make it one's business to visit this studio is part of distinguishing oneself as a serious musician with regard to the men's self-perception and self-confidence, which is associated with their musician and male standing in their everyday Aboriginal settings. When in bush communities, I witnessed many occasions when men told fellow musicians and men in a somewhat important manner that they were going to Alice Springs to 'see CAAMA'. It implied that they had an appointment or recording deal with the studio. When I queried these men on the side, none of them had been in contact with the studio recently. Most of them did not have enough songs to record an album. Some did not even particularly wish to record with CAAMA. These types of 'bonding' references to the studio are thus principally a way to create an image of their musician and male position on an elevated, more professional level of recognition, compared to other music makers in their home settings.

In negotiating the 'blackfella way' and professional approaches to music production in the studio, Aboriginal men also put into play different norms for accruing male respect and worth, as seen in the following recording session.

Bush men playing the studio

It is the second day of recordings with the Haasts Bluff country-gospel band. Steve is trying to make an old man out in the studio synchronize his singing to the music coming through his headphones. The man is simply called 'the

Pastor' and is a small, weather-beaten, dark-skinned man who never takes off his black, well-used Akubra hat. He keeps getting distracted by the music in his ears and fails to sing when he is supposed to. Steve stops the tape for the sixth time on this particular verse. He says nothing, but his body posture signals that he would rather be somewhere else.

About twenty Aboriginal men are cramped together on the seats behind Steve in the control room. One man is fast asleep and snoring. The others keep gesticulating and instructing the Pastor, forgetting that they cannot be heard through the soundproof glass. The band comes from the Pintupi-Luritja community Ikuntji, close to the dramatic Haasts Bluff mountain peak, some three hours west of Alice Springs (Map 2). Formed seven years ago, the band has included a succession of different members. In this version it is a five-piece set, but twelve different men take turns singing and playing on the recording, the youngest in his mid-twenties and the oldest, the Pastor, in his sixties. The rest of the men in the control room are musicians from other desert communities who happen to be in town, heard about the recordings and want to check out what 'the competition' is up to. One man is dressed in a hospital robe and has a disconnected nose-tube taped to his face. He has obviously walked off from a hospital ward to be part of this happening.

The Pastor gets his singing wrong again. The men in the control room exclaim a unison 'aahhh!' They laugh and shake their heads and direct instructions in Luritja language at him that he cannot hear. The atmosphere is generous and supportive. Every man is allowed to make mistakes and others are keen to help him to get it right, without appearing superior. When I took some band members to the kitchen for a cup of tea earlier, they told me how exhausted they were last night after the first day of recording. All the men have played music since their childhood or teenage years in Aboriginal bush settings and some have recorded out there. This is their first professional studio experience, which means it is the first time they have been asked to break up their songs and play them individually, and to do several re-takes of bits and pieces separate from a group playing. Ian, who played with the Warumpi Band in its earliest days, laughs and shakes his head: 'We're not used to doing music this way, cut'em up!' he says. 'We finish them songs!' agrees Douglas, an original band member. John, former lead singer in a Papunya rock band, is mostly impressed by the sound they can produce when playing with 'proper' equipment.

Back on the studio floor, the Pastor finally cuts the song, almost right, and Stan now takes over at the sound-desk. In contrast to Steve, who tends to limit his role to that of a recording technician, Stan often acts as a producer and professional coach, actively advising and instructing musicians to make them expand their musical expressions. He now frequently stops the tape and makes the men take songs from the start several times because the drummer slows down, the bass player makes a slight mistake and the singers get their words wrong. A few band members correct their mistakes in the next take, but most, and especially the Pastor, show no signs of having heard Stan. Without words, they keep doing their own thing.

By lunchtime, they have recorded four songs. The men gather outside the back door. Stan explains to them how important it is that they all keep the same and right tempo throughout a song. They nod, chuckle at their own flaws and comment in Luritja and with hand gestures. The Pastor seems more interested in the good condition of the four-wheel drive vehicles in the backyard. Stan asks how they plan to make this recording 'work for them'. The men look nonplussed at each other and make hand gestures to indicate to Stan that they do not follow his English. 'Are you going to sell some?' Stan rephrases his question. 'CAAMA, you mean?' Ian asks. 'Well, that may be one option, but ...', Stan replies. Like many community bands, the men take for granted that if they record with CAAMA their CD will soon be on the CAAMA Shop shelf. Also, to record an album is often in itself the end goal for many of these bands, since it achieves the desired elevation of their status as men and musician in their home community and the larger Aboriginal desert region.

Stan proceeds to tell them that when the recordings are done he will make them a cassette copy each to take home. He will send them a CD when it is mixed in a week or two. 'You then *own* this music. This sound is yours, to *do* something with,' he emphasizes. The men watch him, waiting for his advice on what to do with it. Stan hesitates. He then says that he thinks they should sell it. Through CAAMA, maybe, but better still, they could sell copies for cash when travelling around and performing among their own mob. More importantly, he advises, they should sit down and really listen to their own playing and arrangements and think about how they could do it better when they make new songs. When they have a bunch of new songs, they can come back to the studio and 'this time we'll do it properly', he holds out to them. He describes how he will put them on a click-track to structure each song from start to finish, and how they will work on getting every single note right to produce an album that will 'cut it anywhere'. The men nod at each other, excited at the prospect of producing an album of a real professional standard.

When Steve and Stan work on the recordings a week later they like what they hear. 'It has a full sound from the start. They know what they are doing,' Stan nods approvingly. Steve suggests that CAAMA should release it as a 'community release', which is a cassette version aimed for the Aboriginal community market and for which the studio puts in less mixing time than for a national CD release. Stan disagrees. The recordings require much more work to reach the standard he sees fit for any CAAMA release. If it had been a CAAMA Music project, he would have worked plenty more with the vocals and arrangements, and he thinks that the men need more professional coaching of their instrumental skills. However, the recording is funded by a community health project and the three days paid for do not allow for any of that. 'And that oldfella …'. Stan chuckles and shakes his head, realizing that the authority that the Pastor commanded in the group probably would not allow for much outside interference in their music anyway.[7]

Accruing blackfella male respect

Many bush musicians who work in the studio, like the Haasts Bluff band members, tell me that they greatly appreciate working with a 'professional' who takes them and their music making seriously. At the same time, the studio experience tends to leave them feeling somewhat inadequate as the studio men always ask them to play their songs differently, and in many takes. Their musical skills are, therefore, constantly questioned. In the studio, Stan and Steve are, moreover, on their home turf, possessing expertise and authority that make them the superior, and the bush musicians the somewhat inferior, men. This is not a comfortable position for any of these men. They are used to command certain respect as musicians and initiated men within Aboriginal regimes of accruing male status in their communities and the wider region. Douglas, for example, is a respected, knowledgeable senior man who guides other men in ritual matters. The Pastor commands a high degree of respect also because of his senior age and religious standing. Aspects of these forms of social and male worth and authority are neutralized, or reorganized, in the studio setting, where professional regimes of gaining male status are the more dominant.

Stan clearly demonstrated the professional studio regimes when he intentionally pursued the issue of what the men planned to do with their recordings. He tells me he wanted them to understand that studio processes and the recorded product are separate matters. More importantly, he wanted them to reflect on their studio work as a phase in their professional development as musicians. By making them imagine themselves at a more advanced stage of music making, he wanted to inspire them to want to move in that direction, and aspire to achieve increased male respect and worth through recognition in a professional realm.

In response to such attempts, bush musicians may use their particular forms of male and Aboriginal knowledge in order to manipulate their inferior male and musician position in the studio. For instance, they may make use of imagery of bush people as less 'sophisticated' to evade the superior, expert position of the studio engineers. Like most bush musicians, the Haasts Bluff men do not argue against Stan's directives on how to change ways of playing even when they disagree. They instead tend to adopt an almost childlike, jovial demeanour as if they are too naive to understand technological processes, and then keep doing their thing. They may also act as if they do not understand the studio men's Standard English, while persisting with their preferred way of playing. They commonly discuss the studio proceedings with each other in their local language, well aware that the studio men cannot understand them. We saw all these 'strategies' in action in the Haasts Bluff band recordings. Meeting the same musicians in other settings, they may speak fluent English, and I have found some of them busy recording and editing their music on computers in their home community, as well as sound-engineering stage performances. In this, they show plenty of knowledge about recording processes and sound technology.

The studio men do, however, need to accommodate certain regional Aboriginal norms for interpersonal male respect when working with bush musicians. For instance, Stan mainly directs frank critique and advice at musicians younger or about his age. He rarely directs Aboriginal men older than himself, such as the Pastor, regardless of how poorly he thinks they perform. To do so would be highly inappropriate in regional norms where Aboriginal men are to show deference for, and not openly criticize or contradict, men older than themselves. If the studio men were to breach such norms, ongoing work and the studio's reputation could be jeopardized because they would be seen as ignorant and not worthy of respect among regional Aboriginal men.

Certain 'blackfella way' sensitivities are, in these ways, required between the studio workers and musicians, and between recording musicians, and can be equally or more important than the professional dimensions or technological expertise. At times Steve and Stan have to tread a fine line between showing respect for traditional norms and producing recordings that meet reasonable technological and professional standards, and bush musicians sometimes complained to me that they experience a lack of respect (for their male status) around the studio. However, most of them tend to accept, or at least tolerate, the unequal studio relationships as site-specific and, as we saw in the described recordings, they variably accommodate, are inspired by and manipulate the situation in order to maintain their sense of male worth.

As the men work with each other in the studio, they not only negotiate different forms of musical and technological knowledge and experiences, and different regimes for gaining male worth and respect. Each encounter is also an occasion for mutual recognition and partial borrowings of their different as well as shared male, blackfella and musical forms of identifying. The studio ethos, in these ways, constitutes a mediating dynamic in which the men rework and assert their individual sense of self. At the same time, they reproduce a distinctive blackfella and male 'ownership' of this socio-musical space. Aspects of this ownership are anchored in the regional Aboriginal topography that the studio is part of, as introduced in Chapter 1. Other aspects have a legacy in the history of CAAMA, which was formed to represent and empower Aboriginal people in Central Australia. It is also constantly reformulated through the transfer and reworking of ideas of distinct, actual and imagined 'blackfella ways' of operating. The next chapter explores how the blackfella and male ownership of the studio emerges, too, from the negotiation of competing notions of manhood and indigeneity associated with musical forms of identification, and in relation to women.

4

Men making the studio

The comfortable sound of gentle acoustic guitar-picking of a slow country love song fills the dimly lit control room. Stan carefully adjusts the knobs on the sound-desk to shape the vocals. The singer in the studio is Lyndon: short, dark-haired and dressed in work boots, jeans and a ripped, chequered flannel shirt. Over the last few months, he has recorded his debut solo album – a mix of his original bluegrass, country ballads and country rock songs. This is one of the final vocal overdubs. Or so we think. Lyndon will, in fact, insist on doing all the vocals again some weeks later. Today, however, he feels right on target.

Stan stops the tape. 'You sing like a fucking cow, fuck you!' he says quietly and matter-of-factly into the desk microphone. Hearing him through his headphones, Lyndon grins and turns his backside to the window, showing with a gesture where Stan can 'fuck' him. 'Cunt!' he responds with a smile and thrusts a rude finger at the control-room window. He then turns the finger in a circling gesture. Stan nods, backs up the tape and pushes the blinking red 'record' button. The sound of soft guitars again fills the control room. Lyndon digs his hands deep down in his pockets, waits for the intro to finish and starts to sing, the lyrics urging his woman to make a new start with him.

The control room door opens a tiny fraction and Warren peeps in, careful not to interrupt recordings before entering. Tall, dark-skinned and dressed in a red sports jumper and jeans, and a dirty baseball cap over black hair that hangs loose down the back of his neck, he sits down with a big smile beside me on the sofa along the back wall. He looks at me with an air of amazement, slowly shaking his head. He is obviously bursting to tell me something but waits for me to ask what is up. When I do, he says that he just cannot believe that 'this is all happening to me'. His latest album has climbed to the top of the Australian independent country music charts and he keeps shaking his head with a wondrous smile, looking humbled by his increasing success which he often talks of as 'good fortune'. He goes quiet and listens to Lyndon. He asks if the harmonies are done yet. We shake our heads. Warren smiles and makes a tongue-smacking 'that's-what-l-thought' gesture. He picks up an acoustic guitar on the sofa and casually strums a few chords and finger-picking lines to Lyndon's love song. It adds a distinct 'sweet' Warren H. Williams-feel that is considerably different from the more edgy, rustic bluegrass that characterizes Lyndon's style of playing (Reid 2002). Warren casually asks where Lyndon is actually planning to sell this album. 'To his Port Augusta mob?' he chuckles jokingly, implying that Lyndon's debut album is destined for an audience of friends and relatives in the small town where he grew up. 'Well, we're thinking of flogging it in Tamworth,' Stan says, his focus never leaving Lyndon out in the studio. Warren waits but Stan does not elaborate on this rather surprising statement.

Tamworth is Australia's country music capital, 500 km north-west of Sydney. Every January the small rural town is inundated with about 50,000 country music fans, bush poets, line dancers, rodeo riders and urban as well as rural cowboys for the ten-day-long Tamworth Country Music Festival. The event attracts Australia's country music elite and upcoming artists who perform round the clock in more than 100 venues. The cream of the country music industry can be seen here, and the annual Australian country music awards are presented at the festival. When the festival started back in the 1970s, indigenous musicians were often met by racist attitudes and were not invited to perform in festival venues. Nowadays, the Tamworth Festival usually includes dedicated Aboriginal concerts.

At times, CAAMA Music sends employees and artists to promote the label at indigenous music festivals in other parts of the country, but the Tamworth Festival has not been on their agenda. It is hard for an organization serving Aboriginal people to justify the cost of sending people to a mainly non-indigenous spectacle. However, with Warren's growing fame and an increased nationwide interest in Aboriginal country music, there has been some talk of maybe sending the studio men, a few musicians and a salesperson next time around.[1] Launching Lyndon's CD at the festival could be a focal point for CAAMA's presence. It would obviously be a scoop for Lyndon to have a first album launched at this pivotal country music event, a privilege that CAAMA has not as yet offered Warren. At this time, however, nothing has been decided. Stan's tentative 'thinking of' indicates that it is one of the many possibilities that circulate around the studio all the time.[2]

When Lyndon notices Warren in the control room, he straightens his back slightly and sings in a more focused way. After finishing the song, he comes into the control room. Warren has already left to start his shift at CAAMA Radio. Lyndon asks if it sounded alright. Stan hums vaguely, reluctant to settle for 'alright' if Lyndon can do better. Next, Lyndon asks casually what Warren had to say. Stan shrugs his shoulders and concentrates on forwarding the tapes to the next song. I make a similar non-committed gesture. Stan then stands up, looks at the clock on the wall, declares 'one o'clock sharp!' and leaves through the studio back door. Swearing, Lyndon watches him through the control room window. The fact that Stan does not respond seems to convince him that Warren did, in fact, say something substantial about Lyndon's recordings. When we part company outside the studio, with him taking off to the air-conditioned public library for a midday nap and with me going for lunch, he shrugs his shoulders and declares that he does not care what others think. He knows what he wants it to sound like, that is all that matters, he states defiantly.

'Healthy' competition

Lyndon's recording moment illustrates some of the dynamics of allegiance and competition in which the male musicians around the studio assert distinct and shared senses of manhood and indigeneity. Lyndon's changing his musical posture in Warren's presence, the comments on Lyndon's work and aspirations, Warren's downplaying his success as 'good fortune' instead of as the payoff for his hard work over many years, Stan's response to Warren's implied superiority, Lyndon's frustration over not knowing how a close colleague and competitor judges his work, and Stan and myself staying out of this sensitive issue are all part of what the musicians around the studio usually talk of as 'healthy competition' between them.

The role of reputation, prestige, respect and competition for the shaping of musical careers, cultures and styles is recognized in many parts of the world, as Gerstin's overview shows (1998). In his detailed study of reputation-building as a central force for constructing hierarchies of authority in musical networks in the West Indies, Gerstin argues that it is in the interactions between musicians who know each other personally, and who are directly involved with each other's musical work, that they incorporate and filter ideas about identity and the wider public discourse into their own immediate social and musical worlds. A major factor in this mediation of ideas, Gerstin suggests, is 'the micro-politics of authority and hierarchy that arises from musicians working together, depending on one another, and competing' (386).

Gerstin's observations are relevant to the negotiation of male, blackfella and musical forms around the CAAMA recording studio, where Aboriginal men like Lyndon, Stan and Warren have recorded, played, toured and made music with and around each other for years. They know each other's musical skills, techniques and preferences as well as their personal idiosyncrasies from having been involved in the musical and personal dramas, and the good and the bad turn of events, that mark their respective biographies. These musicians depend on each other's help and support. At the same time, they each forge and guard their own reputation, integrity and relative position in competition with each other. While competition and allegiance characterize the Aboriginal music scene as a whole in the region and beyond, these forces are particularly accentuated around the studio, where the men are at their most vulnerable. When recording, they are fully exposed to fellow musicians and the sound engineers' close scrutiny and evaluation of their musical skills and choices, and every single mistake they are bound to make is amplified through the sound-desk for everybody present to hear.

In the case of Lyndon and Warren, they are both well-established and skilled country music artists with extensive stage and recording experience. Lyndon originally came from South Australia, was fathered by a non-indigenous man and grew up with his Aboriginal mother, a habitual drinker, and siblings of different fathers. He was taken to a Central Australian Catholic Aboriginal mission as a kid to be raised away from his home environment. He has moved between South Australia and Central Australia ever since, working and playing music. Warren is firmly grounded in regional Aboriginal kin, social and musical networks in Central Australia, as described in Chapter 2. He grew up and was initiated in Hermannsburg mission as the oldest son of the highly respected Gus Williams and his Arrernte mother and non-Aboriginal stepmother.

Lyndon has been Warren's main lead guitarist for the past five years, and they have recorded, performed and toured together. During this period, Warren's career has taken off substantially. Apart from their different status in local Aboriginal regimes, their relative professional status has, thus, changed to one of increasing inequality, which inevitably creates tensions. Any word from Stan or me on Warren's comments about Lyndon's recordings is likely to be interpreted by Lyndon in ways that fuel these tensions. The positive concept of 'healthy' competition is no doubt used to neutralize such tensions, and it helps the musicians to maintain, or keep up the appearance of, a productive musical, male and blackfella congeniality and solidarity. I still want to open up the concept in order to explore how wider musical and extra-musical norms and conventions are engaged and become entangled as the musicians negotiate their relative positions around the studio.

A distinct feature of the 'healthy competition' as it is played out in the Aboriginal music studio is how rarely interpersonal tensions or negative opinions of each other's musical skills or styles are expressed directly between the musicians concerned. Such critique is, in the main, implied or indirect. As when Warren strums the guitar to Lyndon's song, opinions and critique may be conveyed by playing a musical piece differently when the songwriter or instrumentalist in question is present. Or, as in Lyndon's session, such implied critique may be played on an instrument in the soundproof control room in the presence of the producer and other people, who, in turn, can pass this on to the recording musician(s). Critique and opinions are also expressed through bodily gestures, joking manners or evasive silences, all of which we see in Lyndon's session.

The talk of possible future music events that circulates around the studio is also put to work in creating allegiances, for personal positioning, and to deliver critique in indirect and non-confrontational ways. As when Stan and Warren suggest unequally valued scenarios for the launch of Lyndon's CD, possible events may be brought up by musicians to mark out different professional and male status, as Warren does, and that Stan then reverses in order to unsettle a man who appears a bit too sure of himself. These indirect and non-confrontational means of evaluating, critiquing and competing with each other draw on certain enduring norms for congenial sociability and for male status in Aboriginal Central Australia.

Blackfella congeniality

The avoidance of direct expression of critical views between individuals and other non-confrontational practices are characteristic for interactional customs in Aboriginal Central Australia, where day-to-day social relations are to various degrees organized by traditional norms for producing and preserving harmony and congeniality. Myers (1986), Liberman (1985) and others suggest that such normative structures have emerged as pivotal for the maintenance of larger, enduring systems of cooperation and mutual help among many hunter-gatherer peoples. Such norms, they propose, have effectively maintained binding associations between people who lived in smaller, dispersed, highly mobile and temporary groups without formal leaders or political structures, and where the autonomy of the individual was highly valued.

Today, most Aboriginal people in Central Australia live in larger, permanent and socially dense settlements or towns. People often are deeply divided according to, for instance, family and language groupings. Long-running feuds and at times violent conflicts between families and individuals are commonplace. Principles of unanimity, consensus and 'sharing and caring' for each other are nevertheless fundamental ideals that most Aboriginal people in the region identify with, and that are objectified in their ancestral bodies of knowledge. Direct criticism and open contradiction challenge these principles and may be perceived as both an encroachment upon a person's integrity and autonomy and endangering relationships of mutual obligations and rights that are the substance of desired and necessary relatedness. Open disagreement can be seen as somebody forcing his or her own ways upon others, which is perceived as acting egoistically, self-importantly or in a manner lacking in control. In the ideal state of congeniality, all this is deemed unacceptable, at times offensive, or at least inappropriate (Liberman 1985: 25; Myers 1986: 271; von Sturmer 1981). To win respect and sustain autonomy in the ideal blackfella fellowship, a person should be seen to be generous, unselfish and self-deprecatory and should moderate his or her own activities in public accordingly.

Such ideals are reflected in the ways in which 'healthy competition' is acted out around the music studio. Here, Aboriginal music makers rarely speak of their own importance even when they are bursting to share good news for which they want recognition. Instead, as we saw Warren doing, they may make gestures to prompt others to ask before they utter self-amplifying news. When the expected praise is delivered, they tend to accept it humbly and often redirect it to a third party or impersonal force, such as 'good fortune'. The frequent resort to indirect and nonverbal means for communicating opinions on each other's music making is also part of regional blackfella 'etiquette'.

Blackfella etiquette

A group of 'bushies' wander in to the studio area. The black men wear dusty Akubra hats and baseball caps, dirty shirts and jeans, and hard-worn boots. The women walk a few barefoot steps behind in floral-print long skirts and richly coloured T-shirts. The children, in torn T-shirts and dresses, stay close to the adults. One of the men pokes the brim of his hat with a finger as a greeting towards the office where I sit. He does not say a word and avoids eye contact. After a few minutes' silence I ask what I can do for them. The man in the hat moves closer and mumbles what I assume is the name of Stan or Steve. I tell them that the studio men will be back soon and suggest that they wait in the sofa outside the office. No one responds verbally or makes any sign of having heard me. The women stroll out again and the girls follow. The men and boys hang around, commenting in hushed voices in Pitjantjatjara language on artist photos on the walls. They move restlessly but without hurry, occasionally glancing at me. After about fifteen minutes the man touches the brim of his hat again and mumbles what sounds like 'later'. They walk out, leaving only the distinct smell of desert bush: sandy dust and a strong odour of kangaroo meat cooked over open fire.

In my first month at the studio I tried to make what I perceived as ordinary conversations with the bush musicians who frequently appeared at the studio. I would ask where they came from, if they were in town for long, and introduce myself. I soon gave up these attempts at politeness. The response, if any, was usually monosyllabic sounds. I could not detect any signs of interest in making conversation. Typically, bush musicians who visited again after a few weeks or months would declare abruptly that they 'know' me. That is, they recognize me. They might then start to give sparse answers to the questions I must have asked months back. When I got to know some of these men better, and especially in their home settings, they never seemed to tire of being social, albeit not necessarily through constant chatter but by doing and experiencing things together.

The discreet behaviour characterizes the ways in which many Central Australian Aboriginal people act when meeting new people and visiting other people's places. Liberman, among others, notes how 'shyness is institutionalised in a variety of social settings' in Aboriginal Central Australian societies, where many people find it 'discourteous to ask direct questions without first establishing some sort of congenial relationship' (1985: 28). He notes how the people he works with commonly avoid looking into the eyes of others and are visibly uncomfortable when exposed to the gaze of others. The way they initiate communication is usually subtle, such as making small gestures or sounds, seldom addressing a person directly, and not responding much to questions or talk. Von Sturmer likewise elaborates 'the high degree of diffidence' (1981: 1) that characterizes Aboriginal people's ways of interacting with people they do not know. Myers describes this somewhat restrained behaviour as part of 'an etiquette of "asking"' (1986: 99) among Pintupi people, who 'exhibit "embarrassment", "shame," or "deference" at seeming to assume too much' (100) when moving into other people's range.

Similarly around the studio, bush people rarely walk right up to somebody and state their business, even when they are familiar with the place. They usually stay outside the control room or office, do not look directly at any of us working there, just kind of announce their presence and, through this, ask 'to be admitted to the group' (Myers 1986: 99). They may stand there for a considerable time until someone 'invites' them by approaching them. If nobody does, they may leave without having stated their business. As is expected in this unassuming etiquette, the studio men may take some time to respond to people's presence. The delay not least allows the studio men to assess people's possible intentions before deciding if they should invite them to bring up their business. The bush etiquette is also observed by most town musicians and, to a lesser degree, by the core group of men around the studio. They may knock or just walk into the control room, office or studio, but they, too, usually wait for the people present to recognize them with a 'what's up bros'?' or similar gestures before saying what is on their mind. At times, it takes half an hour, or even an hour, before they are addressed directly. Sometimes it never happens.

The ways in which the blackfella etiquette is performed around the studio involve many tacit meanings. Individual musicians at times complain to me about occasions when they think it took too long before they were addressed by certain men around the studio. On some occasions they experienced that they were not 'invited' at all. They tend to interpret such delays or non-inclusions as intentional and as communicating some hidden meanings and strategies. At times they are correct in thinking so, at other times it has nothing to do with the man in question. Either way, the Aboriginal men around the studio both read and exploit this blackfella interactional etiquette to negotiate their relative musical and male positions and recognition in the competitive studio dynamic.

During music work and in everyday interactions around the studio, moreover, elaborated or continuous verbal exchanges are rare. As with Stan and Lyndon in the recording session described, the men typically limit their verbal exchanges to a few crude words that are interpreted in relation to ongoing work and the people present. Various states of mind, opinions and tensions around the studio are instead expressed through eye, facial, hand and bodily gestures, and through silences. These gestures are interpreted through shared knowledge of local and personal histories, and of ongoing tensions and changing allegiances in musical and interpersonal relationships. It means that the blackfella etiquette and 'talking without words' require a certain level of shared, blackfella and male experience. It relies on shared standards of what is, and what is not, appropriate, expected, acceptable, valued and normal. It is also a means to exclude, or it works to exclude, those without such knowledge. People who are used to verbal responses and perceive attentive verbal feedback and small talk as essential for their experience of a congenial interaction may find the silence, avoidance, implicit meanings and nonverbal communication confusing, frustrating and at times offensive.[3] Around the studio, these people are, in the main, non-indigenous or from other Australian regions. They occasionally comment to me (probably seen as a fellow whitefella and non-local) how they find Aboriginal people in Central Australia 'unresponsive' and 'hard to talk to'.

Conversely, in terms of local interactional norms, non-indigenous people often appear somewhat rude, intrusive and self-important. They normally walk straight up to anyone around the studio, stretch out a hand, look people straight in the eyes and introduce themselves and their business without further ado. Even if they have never been in the studio before, they may sit down in the control room and ask questions or comment about ongoing music work. Such whitefella ways of showing interest and friendliness are commonly met by a collective embarrassed or dismissive silence from local Aboriginal musicians.

The only person I occasionally see challenging these unwitting transgressions by outsiders around the studio is Stan, who, as a studio manager, has a certain authority to do so. Typically, he gives such whitefellas a long, intense look, which usually makes them acutely self-conscious of their own talk and whiteness. At times, this look is not effective. On one occasion, for example, a number of non-indigenous musicians and technicians from the interstate worked in the building in preparation for a big festival in Alice Springs. A group of Aboriginal musicians, along with Stan and me, sat talking in the control room when the door suddenly opened wide. A white man none of us had seen before walked right in, said 'g'day' in a forthright, cheerful manner as he tried to pass Stan, who sat in the narrow space between the sound-desk and the editing modules. Stan made no sign of moving his chair. He just looked at the man. Too hurried to acknowledge any of us, the man said he needed to use the computer at the end of the sound-desk. He continued his attempt to wriggle past Stan. When he realized that he was, in fact, blocked intentionally, he finally became aware of the complete silence. He looked up at Stan. Then at us. Irritated, he asked 'What?' He got no answer. He now lost his momentum and let his arms hang. After a few more moments of silence Stan said coolly: 'Let's try that again, mate. From the start,' and nodded at the door. The man looked confused. 'Just do the whole thing from the start, beginning with knocking on that door from the outside,' Stan said calmly. The man looked shaken but did what he was told. Stan called 'yeah?' to the knock. The man re-entered, stopped in the doorway and waited. Stan nodded. 'That's right, mate, you wait,' he said. Without raising his voice, he then made it clear in a few words that left little to the imagination that this was a blackfella space where whitefellas cannot take their presence for granted but should feel privileged to be invited.

If, on the other hand, non-indigenous strangers show restrained respect, deference, patience and wait for people to approach them, it is normally reciprocated with helpful gestures from the Aboriginal men around the studio. Aspects of regional Aboriginal norms for communicative and interactive behaviours are, in these ways, put into play, reaffirmed and reworked in 'healthy competition', investing the studio dynamic with particular shared blackfella values and meanings. In passing on competitive judgements, the men also draw on competing and shared masculine models.

Competing masculinities

One afternoon, Steve and Stan are setting up the studio for a recording session the following day. Steve plays the various instruments while Stan sets the levels in the control room. When Steve is struggling to get a riff right on a guitar, Stan comes out, picks up the bass and starts to guide him. Two of the band members who are due to record turn up and Stan nods them towards the drums and another guitar. After closing the studio doors, they all get into a playful jam session with increasingly wild, extended and loud guitar solos, with bass and drums churning out thumping, exuberant rock beats.

From the control room, from where I can control the volume on the sound-desk, I watch the men enjoying themselves. Lyndon and Warren turn up and join me. They shake their heads and comment that this was a kind of music they played when they were 'angry youngfellas'. These two country musicians then start to imitate an exaggerated guitar-playing style and a robotic head-banging act while looking bored 'cool'. They chuckle and Warren says that anyone can play that kind of music. Country music, on the other hand, they agree, is more demanding because you have to create different moods with fine-tuned skills.

It is fairly common for country musicians to, in this way, mock their colleague rock musicians as fairly immature musicians and men. The rock-playing men out in the studio, in fact, behave nothing like the head-banging figures that Lyndon and Warren exaggerate. Aboriginal desert musicians have not adopted the physically overt gestures of global rock convention, and while the men in the jam session may produce wild, loud and thumping rock music, their physical movements are minimal. The only evidence of their emotional involvement is their exchange of wide grins. The country musicians still use the gestures of global stereotypes of rock musicians' physically showy performance styles and male figures in order to demonstrate the contrasting blackfella masculine models they associate with these two genres. That is, they wish to present country music making as more mature with its more composed instrumental and vocal styles, which they associate with a male imagery of 'real' country musicians as more complex and sincere men.

Aspects of such competing, genre-related male imagery emerge from the different ways in which country and rock music playing works in the making. In country, the main role of instrumentalists is to submerge their contribution to the melody and stay attentive to, enhance and counterpoint the lead vocalist's expressions.[4] If instrumentalists do this too busily or too loudly, they are seen as incompetent, no matter how technically skilled and ingenious they might be. Musicians schooled in rock music expressions are, in contrast, valued for a narcissistic virtuosity on their particular instrument, and they are expected to grab any space to show off in protracted solo playing independent of the vocal melody. As this regional Aboriginal music scene demonstrates, though, such strong musical and masculinist gestures are not necessarily executed with large physical gestures.

When put to work in Aboriginal socio-musical traditions in Central Australia these differences in executing rock and country music become entangled with norms and values regarding ideal male behaviour. The non-assertive way of playing respected country music with selfless attention to other band members resonates with Aboriginal norms for gaining respect as mature men, who ideally appear generous and unselfish and downplay individual assertiveness in public. Youngfella men, in contrast, are expected to behave, and may be admired for behaving, in more selfish, rebellious and irresponsible ways, as if proving themselves through self-amplification. They are not expected to have yet mastered the skills of more composed and knowledgeable men (e.g. Myers 1986: 238). Country music male imagery thus resonates with that of Aboriginal norms for how adult men ideally behave and present themselves, having learnt the art of dignified calm. While the biological age of rock and country musicians may not differ, such generational ideals are still employed in making evaluative distinctions between music-related masculine styles.

The distinctions between indigenous country and rock male imagery are also associated with the historical development of these two genres. As described in Chapter 2, country music styles have come to form an expressive core of Aboriginal desert life over several generations. Country can, therefore, be said to constitute a sonic 'oldfella' of regional musical styles. It is also literally embodied in the many older country musicians across the region. As such, country has accumulated a kind of respect that is related to the higher authority and respect that is (ideally) attributed to older, (ideally) more mature, responsible and wiser men in regional Aboriginal social regimes. As a more recent socio-musical tradition, rock music has yet to earn such a male and social status. Middle-aged rock musicians are certainly accorded a high degree of respect in many settings, too, but this respect is earned on an individual basis, for a man's personal skills or selfless contributions to community life, for instance. Country musicians tend to command a certain degree of respect simply by associating themselves with the long-established social history of this Aboriginal genre.

In all this, it is important to distinguish between aspirations and actual practice. Most of these men do not live as they preach and cannot live as they desire. They live as they can, with the resources and conditions that structure their day-to-day lives and histories in Central Australia, as outlined in Chapter 1. Their aspirations and desires take form through their identification with country or rock music imagery and styles, but do not determine or even guide their actual behaviour. Things are further complicated by the fact that most Aboriginal musicians in the region are not exclusively committed to one genre of music, as mentioned in Chapter 2. The ways in which these men express and identify with blackfella and male modes of being are, therefore, often ambiguous, contradictory and intermingled, and tend to shift depending on present circumstances – the set of musicians they play with and the kind of music event they participate in at any given time and place.

Judgements about, and competition between, musical, blackfella and male styles, status and worth around the studio are, in these ways, often closely intertwined. The healthy competition among the men involves a mediating dynamic in which the men engage aspects of different and overlapping forms of valued Aboriginal manhood, which become associated with aspects of a range of masculine and musical styles that circulate in a continuum from the local to the global. Any of these differences in musical and male identifications are also often secondary to the primary value that the healthy competition is thought to reproduce – a sense of blackfella male and musical allegiance.

Blackfella allegiance

The Aboriginal musicians usually argue that through their mutual critical scrutinizing of each other they challenge each other to do better musically. The line of reasoning is that criticism motivates and pressures them to never be complacent about their own level of skill, which results in better-quality music and recordings, which leads to more career opportunities and increased recognition for all. In practice, this competitive model for producing increased reputation and status is racially exclusive. The musicians compare themselves almost exclusively to other blackfella music makers during ongoing music work. The rivalries and recognition that impact most on their aesthetic choices and crafting of male styles are those within and between blackfella musical networks. The core musicians around the studio make up one such network, while these musicians also belong to different musical groupings outside the studio, and they move between such groupings.

The 'healthy' musical rivalry is, in other words, seen as a productive mode for recognizing and improving blackfella musical skills, for the betterment of a distinct blackfella musical collectivity. While the musicians at times include themselves in a national or even global community of black music making, it is the local and regional Aboriginal music scene that the men address in the black musical 'brotherhood' rhetoric of healthy competition. The overarching value that is constituted through the concept and practice of their 'healthy competition' is, in other words, a blackfella allegiance, which is part of the dynamic of the blackfella and male studio ethos and ownership explored in the previous chapter. It involves the connection and reformulation of co-existing, at times contradictory, at times partially resonating, but always co-productive, intercultural and blackfella norms, ideas, practices and imagery. Whether primarily on an ideational level or a practical level, those sources of identification are engaged in ways that bond the musicians even when they are deeply divided, dislike each other, disagree fundamentally with another man's behaviour or convictions, and when they let each other down badly. A man who rubbishes a fellow musician in an unforgiving way can declare a day, or even just an hour later, that he is going on tour with this same 'wanker'.

The gist of the justification for such radical turns of emotionally charged tensions is that those being rubbished are, after all, fellow 'mongrel' musicians and blackfellas. It is, in other words, explained as part of the 'healthy competition' among men and musicians who not only are dependent on each other but also share an idea of themselves as members of a blackfella historical and sociocultural fellowship.

This racially inclusive and 'mongrel' 'family' image is normally talked of in gender-neutral terms. In practice, however, the rivalries that count around the studio are those between male indigenous musicians. I have never heard or seen the musicians compare themselves with, or refer to, women musicians in their music making. The ways in which musical and non-musical knowledge and activities are put to work around the studio, in other words, reinforce the regional Aboriginal music scene as overwhelmingly male, which I explore next.

Blackfella male studio vernacular

It is 8.30 am and Stan walks in the studio back door with fast, heavy steps and his head hanging. 'My head is fucked, my hands are fucked and my life is fucked. I'm fuckin' fucked! This is what happens when I don't take drugs in the morning!' He glances at me from under depressed eye brows. 'You look fucked too!' Shaking my head I respond 'Sure. Good morning to you, too!' He continues growling while checking the e-mail. Steve walks in and, like most mornings, checks the mood of his 'boss' before saying much. He nods a good morning to me. I respond with a gesture towards Stan and make a 'he's hopeless' face. Steve makes a half-smiling gesture as if saying 'Oh, one of *them* days?' Stan rises abruptly. 'You quails should be careful making faces behind people's backs,' he growls and we all laugh. He then briskly walks out through the studio stage. 'Are you coming or not?' he calls back to Steve, who shakes his head and follows to the coffee shop down the street where they usually talk about the day's work over their morning cappuccinos.

As in this interaction, the core of Aboriginal men around the studio commonly communicate with each other through a somewhat limited repertoire of crude, sexualized terms and profanities, with 'fuck' being the operative expression for a range of different feelings, things and actions. As we saw in Lyndon's recording session earlier, the nonverbal communication between the men also frequently consists of bodily gestures suggesting both hetero- and homosexual acts, or referring to sexualized parts of the body. While only a few of the men revel in more graphic sexualized talk and gestures, it is common practice that if a connection can be made between ongoing music work and sex in any form, it will be elaborated, often in clever, funny ways. This kind of bantering at times develops into a happening in itself when a couple of men perform a kind of duel with increasingly rough insults, with other men energizing the battle with laughs and comments. The men clearly recognize their bantering as part of a blackfella and 'blokey' thing that is inappropriate and can be perceived as offensive beyond their male and blackfella sociality. They tone down or cut out altogether their use of profanities and sexualized gesturing before outsiders, and especially when women are present.

The way the men change their behaviour depends on who the women are and what they are doing at the studio. The Music manager and the administrator are women who have reason to come by most days for work issues, and women from other sections of CAAMA may turn up to get information about music projects or to get sound jobs done. These women normally stay around only as long as their specific errand requires. The men seldom encourage them to stay either. If a woman happens to walk in on a group of men carrying on their usual exchange of good-humoured insults in the control room, for instance, the men normally go quiet and some may leave. It is usually left to the woman to break the silence, which may be a rather intimidating experience and hardly encourages relaxed small talk.

Many Aboriginal town women act rather self-consciously around the studio when the men do not pay much obvious attention to their presence or to what they say. Non-indigenous women are usually more straightforward but may also seem somewhat intimidated, and are at times clearly frustrated, by a lack of overtly 'friendly' gestures from the men, such as smiles or voluntary imparting of information beyond answers to direct questions. The men do, in fact, pay full attention, as discussed in relation to the 'bush etiquette', but they usually do not confirm people's presence with many words or gestures.

Quite a few women, both indigenous and non-indigenous, who know the men around the studio fairly well, tend to adopt a more or less seriously joking, teasing, flirty and flattering style of talking and acting around the men. It is usually the most rewarding approach if they want more verbally rich responses from the men, who usually catch on to, and at times revel in, these kinds of heterosexual word games. The interactions are on the men's terms, though. If they do not feel like 'playing', or if they think the woman 'tries too hard', as in adopting a style of talking they know she is unfamiliar with, they may respond with silence, especially if she is an Aboriginal woman. This effectively tells her that she is out of her bounds, or that she is acting inappropriately according to expectations that Aboriginal women do not answer back in rude ways to men in public. Even when a woman adopts more crude language as a way to parody the men, and thus implicitly discipline the men's vernacular, these exchanges still reinforce such vernacular as a distinct feature of the male studio sociability where women are basically defined as outsiders.

Bush musicians at times bring wives and female relatives with them to recording sessions. There is rarely any communication at all between these women and men who are not related to them. Both the men and the women, here, adhere to regional Aboriginal norms of appropriate gendered behaviour in public and tend to keep a respectful distance from each other. When both men and women from bush communities record, the studio space is soon spatially divided up in gendered ways, with women and men gathering in areas apart. While the control room, corners of the studio, and the studio hallway may gradually shift from a male to a female space and back again during a day of recordings, the gendered division largely remains.

On one such occasion, close to twenty bush community women recorded gospel songs with a male backing band. During the days of recordings, the women frequently gestured for me to come over. They explained their concerns about the way the recordings were proceeding and then instructed me 'you tell'im!' and nodded towards Steve in the control room. After a few mediating efforts that Steve did not seem to appreciate because I interrupted the work and prolonged the recordings, I suggested to the women that they could tell him directly. 'He'll listen, that's his job!' I tried. The women responded with laughs and giggles, jerking their heads backward. 'No, no!' they exclaimed embarrassed, telling me that he would not listen to them. He did not know their language (which I did not, either), and they would not understand what he told them because they did not know 'them fella' machine talk', they argued. The women, in these ways, recognized and reinforced the unequal power relations that come with being visitors on other people's spatial and social grounds, and the male-related technological authority inherent in the studio relationships. They also extended the gender regimes of their daily lives to the studio space by taking for granted a gendered organization where adult Aboriginal men and women largely operate within parallel realms, and where the realms of men are invested with relatively more public authority.

The ways the vernacular and masculinist behaviours reproduce the studio as a male domain are in many ways similar to gendered language behaviour in other all-male spaces.[5] In Fine's (1987) study of restaurant kitchens as male institutions, for instance, he shows that women have to negotiate a range of sensitive and difficult issues to become 'one of the boys'. First and foremost, he argues, women have to learn to respond appropriately to sexual insinuations, either through sexual innuendo or by sexual joking. From this he proposes that it is through sexuality that men demarcate their social world and keep women out. An implied assumption in Fine's and other writings on women in male institutions is that women, in fact, aspire to become 'one of the boys'. I hesitate to suggest this for the gender relations around the Aboriginal music studio. For instance, Aboriginal women from more traditionally oriented settings do not seek to engage actively with this male realm. They are mainly concerned with acting according to norms for appropriate female and male public behaviours in separate realms. More publicly assertive Aboriginal women do not seem to attempt to become gendered equals either. From their bodily gestures and talk, my lasting impression is that they more often are interested in being attractive in feminine ways to particular men.

Only a couple of non-indigenous women worked in the studio when I was there. These sessions were very different from most other recordings I witnessed, in that the men completely abandoned even their moderated coarse language and gestures. It was unlike the few instances when local Aboriginal women participated in recordings or band rehearsals, too. They frequently apologized, fidgeted and required a lot of supportive affirmations from the men if they were to perform well. In contrast, the non-indigenous women musicians carried on with the job with relaxed confidence. At one occasion when a woman fiddler from Darwin played on one of Warren's recordings, an Aboriginal musician in the control room suggested that the woman must be a 'lesbo' because she did not put on any kind of feminine, flirty act. He nodded approvingly and said that he could not blame her. In fact, it was a rather smart strategy, he thought. If he was a woman trying to cut it as a musician, he continued, he too would make himself out to be a lesbian. That way, he would have a better chance to be taken seriously by the men in the business and could escape being constantly sexually harassed by them, he concluded.

While in some general respects similar to the reproduction of male social worlds in other sociocultural settings, then, the demarcation of the studio as an all-male space also emerges from a mutual recognition on the part of men and women of particular regional Aboriginal norms for gendered interactions and homosocial activities. A means for excluding women from this space is a rather crude and sexualized vernacular. Such talk is also a means of male bonding, as it is the men's relationships to other men, not to women, that are of primary interest.

Studio sex – between men

A few musicians and I sit talking in the control room while Steve is busy copying a recording at the sound-desk. We have a full view of the studio through the control room window. Many employees walk through the studio on their way to and from the staff parking outside the studio back door. Right now an Aboriginal woman who works upstairs walks past. The men go quiet and follow her movements. She is a town woman dressed in an office-style sleeveless shirt and a modest skirt. When she disappears out the door, one of the men remarks, 'nice pair of legs'. 'Shows them well, too,' says another with approving tongue-smacking. A third man wonders aloud if she is still with a particular local Aboriginal man. The others seem to think so, somebody saw him the other day. 'Must enjoy having those legs around him,' chuckles the man who first commented on them. 'You wish!' chuckles another, with a face indicating that he would not mind being in her man's position.

The men proceeds to deliver a few imaginative descriptions and begin to imitate how this woman's male partner (and by their performance of these acts, by implication themselves) cannot take his eyes of these legs, and wants to be trapped between them. The men laugh at and with each other. One of them wonders what her man would feel about them adoring his missus' legs. Somebody now gives a brief account of a drunken night when this man ended up with another woman. The others nod and chuckle in consensus over their 'mongrel', sexual nature; 'once a dog, always a dog', one of them mutters, to which another man responds by yelping, causing another round of laughter. The men go on to exchange more rumours about this particular man's sexual habits, and a couple of them throw in comments on their own sexual abilities, which they complain lack any exciting features. This is taken as meaning the opposite, and the others now try to get one of them to confirm rumours about some old sexual 'sins'. He responds with shaking his head in silent denial but his grin indicates the opposite. 'You mongrel!' exclaims the others, as if the rumours are now confirmed.

Men around the studio often comment, in this way, on women they see. They may evaluate the way a woman moves, dresses and is shaped in both flattering and critical terms, and at times with an erotic tone.[6] The one exception to this kind of commentary is the current wives or partners of the men present. The male studio sex talk is, in this way, largely separated from intimacy, and the men usually take care to show respect for each other's private relations and emotions. While initially experiencing the crudest forms of the men's sexualized commentary about women as both sexist and offensive, I soon realized that it is only secondarily about women, and mainly concerned with and directed at men, and in particular Aboriginal men.

As on the occasion described, speculations on Aboriginal men's sexual adventures, preferences, techniques and mistakes are much more elaborated, graphic and take up more time than any sexualized talk about women. Women are largely represented as mirrors for, or a kind of 'starter' to get to the main subject of interest: Aboriginal men's actions, sexual rivalry and relationships. Non-indigenous men's sexual lives are seldom the subject of much elaboration unless they involve indigenous men, such as a non-indigenous man having a relationship with a woman who is, or was, the partner of an indigenous man. The indigenous man is then usually the focus of the discussion.

This conjures up a racialized version of what Kimmel describes as 'masculinity as a homosocial enactment' (Kimmel 1994: 128). It suggests that men mainly prove and define their manhood, and in this case the sexual aspects of blackfella manhood, in relation to and under constant scrutiny of other men: 'Manhood is demonstrated for other men's approval. It is other men who evaluate the performance,' while women 'become a kind of currency that men use to improve their ranking on the masculine social scale' (128–9). Around the studio, the men's sexualized talk articulates competing male status within a male indigenous realm, and also works to bond them. In the process, they reinforce the all-male blackfella domain of the music studio, and of the realm of blackfella music making beyond this particular space.

The simultaneous bonding and negotiation of differently valued masculine behaviours through sexualized talk emerge, not least, from the men's frequent narrating of past musical events. One afternoon, for instance, we are setting up the studio for a recording and I ask the men present what they think of a particular Koori percussionist from Melbourne. Is he any good? One of the musicians knows the man from playing in interstate bands in the 1980s. He responds with a short, graphically detailed story about the percussionist in an embarrassing sexual situation that involved various plastic devices, some homosexual tendencies, and, not very significant for the story line, a woman. When he is finished he adds, 'I guess he's OK.' As a percussionist, that is.

A lot of the sexualized talk evokes the idea that Aboriginal men are victims to their natural, sexual urges, which is repeated in different forms and with ill-concealed pride by several of the men. They may use this perceived lack of control for explaining why musicians miss an important performance, why they end up in jealousy and family conflicts, or in prison and other kinds of trouble. In this they draw on globally well-established colonial and primitivist stereotypes of black men being closer to nature and therefore possessing a more powerful male virility compared to cultured, civilized white men, who are thought to be more in control of their natural instincts (Bederman 1995; Kanitkar 1994; Moore 1998; Segal 1990). A range of scholars have explored how such originally Eurocentric racist and imperialist ideas have been co-opted and cultivated worldwide in positive, affirmative terms by Black rights advocates and in black expressive cultures, including music (Carby 1998; Booker 2000; du Bois 1982 [1903]; Gilroy 1993; Mac an Ghaill 1994; Majors and Manchini Billson 1992). The frequent narrating around the studio of past activities and experiences through imagined and real male sexual practices works to link the all-male studio sociality to such broader racialized and sexualized male realms.

In their narratives, the men also put into play music genre-related male sexual morality. For instance, and as I analyse in more detail elsewhere (Ottosson 2012), on one occasion, a highly experienced and non-drinking guitarist in the circle around the studio is dropped from a tour to a big country music event and is replaced by a less skilled guitarist who usually drinks when on tours and therefore cannot be trusted to play well or even turn up for performances. The first guitarist mainly plays and identifies with rock music genres but is also skilled in country music playing, and he can always be trusted to turn up and do a professional job. The country musicians' doubts about bringing him are instead shaped by their suspicions that the rock guitarist will be successful in 'scoring' sex among the 'less streetwise' indigenous women in the country music scene. This, one of them argues, will jeopardize the country musicians' reputation because 'us country mob are more like family' who know and respect each other, including not going after each other's women.

The employment of a 'country music family' imagery of morally responsible men who protect the (also sexual) innocence of their women is particularly effective in distinguishing blackfella country musicians as men of higher moral worth, because it resonates both with the all-important value of maintaining affective kin relations in Aboriginal normative regimes and with Christian values that emphasize male family responsibilities and monogamy (Ottosson 2016). This model of valued male behaviours is contrasted with an 'anti-domestic' global imagery of rock music culture, populated with rather sexually indiscriminate, promiscuous and predatory men and women (Reynolds and Press 1995). By mobilizing distinct and competing, locally meaningful and interculturally mediated blackfella male models, the musicians put into play globally widespread music-related male imagery as they craft particular shared and competing blackfella musical identifications.

As pointed out previously, the ideas and convictions that the men express do not necessarily coincide with how they, in fact, behave and live. These ideas can nevertheless have real and practical consequences for their personal and professional relationships and relative status, as when a reliable professional guitarist is replaced by a less skilled and unreliable band member, who did indeed cause problems because of his drinking during the country music tour.

The all-male blackfella studio ethos is, of course, not only reproduced by internal dynamics but also constantly reformed in broader processes. The most obvious attempts to reform the studio sociality are shaped by aspirations within CAAMA to cultivate what can be called a 'modern' and 'tidy' Aboriginal public profile. This profile does not map neatly onto the social and male life of the studio.

Tidy Aboriginality and modern black males

In the process of expanding and moving uptown in the 1990s, CAAMA restructured its operational aims more in line with a mainstream industry, including a respectable and modern public Aboriginal profile. As an Aboriginal organization in a regional setting where Aboriginal people are commonly associated with negative stereotypes, CAAMA has been important for both acting as a role model for Aboriginal people and presenting a more 'sophisticated' Aboriginal presence. A sophisticated, professional image is also crucial in negotiations with funding bodies and sponsors on which CAAMA depends for its continued operations.

The studio, however, has in some respects upheld the congenial and informal blackfella praxis that characterized CAAMA's earlier days. That is, parties of weather-beaten, ruffled bush visitors and untidy musicians wander about the studio area, gather at the studio back door and at times spill over to other parts of the building. They do not fit well with the efficient and cleaned-up Aboriginality that the organization wants to present to the outside world. The traffic of blackfella strangers also worries staff in the building more directly. Bags, money and other things have gone missing from desks in the radio area, for instance, and the drinking-water fountain and toilets between the radio and studio areas are found in rather messy states at times.

The historically all-male and masculinist character of studio activities, including the male vernacular and 'slack' blackfella organization of work, further diverges from upstairs aims for a modern operation. The new CAAMA Music manager, for instance, tells me that indigenous music making in Central Australia, and as an extension, the studio, reminds her of the highly male-dominated music scene in larger Australia back in the 1970s and 1980s. She hopes to see the desert scene move in the direction of the mainstream music industry, where, she notes, men can no longer get away with patronizing and chauvinistic behaviour, and where more women are involved. Several people in the management and the other more gender-mixed sections of CAAMA similarly wish to open up the male reserve of the studio and modernize it by encouraging more equal participation of men and women and more presentable people and practices.[7]

Concurring with such more general aims, senior staff members at times advise musicians on their appearance. A few days before a community event that CAAMA Music takes part in, for instance, somebody suggests to Lyndon that he should get a haircut and better clothes. He is told that 'out there' he will represent CAAMA, which requires that certain standards are upheld. On another occasion, a bush community band arrives at the studio after travelling for a rough day and a night. They are taken upstairs and introduced to the new manager of the CAAMA Group, an urban Aboriginal person who soon comments on their 'smell' and suggests that they should go and clean up.

In these and similar cases, the men find the direct criticism of their appearance inappropriate. Some experience it as patronizing and as suggesting that they are too uncivilized to realize how they appear to others. Most of the regional musicians I have met are fully aware and often self-conscious about the way their appearance differs from that of a middle-class, mainstream Australia. I find that many bush musicians make an effort to renew their sparse wardrobes when in town, and all of the men want to look clean and attractive on stage, although the model for attractive male demeanour that they adhere to diverges from that of mainstream, non-indigenous Australia. I described some aspects of such differences in Chapter 1 and discuss a related 'too much' and 'mongrel' blackfella quality in Chapter 6.

Other upstairs interventions to reform the characteristics of the studio sociality include attempts to discourage the traffic of people to and from the studio. For instance, a door is installed that close off the front entrance from the rest of the building and Stan and Steve are informed that from now on only people who participate directly in ongoing studio work should be there. This is not in the professional or personal interest of the studio men. As we saw in the account of a studio day in the previous chapter, it is an advantage for the creative, ad-lib studio ethos of music making to have a steady flow of different musicians through the studio. Their skills may become useful at any moment. The traffic of blackfella musicians from all over the region in the studio, moreover, underpins the CAAMA Music record label's continued existence as the producer of distinctive forms of regional Aboriginal music. Because few people in the rest of the building are familiar with the regional musicians or with the intricacies of studio work, the studio men can and will evade the restrictions by simply acting as if nobody is illegitimate.

Other aspects of the studio are somewhat easier to interfere with. For example, the studio back door is commonly left open or unlocked and the studio men and musicians often gather at the door for smoke breaks and to discuss ongoing work. As in any studio, recording sessions, mixing work and rehearsals do not always follow a nine-to-five schedule, and at times, Stan and Steve, as well as studio equipment are engaged for events at night and weekends. The back-door area often turns into a socialized male space in relation to these activities, too.

This door is a recurrent issue between upstairs management and the downstairs studio staff during my time at the studio. The management wants it closed and locked at all times. Their concerns are put in terms of security and insurance requirements. From the studio men's point of view, this is not an issue. They think that they have sufficient control of who walks in and out of the studio area. They are fully aware that some studio equipment has gone missing over the years, and they can guess where some of it has gone, and it is not with people who wander in because the back door is open.[8] The studio men, moreover, consider it beneficial to keep the door open. It would be a major obstacle for ongoing work if keys had to be produced every time they and musicians use this entrance. To be able to enter the studio more informally from the back is also important in making the studio an accessible and relaxed space for many indigenous musicians. The alternative entrance from the main street door involves passing the scrutinizing eyes of the shop and radio staff, all of them wary of potential shoplifters, thieves and drunks. For the studio men and musicians, their back-door gatherings are furthermore productive social sites for music work. Most back-door talk, crude or not, concerns musical matters and people in this studio and elsewhere in the region, the country or the world. In an expanded sense, these gatherings thus contribute to the maintenance of the studio as an important place for exchanges and connections with broader musical realms. For these reasons, instructions to keep the door closed and locked are frequently ignored. When a spring is installed to close the door automatically, various heavy objects can soon be found at the door to stop it from closing. The spring eventually breaks and the door is left open as usual.

Mundane issues such as these highlight the contestation over the right to define appropriate gendered and blackfella behaviour around the studio. Many of the men around the studio see the increased disciplining of the studio practices as interferences in the way their music work is organized, which means they are intrusions on the values and ideas that constitute the blackfella and male studio ethos. Individual musicians may still comply with some of the upstairs instructions when it benefits their social and musical position. Some of them also support some of the changes the management wants to introduce. Not all of the men agree with every aspect of the male studio ethos, even if they do not voice their objections in the male groupings around the studio.

While the men around the studio continue to employ a variety of low-key forms of resistance to undermine and evade upstairs directives, they never seriously question the overall aims and purposes of CAAMA. As Scott observes, struggles of everyday forms of resistance take place, and emerge, almost entirely within the values of an existing hegemony (1985, 1990). These forms of resistance draw on values that are shared by the superior and subordinate parties, whose actions depend upon that fact for their effectiveness. Applied to the CAAMA downstairs–upstairs tensions, this inter-dependence is most obvious when outsiders criticize CAAMA. On all such occasions I have witnessed, the core of men around the studio will express their allegiance with the organization and will at times adamantly defend its professed vision of Aboriginal empowerment and self-representation.

The day-to-day types of resistance in the studio instead concern the right to define the parameters for gendered and indigenous practice and authority within the organizational and normative structures of CAAMA. In this, the studio men and musicians assert their own, internally differentiated interpretations and understanding of what constitute appropriate and beneficial practices in the advancement of indigenous and male music making. They assert a socio-musical male space of knowledge and experience that increasingly diverges from broader societal and ideological changes concerning more equal gender relations and better dressed and spoken Aboriginality that the management increasingly embraces.

As upstairs attempts to reform the blackfella all-male studio practices intensify during my time at the studio, these very practices become increasingly important for the musicians. And as the men's resistance becomes more obvious, upstairs interventions become more formalized and non-negotiable. In a dialectic dynamic of increased tensions, the space for ambiguity, flexibility and heterogeneity tends to shrink. Instead, two largely opposing models for male and indigenous ways of being are increasingly sharply defined and defended, both of them increasingly at odds with the lived, multilayered experiences of Aboriginal musicians and men in the region.

Having established how a diversity of indigenous ways of being and identifying as men and musicians are mediated in the daily work, male homosociality and blackfella ethos of the Aboriginal recording studio, other aspects of the making of men and music are played out in the setting of Aboriginal bush communities, which is the subject for the next chapter.

5

Playing Aboriginal communities

Come Easter, the cold season has arrived in the Australian desert region and the Central Australian Football League season starts. A Country Cup is also battled out between Aboriginal community teams that travel with their home crowds to each other's community Sports Festivals. The daytime attraction of these Festivals is the football, but just as important are the music activities at night. After sunset, everybody moves over to the community hall or outdoor stage to enjoy and dance to a succession of regional Aboriginal musicians and bands long into the night. Many aspiring bush musicians make their debut as performers before larger audiences in this circuit of community concerts, and it is in this hinterland music scene that most community bands and musicians establish and maintain their regional reputation. A night of a Battle of the Bands is mandatory for any respectable community Sports Festival and it is often the highlight of the weekend. In this chapter, I will explore how male and indigenous distinction and shared sentiments are played out in such a musical battle.

As described in Chapter 1, desert communities were established through colonial and missionary regimes of racial segregation. They continue to operate rather isolated from mainstream society, a segregation that is now mainly justified by ideas of cultural protection and self-determination (Rowse 1998). Accordingly, invitations to most Sports Weekends are usually limited to Aboriginal communities and organizations, and are issued by word of mouth through Aboriginal networks. The fact that these events often are announced a week or just a few days before they take place, and may be cancelled, postponed and then on again within the same time frame, also excludes most people who are not part of an Aboriginal network. With a few exceptions, non-indigenous visitors also need a permit that can take more than a week to process, and people who are not known by community residents are not always granted visitor permits for Sports Weekends. The gatherings of Aboriginal people from all over the desert create opportunities to carry out cross-regional ceremonial activities, which are not for general public viewing. Some community leaders tell me that this is a main reason why they are reluctant to approve visitor permits for Sports Weekends.

A Battle of the Bands is obviously about competing musically, but this may not be the most important issue at stake. Through performing at these events the musicians claim particular positions as Aboriginal men of particular families, communities and language groups, as distinct from other Aboriginal individuals and groupings in the region. The musical battles may, therefore, be explored as condensed and emergent performative expressions of cross-regional Aboriginal relatedness and distinctions, in which indigenous and gendered forms of identification are reiterated and transformed. In some respects, community concerts can also be understood as contemporary variations of traditional ceremonial activity. As Myers observes among Pintupi people, 'Singing provides a salient image of sociability ... [and] whenever large groups came together in traditional times, they would sing together at night' (1986: 112). Song and dance, Myers suggests, function as a 'ritual process' that reduces discord and tensions between groups and individuals who do not normally camp together, a process in which participants in effect practice relatedness. In this chapter, I will show how more recent genres of music performance have become an important contemporary medium not only for practising relatedness and for forging regional differences and discrete ways of being Aboriginal and male; these forms of music also provide a rare public forum for articulating shared everyday concerns and intra-community problems.

Lajamanu Battle of the Bands

It is well after sunset and the noise is deafening inside the pitch-dark Lajamanu community hall – a big, tin-roofed structure with wire-netted sides in the centre of the settlement.[1] What sounds like hundreds of children are screaming at the top of their voices in there, while chasing each other, kicking deflated footballs around and dragging sticks noisily against the wire-netting. A couple of boys are banging away like mad on the drum set on the stage, and a number of barking dogs add to the cacophony. One of the two stage- and sound-engineers from Darwin finally finds the power plug in the dark outside. In a sudden flash the hall is brightly lit up by many-coloured spotlights. The screaming reaches panic proportions as kids scramble out through ripped-up holes in the wire-netting. Many of them stop in the dark outside in excited anticipation, but they will have to wait for another hour before the highlight of the three-day Lajamanu Sports Weekend kicks off in earnest: the Battle of the Bands.

The concert was, kind of, supposed to start at 7.00 pm. But, even at 8.30 pm nobody has turned up at the hall except for the kids and dogs. However, as soon as a seductive reggae-beat starts up in a sound check by one of Lajamanu's best-known bands, the Teenage Band, hundreds of residents and visitors are on the move towards the hall. Groups of women carrying babies, blankets and water cans appear from all directions, with dogs at their heels. They spread the blankets on the floor along the darker sides of the hall and sit down. Kids, teenage girls and older women join them, kicking the dogs away. Men of all ages gather in the dark at the back end of the hall. Other men stay around the vehicles now parked outside the wall-netting. They will occasionally contribute to the stage effects during the night by flashing the car headlights with the beat of the music.

The Teenage Band finishes up when the community council chairman, a middle-aged man with greying hair, enters the stage. He welcomes everyone to the Battle of the Bands and urges competitors to come forward and enter. Ideally, a Sports Festival should have a substantial line-up for its Battle of the Bands without organizers having to prompt people. At the same time, it is part of the informal code of conduct, and part of the competition between musicians, not to appear too keen to perform. Some men prefer to be seen as having been talked into entering by relatives and fans, which demonstrates their musical and social status. The council president holds up five hundred dollars; the winner takes it all. The money is probably more a show of how well-organized this Sports Weekend is (i.e., it has been properly funded) than a bait to get those holding back to come forward as entrants. Musicians will enter a Battle that offers no prize at all, as the status of winner and the opportunity to perform is in itself to accumulate recognition.

The council chairman proceeds to speak strongly in Warlpiri language for a good fifteen minutes. The sentences are brief, intense and emphasized with firm hand gestures. He pauses now and then in silences that demand respect from the packed hall. He tells them that they are here to celebrate music and sports and family together. What happened last night must not be repeated. It will not be tolerated. Our own people are all we have, he says, we must take care of each other, not fight among ourselves. So please, he appeals with authority, you married women should not dance without talking to your husbands, and you men should not hurt your women and children.

The previous night was the first night of the festival. Lajamanu, like most desert communities, is 'dry', which means alcohol is banned within its boundaries. However, many visitors drank on their way here, and during the welcoming concert, married women got up and danced in the bum-gyrating 'sexy dance' that is common in Aboriginal settings all over the desert (and elsewhere).[2] According to local norms of appropriate gendered behaviour, married women should not dance in public, unless in the company of their husbands or in their own groups, and they should always dance in a moderate manner. Married women, of course, do not always do what is expected of them and may still get up and shake their bums, especially when drunk, which can be perceived as sexually inviting. The previous night a drunken musician thought that his dancing wife went too far. He jumped off the stage and started to bash her up. This provoked more fights when other men disciplined their wives, came to their relatives' help and probably took the opportunity to settle unrelated grudges. The night ended with a few injured people.

Tonight, the chairman's speech seems to have the intended effect. During the first half of the night, before most married women and senior people retire, the dancing is unusually subdued. Women, teenage girls and boys form separate groups, shuffling their feet, with serious faces and minimal bodily movements. Also, the Night Patrols – Aboriginal law and order teams – continuously circle the hall and the community in order to confiscate any alcohol and prevent conflicts from flaring up.

The Teenage Band plays a few songs to give musicians time to enter the competition and for a judging panel to be formed. The organizers, a few men in their forties from prominent Lajamanu families, are looking for judges who ideally are not related to any contestants, a criterion which excludes most people present. Two senior Aboriginal men considered wise and respected enough to vote without bias are approached, and so am I. One of the men is soon loudly contested by the audience for being 'too much related', and after some discussion he drops out, visibly offended. The final panel includes a respected community leader from Yuendumu, one of the non-indigenous sound engineers from Darwin, and myself.

It is now after 9.30 pm. In an attempt to manage the time factor, the organizers declare that each entrant can only perform three songs. They know that contestants usually try to make an impression by extending their time on stage, and it is also common that three-minute songs become ten-minute numbers in a Battle of the Bands. A lot of time also tends to pass between songs when band members discuss what song to do next, and they may then proceed to unhurriedly swap instruments and places on stage. The change-over of contestants takes considerable time, too. An entrant may need instrumentalists to back him up and if he has specific musicians in mind, they are called out for, sometimes repeatedly. If they do not appear, it may take some more time before volunteering musicians make their way through the crowd to pick up the instruments, unhurriedly, in order not to seem too keen. Also, people move about the community throughout the night and it can take time to gather all members of a band when it is their turn.

Most community Battles of the Bands proceed in the form of a musical and social three-staged crescendo that I will elaborate on. The night usually starts in a mellow mood and slow tempo with gospel and country musicians, what I call the 'oldfella' acts. It refers to the oldfella status of the music genres and not necessarily to the age of the performers. These acts are followed by what I discuss as the 'hit and miss' section with less experienced musicians or temporary band sets. They are succeeded by the 'headline' acts, which are the more established and well-known bands. These are my terms for making a common pattern clearer. Local musicians or organizers do not call them anything in particular. In lining up the contestants in this order, however, consideration is paid to both local hierarchies of meanings of musical styles and to different Aboriginal groups and regional relationships.

The oldfella acts

Tonight the gospel and country section includes four gospel entrants but, atypically, no country music performers. First on stage is a well-known, older Lajamanu man, who, with a beaming smile, performs a couple of straightforward Warlpiri gospel songs in a crackling but passionate voice, backed up by a local man on acoustic guitar. He is followed by the Yuendumu Choir: two Warlpiri women who sing well and are backed up by a couple of boys and girls and a Yuendumu man on acoustic guitar. Next on stage is *Kumunjayi* Patterson, the smooth-singing founder of the North Tanami Band and a senior Lajamanu man.[3] He performs a gospel duo with his wife, followed by *Kumunjayi* performing a country-gospel version of 'Knocking on Heaven's Door' in Warlpiri. The last gospel act is a middle-aged Yuendumu man. He asks for keyboard accompaniment. After some negotiation, he accepts a young Lajamanu keyboardist. All acts receive equally warm applause, some whistling and appreciative calls from the audience.

During the opening gospel/country section, the younger part of the audience is usually preoccupied with extra-musical matters as boys and girls move about outside the hall. Men in the next generation, between the age of twenty and thirty-five, tend to divide their attention between social and musical business during this part of the night, but usually pay respect to the oldfella music by joining in the applauding and encouraging calls for each contestant. The main support and attention, however, come from the older folks and the women sitting on the blankets in the hall. If honky-tonk country is played, people will also be up dancing.

Gospel and country, as discussed in earlier chapters, are perceived as the oldfella non-ancestral music forms in Aboriginal Central Australia, and other more recent musical styles have gradually developed from gospel. The social meanings of these music forms can, to some extent, be paralleled to the hierarchical social organization of most desert societies, where senior men, the 'oldfellas', are mediators of the enduring ancestral order. One way in which senior men do this is through their nurturing (authority) and looking after men of subsequent and subordinate generations (Meggitt 1962; Myers 1986). In traditional ontology, too, 'just as The Dreaming is the source of the present, so are the older men the source of the younger' (Myers 1986: 243). This generational model can be loosely applied to understand the hierarchy of music making, where gospel and country music represent seniority and can be said to 'look after' and be the source for rock, reggae and other subsequent and subordinate 'junior' generations of musical expressions. Gospel and gospel-country are also, more predictably, associated with the widespread moral authority of Christian values and orders in Aboriginal communities. For these reasons, it is appropriate that gospel and country are staged first, in order to anchor the Battle of the Bands in regional socio-musical hierarchies of authority and knowledge. It is also the part of the night when all generations are present and can pay respect to the senior music and its performers-mediators, even if the extent to which different age-sets engage varies. When the next set of acts begins, younger generations pay more attention.

The hit and miss acts

What I call 'the hit and miss' section includes less experienced but often keen performers. Some more experienced musicians may also form an ensemble for the night that performs in this section. At times, these acts are ill-prepared. Every so often they are not complete sets, either, and have to call out for additional instrumentalists. Willing men soon emerge, and away they go. And it is just as often a musical hit as it is a miss.

In some Battles of the Bands the 'hit and miss' section goes on for hours. Tonight it has only the one act, the Pawu Brothers, made up of two young brothers of a big Lajamanu family. In his early twenties, the older brother sings, and the younger brother plays the keyboard. They call out for a drummer and Alan, one of the Darwin sound engineers and an experienced African American drummer, puts his hand up. The older brother has composed the three, very long reggae-rock style songs in Warlpiri language that follow. He interrupts the songs several times to instruct his obviously less experienced brother in how to play the keyboard. It takes time between songs, too, when the older brother tries to find the right sound and rhythm styles on the keyboard. The young singer's performance style is, however, well crafted.

He introduces the songs with a professional flair and a clear verbal delivery. He also, appropriately, dedicates each song to different relatives in classificatory kin terms. When singing, he looks as if he is appearing on a world stage, looking out over the audience with a confident posture, akin to male crooners like Frank Sinatra. But he never exaggerates; his bodily expressions are composed and humble, and with his introductions and dedications, he anchors his songs and performance, and thus himself, within his kin network and the Warlpiri sociality of Lajamanu. In this, he combines some appreciated qualities in a young man moving into adulthood according to local Aboriginal norms – the ability to carry oneself with modest confidence and a certain style, while showing deference and paying respect to senior people and circles of relatedness. He is rewarded with encouraging calls and applause, especially from middle-aged and senior men and women.

The headline acts

The 'headline' acts move the Battle towards increasingly confident socio-musical grounds, reinforcing the status of already established male musicians in the regional Aboriginal musical and social scene. Tonight, the first entrant in the section is the Balgo Band from across the border in Western Australia. It is now past midnight and most married women, the smallest kids and older people have left. The floor is taken over by dancers. When their band is called up, the many Balgo visitors crowd into the hall and in front of the stage. The lead singer dedicates the first song to 'all family' and their home crowd erupts in ear-banging whistles and rhythmically shouts in unison: 'Balgo, Balgo, Balgo!'

The five men in their twenties and early thirties start up a tight, thumping rock'n'roll beat and they never let the pace down throughout the set. It is true bad-boy, hard-riffing, pumping bush rock. In a black tank-top that shows off his muscular upper arms when working the guitar far up its neck, the rhythm guitarist fits the bill of conventional, global male rock musician appearance, while his immobile bodily style fits the bill of local Aboriginal male stage conventions. The other men are likewise bodily highly composed and they perform in the same everyday desert wear that most men their age in the audience wear – dusty jeans or plain trousers, sports or printed T-shirts, hooded jackets or chequered flannel shirts, and baseball caps or knitted beanies in the colours of football teams.

The Balgo Band's first number is written for their host community. As a competitive strategy to attract support from the locals, it works. Lajamanu people wholeheartedly join in with the Balgo mob in enthusiastic dancing, shouting and whistling. The singer dedicates their second number to specific kin-categorized relatives in Balgo. The band ends their loud set with 'Two-Faced Woman', a regional hit that the singer dedicates to his 'brothers', that is, men in his generational set of initiates.

The line-up placing of the Balgo Band, and the way they carry out their performance, highlights some local regimes for intergroup and interpersonal relations. First, it is appropriate for the host community to put visiting bands first in the headline section. To stage the home community's well-established acts first would be to inappropriately 'show off'. While the ordering is the same as in globalized concert conventions where star artists (in this setting, the host community bands) come on stage last as the climax of the night, the rationale thus differs. Secondly, the Balgo Band, as visitors on other but related people's country, appropriately returns the hospitality by introducing their performance with a song to their hosts and by dedicating it to an inclusive 'all family'. This embraces most people present who are connected through kin networks and cross-regional ceremonial activities that predate colonization and that were intensified through relocations and cohabitation in colonial and post-colonial times (see Chapter 1). The Balgo Band, in this way, starts their performance by reinforcing the relatedness of most people present, before, with their second song dedication, claiming positions within particular descent groups, and, with their final number, within a specific male age-set.

The crowd settles down during the next act, the Kuramindi Band from Lajamanu. The band has existed for some years but has not performed widely in the region. Their songs are classic desert reggae and tonight they are not well rehearsed. The men make mistakes and have trouble beginning and ending the songs, which is probably why they never get around to introductions or dedications. One song is about Lajamanu and gets the locals dancing and singing along, and the band receives supportive applauds and whistling after their final song.

The next contestant is Chris, the lead singer of the well-known Rising Wind Band from Yuendumu. Earlier in the night I found him sitting on his heels in a corner of the hall, disappointed that the other band members had not turned up. When I asked why, he just shook his head and muttered about family problems, but did not seem to accept this explanation. He still entered the Battle of the Bands, partly in the hope that the others would drive in during the night, and partly, perhaps, as an act of defiance and show of autonomy in relation to the rest of the band. The Teenage Band now steps in and backs him up in three Rising Wind songs. It is unusual that a single member of an established band performs its repertoire in a Battle of the Bands, and I return to this atypical performance later. Chris has an engaging, high-pitched singing voice, but he seems a bit off tonight. He receives a good response from the audience, but it may, in fact, be the Teenage Band they mainly applaud.

The Lajamanu Teenage Band stays on as the next competitor. As soon as they start up their characteristic and widely popular reggae-rock beat, every inch of the floor fills up with dancers. Droves of young kids perform the sexy dance in front of the stage, and further back separate circles of men and women dance together. At the back wall, another performance space is created when teenage boys and girls take turns in performing twenty-seconds sets of highly individualized sexy dance versions, after which they, screaming and feeling ashamed, dash back into the cheering crowd.

The last contestant is the North Tanami Band. This is probably Lajamanu's most respected band. They have performed for more than twenty years across the NT, with songs in Warlpiri and English about common contemporary Aboriginal community concerns and (Warlpiri) history (North Tanami Band 1990, 1995, 1999, 2003, 2005). The members are related within an extended Warlpiri family, and the founder of the band is *Kumunjayi* Patterson, who performed gospel songs earlier. He is gradually handing over the leadership of the band to his oldest son, now in his early twenties. He fronts the band tonight. Neatly dressed in long khaki shorts and an ironed, short-sleeved tropical shirt, he dedicates the first song to his wife and sisters, and the band starts up a deep reggae-rock groove driven by rhythm guitar and keyboards. Every person in the hall is now dancing, but unlike the playful dancing to the Teenage Band, the North Tanami men's performance, their music and the audience's response are more 'mature'. Many dancers close their eyes or exchange contented smiles, and instead of screaming and shouting after each song, people raise their arms in a forward and intimate gesture, while calling out for more.

It is close to 2.00 am, when the band leaves the stage and the list of contestants is exhausted. While we judges gather to consider their verdict, the Teenage Band comes back on stage to keep the crowds on their feet.

And the winner is...

As the judging panel gather to pick one winner and two runner-up acts we follow some tacit conventions that usually guide the judging at community Battles of the Bands. We run down the list of contestants and nod in agreement that the Balgo Band gave a very good performance. In the regional norms for personal and group interactions it would look inappropriately self-assertive on the part of the host community if one of their bands walked away with the first prize.

Because both Lajamanu and Yuendumu are Warlpiri centres, it would also be more appropriate if it went to non-Warlpiri visitors. The Balgo Band happens to be the only contestant who is not from a firm Warlpiri setting. We have a winner.

For the first runner-up place we agree that we should select a country-gospel act. It is common practice in community Battles of the Bands to, in this way, pay respect to these more senior music forms. We settle for the Yuendumu Choir. They performed well, and the judge from Yuendumu thinks that we should support women who get up on stage. For second runner-up position we cannot decide between the beautifully singing Patterson country-gospel duo and the North Tanami Band. In the end, we award the gospel act, since it also extends to the North Tanami Band through *Kumunjayi* Patterson's central role in both. We, therefore, pay respect to the host community's socio-musical hierarchy in two ways: by rewarding a local gospel act and, by implication, a senior Lajamanu reggae-rock act – the North Tanami Band.

In considering judging conventions of community Battles of the Bands, we have now taken into account both the musical quality and some extra-musical norms about appropriate intergroup behaviours and relational hierarchies. On this night, our job was made easier because the two aspects largely coincided.

The winners are declared, and the Balgo visitors go absolutely wild. In a noisy chaos the band is called back for a winner's performance, but the band members are nowhere to be found. Somebody from Lajamanu shouts humorously that the guys must have taken off to Balgo, feeling defeated when hearing the superior Lajamanu acts. This is loudly refuted with laughter and howls from the Balgo side of the crowded hall. One of the band members is lifted up as evidence, causing an explosion of laughter. The Teenage Band keeps people on their dancing feet for the half hour it takes to find all the Balgo Band members and they proceed to perform a set of strong, rocky songs to an enthusiastically dancing crowd. The Teenage Band then again returns to the stage, only reluctantly laying down the instruments when sound engineers Alan and Tom declare that enough is enough. It is now well after 3.00 am. An hour later, Lajamanu is quiet. Smoke is rising from the campfires on the outskirts of the community where visitors have set up camps in the direction of their home countries.

Three interrelated themes raised in this musical battle is worth more consideration in relation to popular music making as an important contemporary medium for crafting Aboriginal male worth in bush community settings. The first concerns the performance of Aboriginal distinctions and relatedness. A second theme concerns the role recent forms of music making have come to play in expressing contemporary concerns and forms of identification in remote Aboriginal settings. The third issue is to do with musical careers as an alternative and complementary way for crafting respected Aboriginal manhood.

PHOTO 5 *Lajamanu Teenage Band.*

Competing Warlpiri men

The fact that the Teenage Band backed Chris up in his performance of well-known Rising Wind songs means that a well-established and popular Lajamanu band replaced and played the songs of a well-respected and popular Yuendumu band.[4] This rather unusual performance put into play some intra-Warlpiri dynamics through which the role of popular music in forging Aboriginal difference and relatedness can be explored.

The Teenage Band no doubt collected a few cross-regional Aboriginal social points by generously and professionally helping out a fellow musician and Warlpiri countryman. They also proved their versatile musical skills by at short notice playing the music of another established band well. I have no doubt that Chris was aware that the Teenage mob, who are colleagues and competitors to the Rising Wind Band in the regional music scene, scored important socio-musical points through his decision to go solo with them as backing band. He would be aware that this would cause reactions among his fellow band members in Yuendumu. Hence my previous suggestion that he did it partly as a show of defiant autonomy in relation to the other band members, who, according to him, could not be bothered to turn up.

The musical actions on the night, and their social effects, should be understood in the socio-musical scene in which these bands operate. Apart from being played on local and regional radio and recording albums, the main way for Aboriginal bands in Central Australia to first of all be recognized and thereafter build up credibility is to perform frequently and widely as this particular ensemble. This is how they accumulate increasing respect as a solid act that can come to represent their particular group, whether this group is based on language, descent or a particular bush community. Chris is clearly recognized in the region as Rising Wind's lead singer. The fact that he performs their songs without the band, and, moreover, backed up by another famous regional band, is, therefore, a way to 'talk back' in challenging terms to his own band mob.

At a later date I brought the performance up with other Rising Wind members. They did regret not going to Lajamanu after all, to reinforce and defend the band's reputation and status. While they did not go as far as overtly criticizing Chris' actions, they were very interested in hearing all the details about the performance. I described in general terms how their songs sounded 'different' when played by the Teenage Band. They shook their heads and looked clearly satisfied that their own sound is inimitable, and it was, therefore, confirmed to them that the performance had not damaged their standing as a Yuendumu Warlpiri act, as distinct from being Lajamanu Warlpiri.

These bands' home communities and Warlpiri occupants are tied to each other through ancestral dreaming tracks that traverse the whole of Warlpiri country and beyond, creating 'a network of spiritual bonds among all the descent groups of Warlpiri society' (Wild 1987: 102). Ever since the two settlements were established, Warlpiri people have also constantly moved between them. At the same time, the two Warlpiri congregations have developed distinct practices and attitudes. They now speak recognizably different Warlpiri dialects, the historical trajectories of people in the two communities differ, and their respective geographical settings and Aboriginal neighbourhoods have shaped different social organizations and contemporary ceremonial styles (Laughren et al. 1996; Wild 1987). For instance, Lajamanu people tend to travel north to Katherine and Darwin for shopping, education and various services. This is also where Lajamanu Warlpiri are likely to settle if they leave the community. Consequently, Lajamanu Warlpiri interact mainly with northern Aboriginal societies and music styles. Yuendumu Warlpiri are instead oriented south to the centre of Alice Springs. In contrast to Lajamanu, Yuendumu is also located in a sub-region with a cluster of sizeable non-Warlpiri Aboriginal communities, and Yuendumu Warlpiri intermarry and have ongoing social, political, cultural and musical exchanges with these peoples.

Yuendumu is moreover the largest Aboriginal community in Central Australia and the most accessible and well known in non-indigenous realms. People here have been the subject of internationally published works and ethnographic film at least since the 1930s (Hinkson 1996). The establishment of Warlpiri Media (Michaels 1986), the increasing fame of the community's Warlukurlangu art centre and the widely promoted Yuendumu Sports festival have further attracted media, musicians, visual artists and researchers from all over the world to Yuendumu. Also, while Lajamanu is located about 120 kilometres from the nearest Aboriginal community, and almost 600 kilometres of rather poor roads from the nearest larger population centre, Yuendumu is located 300 kilometres from Alice Springs, by a wide, partly hard-surfaced road that leads to a mining operation, and it is also used as a shorter and considerably rougher route to north-western Australia (Map 2). The high proportion of non-indigenous people in Yuendumu (about 10 per cent, or nearly 100 people) also makes it more accessible for people who lack experience of Central Australian Aboriginal peoples. Other communities can be more demanding to reach and complicated to communicate with, and less interested and experienced in dealing with outsiders.

All this means that Yuendumu and Lajamanu Warlpiri, just like people in any desert community, have engaged with different intercultural constellations and ranges of people, musical styles and activities. Particular localized forms, styles and sounds of music emerge from such different relational histories and geographical locations, and these differences are further cultivated in community music events like the Lajamanu Battle of the Bands. In the ordering and performances of these events, discrete personal as well as shared ancestral affiliations, intercultural experiences and regional relatedness are articulated and negotiated. In this, these forms of music activity continue to provide a space for the elaboration and recombination of musical, indigenous, non-indigenous and gendered practices, values and imagery. To understand why non-ancestral musical expressions have become especially important means for articulating and mediating contemporary experience and distinct ways of identifying, one will need to consider how music differ to other forms of representation in Central Australian Aboriginal settings.

Representing self and relatedness

In the Lajamanu Battle of the Bands, as in similar events elsewhere in the desert, Aboriginal audiences responded with intense feelings to bands and performers from their particular home communities and family networks. It is also, in the main, their own home crowds the musicians dedicate their songs to, and it is principally towards them that they direct their performance. The home crowd and the musicians, in this way, participate in a mutual reproduction of shared identification in which the musicians and their music not only express, but also come to represent, shared sentiments. It is precisely this kind of status that most of the desert musicians I meet principally aspire to, and that motivates them to pursue a musical life: to become worthy representatives for their home communities and people. This motivates them in trying to write and perform music in ways that create strong and shared emotional responses among their home crowds. Other important driving forces for the musicians, such as the sheer pleasure of expressing themselves through music and from mastering their instruments, or feeling attractive as men by the attention they get from women, or gaining professional recognition in mainstream musical realms, amplify, and are amplified by, the desire to be seen as representatives for their people.

Scholars have noted how indigenous people in different parts of the world are reluctant to appear to represent people other than themselves and their immediate family or household (Dyck 1985). One of the explanations provided is that traditional regimes of organizing interpersonal and intergroup rights and responsibilities have been highly specific according to kin positions and categories, gender and age groups, and in relation to specific sites and country. As a consequence, the authority to represent is seldom generalized. Central Australian Aboriginal societies are, to a large extent, organized in this manner. Traditional forms for maintaining social relatedness, for organizing everyday relations and for ceremonial performances are highly specific with respect to a person's realm of authority. Gender, age, totemic affiliation and associations to particular ancestral country are some of the deciding factors for defining and limiting what a person can legitimately do and speak for. In general, and as Stanner notes on political organization and leadership in many parts of indigenous Australia, 'the idea of a man of authority with right and title to command them over a wide range of many things is foreign to their idea of social life' (Stanner 1968: 46).

By being kept separate from the more restricted and specific ancestral forms of knowledge and expressive regimes, more recent forms of music practices have come to establish a complementary and more open expressive and representative space. In musical events like the Battle of the Bands, people who are otherwise dispersed or segregated by gender, age, kin and residence can participate and enjoy themselves in a shared space. By not mixing ancestral and more recent musical forms, these two expressive genres have also come to address different dimensions of people's lives, and aim at different realms for their intended social effects. In his study of Warlpiri ancestral songs in Lajamanu, Wild describes them as 'direct communications from the spirit ancestors' and as providing an 'authoritative guide to social relationships and to relationships with the land' (1987: 106). This authority principally rests on the capacity of ancestral song genres to connect the living and the dead, and to evoke spirits that are perceived to have supreme powers to manipulate people and the environment in both benign and malicious ways. Ancestral song genres are, for instance, used (with singers as the medium for spiritual agency) for singing people to death, to make or stop rain, to assist hunters in tracking game, for healing purposes and to attract lovers (e.g. Bell 2002; Elkin 1974: 308; Strehlow 1971; Clunies Ross, Donaldson and Wild 1987).

Desert country, rock and reggae musicians commonly describe the potential power and authority of their music to produce social effects in similar terms, but the areas they directly address are contemporary sociopolitical circumstances. More or less every desert musician's song repertoire includes songs about drink driving, petrol sniffing, parents abandoning their children for a drunken life, and people leaving the particular people and country they belong to. Bush musicians express an adamant belief that these songs can move people emotionally and physically to stop drinking, return to their children, people and country, and fulfil their responsibilities within kin structures. They also acknowledge that some people cannot be moved, they are too much 'lost', as expressed in the North Tanami Band's 'Nothing We Can Do' (2003). The perceived impact of their songs depends on the place and social situation of a performance, which I discuss in relation to town performances in the next chapter. My main argument here is that country, reggae and rock performances and songs can bring up contemporary socially problematic issues, at times shameful matters, in a cross-social expressive and representational space. Because the lyrics are kept at a general level and do not address particular persons or groupings, issues can also be presented in an appropriately non-confrontational public form.

There are few other fora in Aboriginal desert communities for articulating sensitive interpersonal, intragroup and intergroup issues in non-specific, enjoyable and cross-social ways. Ceremonial and ritual fora are gender and age specific and the activities organized according to kin and other sociocultural categories. The community council, as the formal representative body of a whole community, is the main forum for bringing up communal issues. However, Myers' (1986) and Trigger's (1992) descriptions correspond with my experience of people's perceptions of councils more as individuals (of particular families) acting in community matters vis-à-vis whitefella governments and administrations. There are also widespread expectations that councils (and council members) should 'look after' people in the community and provide them with both services and material things. But I have no impression that people understand the councils' work or public performance as representing, maintaining and giving substance to the moral, emotional and social cohesion of their community as a whole. The forms of music I discuss here provide exactly such an arena for asserting and reforming valued cohesion and relatedness of whole communities. It is demonstrated, for instance, in the emotional ways in which Aboriginal people participate in country, rock or reggae music performances from their community and the larger Aboriginal desert region. It can be seen and heard, too, in the elaborate ways in which people talk about these forms of music as part of their intimate and shared social history and everyday lives. The suggestion that musical expressions represent communities as well as specific groupings within them is further supported by the all-encompassing turnout of people for local music events.

The fundamentally socially productive aspects of popular music making are rarely acknowledged by researchers of remote Aboriginal life worlds. They may occasionally comment on Aboriginal community people's passionate interest in country, gospel and other recent music forms, but few elaborate on the matter. To take one example, in Myer's extensive exploration of the reproduction of relatedness he recognizes in a mere paragraph how communal singing of hymns in Pintupi language gives a 'substance to the relations among coresidents' that the activities of the community council do not (1986: 269). Gospel music certainly produces such forms of cohesion, but mainly with respect to members of particular local Christian denominations. Country, rock and reggae music, on the other hand, are highly inclusive forms for producing relatedness, identification and representation.

Sports, and especially Australian Rules Football, is another form of performance that provides people with the opportunity to participate in the reproduction of a strong sense of belonging to particular as well as cross-regional socialities. Football teams or individuals who distinguish themselves through sports achievements are also thought to represent their home communities and people. Musical performance does, however, add some significant dimensions that sports performance lacks: lyrical expressions and dance. Song lyrics directly express, evoke and reaffirm shared and individual histories, experiences and emotions. Dance is a way to physically engage and identify bodily to various degrees with such experiences and emotions. In this, musical performance constitutes at the same time collective, interpersonal and personal internal 'conversations' to a greater degree than sport does. In sport performances most people are spectators who (however physically and enthusiastically) watch and evaluate the performance of a small group of men, or in softball, women. In musical performances anyone can participate and identify directly on several physical, emotional, individual and social levels in the event and the lyrical themes, as performing dancers and co-singers.

When comparing Central Australian and Top End music practices in Chapter 2, I discussed how desert musicians keep more recent and ancestral musical forms and knowledge separate. As I have argued here, this compartmentalization not only works to preserve the perceived strength of ancestral knowledge traditions; it also underpins the effectiveness of more recent forms of music making as a medium for articulating contemporary problems and 'mongrel' forms of identifications in culturally appropriate public and socially cross-cutting ways. The crafting of country, rock and reggae musical lives is, moreover, an important contemporary means for men to garner respect and enjoy a sense of worth.

The musical crafting of manhood

There are many examples of established Central Australian Aboriginal musicians who become community leaders and representatives for their people, country and settlements.[5] *Kumunjayi* Patterson, for instance, described to me how his music making was a significant factor for his taking on increasing personal and public responsibilities in Lajamanu. When the North Tanami Band began to perform songs about Lajamanu and local matters for Aboriginal audiences across the region, people started to turn up at his house and ask him to write songs about concerns of theirs that they wanted to bring to everyone's attention. Concerns included parents abandoning their children, people leaving for towns to drink, and domestic violence. The band and their music soon became a resource for community members to bring up matters that worried all of them, and to issue moral warnings and preventative instructions.

By listening to people's concerns, *Kumunjayi* and the older band members Hector and Jarmon told me that they became increasingly aware of the extent of domestic and social problems in their community. Many such issues were never brought out in public because they were shameful and intimately associated with internal family problems. By travelling and performing throughout the region, the men also encountered first-hand other Aboriginal communities' and people's situations. This, *Kumunjayi* said, made them even more determined to work to hold together their own people and the Warlpiri ways of living in Lajamanu. On a more personal level, *Kumunjayi* told me that as part of this increased awareness, he came to reflect on his own way of living. He felt that if he sang to others about taking care of family and Warlpiri Law and to live more responsibly, he had to improve himself. He subsequently gave up drinking and smoking and began to actively engage in community matters. Before his untimely death in 2003, he had progressed to the vice chairmanship of Lajamanu community council and he was a senior Law man.

Talking about his musical and personal life journey, Sammy Butcher in Papunya community and a founder of the Warumpi Band similarly describes himself as a man who gained insights through touring, performing and representing his country and people in indigenous and non-indigenous settings around Australia (see Chapter 2). As a result, he gave up drinking and increasingly focused on the many urgent social matters in his home country. During my field research, Sammy was the vice president of Papunya community council and he has since held representative positions in regional Aboriginal organizations. He also continues to use his musical talent, passion and experience to guide troubled boys and young men in developing creative skills and positive self-images, as an alternative to widespread self-destructive activities such as petrol sniffing and drinking alcohol.

Another example is the late Gus Williams, also introduced in Chapter 2. A president of Hermannsburg and Ali Curung Aboriginal councils, and a senior Western Arrernte Law man, his extensive touring as a country music artist from the 1960s until his passing away contributed in important ways to the respect he came to commands all over the desert region and beyond. Just like Sammy, Gus expressed a strong belief in music making as a powerful 'character-building' activity for younger generations of Aboriginal men.[6] Terry Simmons and Geoffrey Campbell of the Titjikala Band from Titjikala community south of Alice Springs, are further examples of men who, through the crafting of musical lives, have become more aware of their male and community responsibilities. Both men were on the community law and order team, where only men (and women) who command a high degree of respect can be effective, since they are likely to be listened to and obeyed even in emotionally charged, drunken or violent situations.

When I travelled back to bush communities to talk to musicians about the chapters in this book, all of them, independent of each other, wanted me to note how they teach their music to young people (i.e. boys). They described with great pride the youngfella bands or musicians they have mentored and urged me to return for the next community concert so I could see and write about these youngfella's performances. In this, the men emphasized the importance of an Aboriginal man's demonstrated ability to teach and guide younger generations for the accumulation of male status and seniority. Their accrued skills and reputation in country, rock and reggae music making is an important means for this intergenerational labour and recognition.

While most bush community musicians are initiated in customary ways, the degree to which they continue to accumulate male status and seniority through ritual activities and knowledge varies. Country, rock and reggae music making have become complementary and less restricted means for these men to earn increased male respect and status. By being performing musicians, the men effectively become mediators of both internal Aboriginal community matters and exogenous worlds, which become central to their crafting of respected and worthy manhood in their home communities and across the desert region.

Performative mediations

The mediating processes I have discussed in this chapter are reminiscent of Gilroy's discussion of the creation of 'mongrel cultural forms' (1993: 3). He outlines this for black musical culture across the Atlantic as a 'history of borrowing, displacement, transformation, and continual reinscription' (102). In Aboriginal Central Australia, just as in the 'mongrel', diasporic black identity formations Gilroy explores, 'music and its ritual can be used to create a model whereby identity can be understood neither as a fixed essence nor as a vague and utterly contingent construction' (102). By being articulated in musical activity, performance, language, gestures and bodily signification, such 'mongrel' forms of identification are 'lived as a coherent (if not always stable) experiential sense of self' (102).

Focusing on another adoptive expressive form in indigenous settings around the world, Turner (2002) suggests that a consistent lesson of indigenous video production has been how these film makers 'tend to draw upon deeply embedded cultural categories and social schemas organizing forms for the complex visual representations they create and produce' (80). He cautions against interpreting this in terms of preservation of a fixed 'culture', and urges us to instead understand it as 'empowerment of social actors, whatever their degree of cultural "purity" as defined by whatever standards, to produce their own cultural mediations' (80). Such mediations, Turner suggests, are processes in which 'cultural forms, together with the capacity and motivation of social actors to produce them, are reinforced, rearticulated, and transformed in various ways through the use of new techniques of representation and new social forms of utilizing and circulating them' (80).

A lesson of rock, country and reggae music making and performances in Central Australian Aboriginal bush communities is similarly that the male musicians draw upon longstanding Aboriginal musical and social norms and traditions when representing themselves, always in relation to particular Aboriginal others and places, and always in intercultural dynamics. In the process, they reinforce, articulate and transform previous, present and possible musical and social forms for being Aboriginal and men in diverse ways. For these music makers, as for the video makers that Turner discusses, the process of music making in itself 'mediates the indigenous categories and cultural forms that simultaneously inform and constitute its subject matter' (2002: 82).

It is within such conceptual frames that one can begin to understand the male and Aboriginal forms of identification that are involved, for instance, in the performance of the Pawu Brothers singer at the Lajamanu Battle of the Bands. Approached as a performance of 'mongrel' and mediated self-expression, it makes sense to the singer and the audience that he simultaneously portrays himself in the figure of a Frank Sinatra on a Las Vegas stage and a young, traditionally initiated and also Christian Warlpiri man and musician of a particular family, and at a certain stage in the lifelong process of becoming an increasingly knowledgeable and competent Warlpiri father, husband and respected elder. In the Aboriginal settings of desert communities, the success of such a performance of multilayered musical, Aboriginal and male forms of identifying depends on the performer's ability to ground it in prevalent and interculturally modified ancestral norms for respected male demeanour, which vary according to the performer's age, position in kin categories, marital status, and more.

In the next two chapters, I explore how the desert musicians put into play further aspects of male and indigenous worth and respect in the socio-musical settings of town gigs and touring ventures.

6

Blackfellas playing whitefella towns

The previous three chapters have explored music practices and ways of identifying in the predominantly blackfella settings of the Aboriginal recording studio and desert communities. In this chapter, I shift the attention to the relational dynamics of blackfella music performances in whitefella-dominated regional towns. Bush musicians who have performed in regional towns frequently bring up these experiences in ongoing music and social activities in their home communities. In this, they often emphasize their encounters with musicians or music workers in town venues who are not 'bush mob'. They will mention how they mingled with this or that more or less well-known regional or interstate non-indigenous or indigenous musician backstage. If these musicians are from 'big smoke' places such as Melbourne or Sydney, it will be elaborated. If big-city sound engineers or organizers are involved, bush musicians usually make a point of this, too. In their accounts of their gigs in town venues they may also refer to, and, in this way, connect their own performance with, certain famous musicians who have performed there in the past.

In some respects, this talk is similar to that about 'going to see CAAMA' discussed in Chapter 3. It is a way for musicians who start out in desert communities to distinguish themselves as music makers who have advanced from just 'mucking around' in the hinterland blackfella performance circuit. However, in drawing on town gig experiences, it is the whitefella quality of these experiences that boosts an image of being situated somewhat beyond and above the social embeddedness of the hinterland blackfella music scene. Town gigs are thought of as connecting them to a mainstream, non-indigenous musical sphere – an artistic community that stands for what their everyday situation is not.

'Town' is, in this way, often created as an imagined stereotype of non-indigenous spheres, and with ambivalent connotations. These spheres may include people who can represent a 'not us' that is thought of as being 'square', 'tight' and effeminate, as discussed in relation to musical creativity in Chapter 3. As mentioned in Chapter 2, Aboriginal people in these places can also be seen as lacking culturally. In the regional blackfella Central Australian topography described in Chapter 1, 'town' can moreover represent something that drains their own sociocultural strength because of its strong association with people leaving their home communities and responsibilities for a life on grog. At the same time, the men recognize that town spheres are part of the dominant mainstream, while their blackfella position in the bush is a kind of backwater of both the music industry and the larger Australian society. The talk of town gigs, in these ways, reinforces an imagery of a desired sphere where they can tap into greater resources and recognition, and that can also offer a way out from the everyday constraints of their blackfella music making and life.[1]

Looking closer at how a set of community band performances in the town of Alice Springs are carried out and evaluated by the people involved, this chapter will show that, in actual practice, these happenings tend to contradict the musicians' imagery of participating and being recognized in positive ways in non-indigenous realms. In fact, the relational dynamics involved in many ways reproduce the historically established relations of disengagement between Aboriginal and non-Aboriginal people outlined in Chapter 1, but relations are also always transformed.

Todd Tavern, saturday

At 9.00 pm, half an hour after the doors opened, a couple of hundred Aboriginal people have gathered outside the entrance to the gig room at the Todd Tavern, one of the oldest hotels in Alice Springs. The crowd spills out across the adjacent parking lot and down a pedestrian mall. They are here for tonight's concert, a double CD launch of the Ltyentye Apurte Band (2001) and the Titjikala Band (2001).[2] There are lots of Arrernte people from town and many people have travelled from Titjikala and Ltyentye Apurte, located about 90 km apart, a good hour south of Alice Springs (Map 2). Both bands turned up for the sound check earlier in the day and all members are in the venue in good time for the performance.

The two non-indigenous security guards at the door are meticulous in their screening of people. They run a metal detector up and down a black man in front of me to detect any weapons, and ask him to show an ID and money for the ticket. The man can only produce a few coins. Before he can ask around for contributions, he is asked to move away. Two Aboriginal women in their best bush wear – clean, brightly coloured long skirts, sleeveless tops and plastic sandals – are turned away for not wearing covered shoes. Three more men are then denied entry when the guards deem them too drunk. I know one of them as a teetotaller and the others do not seem particularly drunk to me, just tipsy and happy. An older woman that the guards turn away for having 'had enough' is not drunk at all. She is red-eyed, though, which is probably an indication of trachoma or another eye condition common in the regional Aboriginal population. When I reach the door, the guards do not scan me with the detector or ask for ID or money, and they let me in with my uncovered shoes.

About fifty Aboriginal people and a couple of non-Aboriginal people are scattered around the bar and tables in the gig room. As the night progresses and the room fills up, people are divided up, with Arrernte people gathering on one side and people related to Titjikala (a mix of Southern Luritja, Pitjantjatjara and Southern Arrernte) on the other. Men move around to talk to other men. Women tend to stay in the group they arrived with, and many stay in the back of the room for most of the night. The five non-indigenous men and women I can spot during the night all work for Aboriginal organizations.

The Titjikala Band is on first. Clean-shaved and dressed in neat, collared sport shirts, jeans and good shoes, they start with a contagious country-rock tune. Men and women immediately take to the dance floor. During the performance, the band dedicates each song to particular relatives. They play their rock number 'Titjikala is My Home' three times, every time drawing an enthusiastic response from the Titjikala side of the room. They play a few of their other more well-known tunes more than once, too. Between songs, the band members have lengthy discussions among themselves and after about an hour, they seem to run out of songs. After another discussion, singer Ronald simply says 'thanks', and they leave the stage.

After a break, the Ltyentye Apurte Band starts up. All but one member wear baseball caps that hide their faces. Only lead singer Farron shows off his hairstyle, having had the ends of his black hair bleached in a trendy look among local young Aboriginal people at the moment. Some of the members wear their everyday chequered flannel shirts, dusty jeans and dirty work-boots, and others are dressed up in new jeans and clean T-shirts. They begin with three instrumental, thumping hard-rock tunes that rev up the dancing audience. The men on stage do not move much, though, and like the Titjikala Band, look fairly serious and disengaged. From the upsurge of dancers and appreciative shouting, it becomes obvious that the majority of the audience are Arrernte people and this is their band tonight. When the band plays 'It's My Home Santa Teresa', twice, the Arrernte crowd goes wild. A few rather drunk women crowd up to the stage, screaming and stretching out to the musicians. The band members at the front carefully back off and do not respond in any overt ways to this enthusiasm.

The band recently returned from a tour in the Melbourne area, and they are more confident on stage tonight than I have seen before. Usually, their singers are extremely shy, seldom looking up and often turning away from the crowd. Tonight, Farron actually looks at the audience and even talks between songs, dedicating them to relatives and friends. They also start up every new number without fiddling around. It seems like the interstate performance experience has made them more professionally aware and relaxed about their stage manners. They also keep up the tempo right through the set, with Chris going off in tricky, well-rehearsed solo breaks. When they stop at midnight, people are reluctant to leave, some of them very drunk and happy. As soon as the lights are turned on, however, the room is quickly emptied. Stan and Steve from the CAAMA studio have sound-engineered the concert and they now speedily dismantle the stage. The band members soon say 'see you' and they are off, driving back home to their communities.

Post-talk

A week later, I meet up with Titjikala Band lead guitarist Terry and rhythm guitarist Geoffrey in their home community. About their lengthy stage discussions, they tell me that they had, in fact, written a song list but forgot to bring it in the commotion before leaving for Alice Springs. It can be a complicated process of negotiations for community bands to first of all organize a vehicle for a town trip. The Titjikala men moreover had to drive several hours south on rough tracks to pick up singer Ronald in Finke community. The reason they repeated the song 'Titjikala is My Home' several times, Terry tells me, was that Titjikala people requested it, and they did not want to disappoint their home mob. They were also restricted in the songs they could do. Ronald wanted to perform their new songs, many of which he has written. The others realized the limitations of their inexperienced drummer who mainly knew their older numbers. They could not rehearse and 'break him in' before the gig either, because some drunken youngfellas had smashed up their equipment a while before.

Terry and Geoffrey are really happy with the gig, though; their measurement being their home crowd's enthusiastic response and joyous dancing. Terry's only complaint is that the wives and the kids could not be there to see them. Kids are, of course, not allowed in pubs, but the men's wives did come to town for the concert. From the stage, the men could see them at the door, 'Trying to get in, you know ... but them two big blokes stood and pushed. "No shoes! No shoes!"' Terry chuckles with resigned head jerks. Geoffrey lifts his eyebrows in a similar gesture of 'that's how it is, but what can one do?'

Talking with Chris from the Ltyentye Apurte Band, I find that he is less satisfied with his band's performance. He is first of all annoyed because their second singer did not turn up. He was too busy drinking somewhere in town. Chris does not think that they played as tight as they should have either. As I discussed in Chapter 3, among the blackfella musicians, notions of playing tight are often associated with more disciplined and professional ways of playing. They often have an ambivalent view of this quality, at the same time admiring and desiring it and dismissing it as too regimented. Chris is clearly inspired by their recent tour and has described to me on an earlier occasion how they received a great response from the mainly non-indigenous audiences and organizers at high-profile festivals. 'They hadn't heard anything like it before,' he said, shaking his head with a satisfied grin. 'Blokes would come up after and carry on about how they really got off on "real" rock. You know, the lead breaks and that. But also different, they thought, good different, because we sing our mongrel English, the Arrernte.' While Chris was proud of being recognized as a classy rock guitarist on par with any non-indigenous guitarist (but not being too big-headed by saying '*my* lead breaks'), it was a distinct blackfella and somewhat untidy and 'mongrel' quality that distinguished the band as unique. Chris had wanted to show their local crowds and regional Aboriginal musicians their best form, which had gained momentum from the appreciative non-indigenous recognition. When I remind him of the passionate response they still got from the Todd Tavern crowds, he nods, clearly proud but not satisfied. 'Can't wait for the next town gig,' he concludes, keen to show what the band really can do.

Moving community and gender to town

From this concert and the musicians' comments, it appears that the social dynamic of a regional town gig in many respects recreates that of bush community performances, as described in the previous chapter. Of course, for such practical reasons as lack of vehicles and long journeys on bad roads, and because of the pub venue, there are not many elderly people and no kids at the Todd Tavern gig, and teenagers have to stay outside. There are no dogs either. The accessibility of alcohol in town, and in this case, the pub venue, also means that town performances often become drinking happenings, which I return to later.

In its social composition, however, it is almost as if a community performance has moved to town, with blackfella musicians performing before a more or less wholly blackfella audience made up by people from their own and other regional language groups and communities. As my conversations with Terry, Geoffrey and Chris indicate, it is also their home mob the musicians primarily address with their music, and it is their response that counts most in the band members' evaluation of their performance, while other regional Aboriginal musicians' and audiences' opinions also play a role.

The gendered dynamics of town gigs are also similar to performances in bush communities. Men and women largely move in separate groups, and (sober) women behave less extrovertly and restrict their movements, while men are the public 'movers and shakers'. As a concession to the requirements of appropriate behaviour in commercial town venues, few women sit on the floor, though. Like Terry and Geoffrey, many community musicians want their wives and children to be present when they perform in town, to 'make them proud'. Just as when they perform in community settings, their stage appearances in local towns and before regional Aboriginal crowds are a means to further assert themselves as husbands and fathers, and as men of particular positions and status in kin and community realms. In towns as in bush communities, the musicians' comportment is also highly tempered on stage, with minimal bodily gestures, which adheres to the regional Aboriginal norms of appropriate and respected adult male behaviour, as discussed in previous chapters.

At the same time, there is an expectation, and some men insist, an acceptance, that musicians and audiences play the extra-marital sexual field to a somewhat greater extent at town gigs. The access to alcohol in towns contributes to more overt and daring sexual behaviours around town gigs,

PHOTO 6 *Town gig audience.*

and jealous dramas and fights are often played out both during and after these events. In the concert just described, we saw how the Ltyentye Apurte musicians stepped back when pursued by dancing and drunk women. The men are well aware that any indications on their part that they enjoy the women's attention can be interpreted as sexual invitations. This is likely to cause jealous conflicts with wives, girlfriends and relatives, and with the female fans' husbands, male partners and relatives. While big concert nights in remote communities are also framed by a heightened sexual dynamic, behaviours tend to be more closely monitored in these socially dense settings. As we saw in Lajamanu, though, when people are drunk, sexual jealousy can cause fighting around community music events, too.

Hence, while people adapt some conduct to rules and expectations of town venues, and while the drinking creates somewhat more permissive conditions for sexual and other behaviours, town performances by bush musicians largely reinforce gendered and behavioural regimes of their everyday socialities. The musical articulation of relatedness and distinctions, and of male worth, does, however, take on expanded meanings in regional town gigs. This is most evident in the performance of 'community songs', such as 'It's My Home Santa Teresa' and 'Titjikala is My Home', which the bands played several times.

Performing place and people in town

Most Aboriginal community bands of any standing in Central Australia have what I call a 'community song' – tunes named after their particular desert community and with lyrics that may describe its history, celebrate features in the landscape around the place and express particularly strong feelings for this specific place and its people. The musical styles of these songs vary. A common format is very long and emotional country-rock ballads, such as the Teenage Band's 'Lajamanu' which is eight minutes long in its recorded version (Lajamanu Teenage Band 1999). Other community songs are fast, catchy rock tunes, such as Ltyentye Apurte Band's 'It's our home – Santa Teresa' (2001) or Lazy Late Boys' 'Daguragu/Wattie Creek' (1999). Community songs may be set to a desert reggae beat or a country tune, too. Some are sung in a local language, others in English, and there may be a mix of both.

Most musicians tell me that they write these songs to make their own mob 'happy and proud', and these tunes always evoke strong emotional responses among people from the community in question. In this, the performance of community songs reaffirms a sense of intimate relatedness among people from a particular place, and becomes dense occasions for expressing and experiencing shared sentiments, social memories, history and place.

When performed outside the community, an equally important purpose of community songs is emphasized by the musicians – to make their particular place and people 'heard'. In this respect, a community song is a public statement of a community's people and country, representing and placing them on the regional Aboriginal social map and beyond. Especially when sung in a local Aboriginal language, community songs are moreover described by the musicians as a way to prove to other Aboriginal people that their community is 'strong' – that their particular sets of local Aboriginal social relatedness and ancestral Law are actively practised. Community songs, in this way, become contemporary forms for representing bodies of customary knowledge and practices, by using and displaying the language of particular ancestral Laws. At the same time, the performance of these songs is described as a way to reproduce the strength of such local Laws, by using the language of ancestral Laws and therefore encouraging people (and especially younger generations) to use and actively keep the language/culture alive.

The aspirations to make particular indigenous collectivities 'heard' through community songs make these pieces of music especially important for marking out and reinforcing differentiation and relative strength between different Aboriginal desert groups and communities. Anybody can certainly enjoy a community song of other groupings as a great piece of music, but they can never share its sentiments of belonging in the same emotional and socially meaningful ways as people from that particular community and Aboriginal grouping (which may include different language groups). Performed community songs, in this way, musically define Aboriginal exclusivity, just as they are inclusively 'owned' by particular Aboriginal performers and their social groups. I have never heard a community song performed by musicians other than those of the community referred to. And while audiences can respond emotionally to other types of songs, the community songs confirm the highest degree of exclusiveness and inclusiveness of the non-ancestral song genres.

To perform community songs in regional towns has a third, important purpose and power for many musicians, which can be described in terms of the 'gathering power of place' that the songs are perceived to perform. Casey (1996) describes this power as working in many ways and at many levels to conjoin our experiences of time and space with a specific place. This place provides a scene for the experience of our past and present feelings, thoughts, expressions and actions, regardless of our immediate locus. The perceived 'gathering power of place' of community songs is especially important because most Aboriginal desert communities have 'lost' people to regional towns. While people leave for towns for many reasons, when people talk of a person being 'lost' to town, they commonly mean those who get caught up, sometimes for life, in drinking alcohol in towns.[3]

The migration to towns is often experienced as a major problem for those left behind. The continued existence of functioning Aboriginal social life within customary cultural frameworks fundamentally depends on individuals being present and practising specific responsibilities and rights in relation to particular other individuals, groups and tracts of country. Numerous songs by community musicians, therefore, address this issue by, for instance, describing children as crying for their mothers or urging fathers and husbands not to go to town but to stay and care for their wives and children.[4] However, these kinds of songs mainly take the form of precautionary advice directed at people who live in bush communities. When it comes to convincing countrymen and women in towns to return to home country and responsibilities, it is the genre of dedicated community songs that the musicians think are the most powerful. These songs are made and performed to act on people in order to move them emotionally, morally and physically to return to their people and country. Musicians are keen to provide me with concrete examples of the effectiveness of these songs by naming men and women who have returned after being 'lost' for years to town life. From hearing or seeing them perform their community song, the musicians insist, the lost ones got so homesick for their country and people that they managed to give up the grog and town life, and returned home.

To perform community songs can, in these ways, be understood as performing a kind of 'gathering power of place'; a power to emotionally and physically move and transform people and their sense of belonging to a particular place; a power that is sourced from the specific social and physical place that is musically evoked in its multiple social and cosmological meanings. The musicians, as mediators of such performative forces, moreover accumulate status as men and musicians through re-performing community songs. As mentioned in the previous chapter, several bush musicians become leaders and representatives for their communities. The performance of community songs is especially important in reinforcing such representative male authority, because of the perceived power of these songs to act on others.

The particular forces created by blackfella town gigs resemble the 'embedded aesthetics' that Ginsburg elaborates as an orientation for indigenous video producers, who judge the quality of work 'by its capacity to embody, sustain, and even revive or create certain social relations' (1994: 368). It leads her to propose that they understand Aboriginal media 'to be operating in multiple domains as an extension of their collective (vs. individual) self-production' (368). The musical power exercised by community bands in town performances, and the social dynamic of these events, similarly extend and amplify specific social relations, gendered regimes and individual and collective senses of place that form the substance of self-production in the participants' everyday Aboriginal settings. As an effect of the ways in which many blackfella town gigs are performed, then, distinct and internally differentiated Aboriginal ways of identifying are reinforced. The organization of town gigs also reinforce a distinct realm for blackfella identity formation that is demarcated from whitefella orders by certain blackfella 'too much' ways of behaving and appearing.

Organizing town gigs

Driving to the Ltyentye Apurte and Titjikala bands concert, I tune to the Aboriginal CAAMA Radio station. The DJ repeatedly promotes the event and urges listeners to turn up to support their local bands. According to the organizer, CAAMA Music, plenty of copy-machine flyers about the concert have also been distributed around town. I have not come across any in public spaces around Alice Springs but saw some on in-house notice boards of Aboriginal organizations earlier in the week. The local paper mentioned the gig in a few lines in the entertainment pages, merely stating the names of the bands (misspelling Ltyentye Apurte) and the venue. The Todd Tavern did not put up any posters or advertise the concert. As is often the case with community band gigs in Alice Springs, then, this CD launch is not promoted widely in public town spaces, and is not attracting much whitefella attention. In contrast, performances by non-indigenous or interstate (indigenous or non-indigenous) musicians are usually listed in the local papers' events diaries, promoted in separate ads in the papers, and the artists are often featured in news stories. The venues normally promote these performances, too, with posters on town. The existence of a lively Aboriginal regional music scene can, in other words, easily escape the notice of people not connected to Aboriginal networks or life worlds, which includes a large part of Alice Springs' population and the many tourists that visit town.

The often segregated music performance situation in Alice Springs is maintained by both Aboriginal and non-Aboriginal parties. The lack of promotion of blackfella music events in the whitefella realms can be partly explained by the tight financial situation of many Aboriginal organizations, which usually stage such events. They basically rely on the informal blackfella network to do the promotion work for them, and it usually does. At the event described, for instance, approximately five hundred Aboriginal people turned up outside the Todd Tavern without wider public promotion. These strategies obviously exclude most non-Aboriginal people from even knowing about the event, which was evident at the gig described, where the handful of whitefellas in the audience belonged to a particular category; all worked in local Aboriginal organizations.

More importantly, Aboriginal organizers usually do not show much interest in attracting non-Aboriginal audiences. When I asked different organizers about the lack of promotion in non-Aboriginal places, some raised their eyebrows as if they had not given it much thought. These events draw enough people without such promotion, anyway. Others merely stated that it is, in fact, an event put on primarily for blackfellas, who, compared to whitefellas in town, do not have that many happenings put on for them. These organizers did not mind whitefellas turning up, but they also recognized that most non-indigenous people probably would feel uncomfortable in the large gatherings of often rowdy blackfellas.

The absence of whitefella audiences does not concern the Aboriginal musicians much, either, which seems inconsistent with their talking-up town gigs as opportunities to gain increased recognition in a mainstream, non-indigenous realm. In practice, Aboriginal musicians, organizers and audiences instead assert a distinctively 'too much' blackfella presence that tends to limit engagements with whitefellas.

'Too Much' blackfellas

Because I thoroughly enjoy the music of community bands myself, I suggested on a few occasions to different musicians that whitefellas, and especially tourists, probably would be interested in attending a blackfella concert if only they knew about it. This, I argued, could lead to a wider interest for Central Australian Aboriginal music and increased sales of their recordings. The musicians usually responded to this with curious looks, as if such a proposition was unimaginable or perhaps just irrelevant. Resonating with some of the Aboriginal organizers' assumptions that blackfella gigs may be somewhat intimidating for many whitefellas, quite a few of the men also stated, with a certain degree of assertive pride, mixed with self-irony, that their gigs are just 'too rough', 'too drunk', just 'too much' in general for most whitefellas. This 'too much' blackfella quality is often a defining feature of the musicians' self-declared, and ambiguously valued, 'mongrel' status.

When used in relation to town gigs, the 'too much' quality refers to the ways in which many Aboriginal people behave and look in ways that tend to unsettle the non-indigenous town order of appropriate conduct and appearances. It is also precisely such non-indigenous modes of making their presence known that tend to be the subject of non-indigenous complaints, disciplining, interventions and at times fear and disgust. This informs the attitudes of many town venues. Alice Springs has 10–15 public pubs and member clubs that can provide a performance space, and all venues that regularly put on live music are operated by non-indigenous people. Only two or three of them are, to some extent, open for staging Aboriginal performers. When I have called around to find a venue for community bands, some managers explain that Aboriginal bands 'do not suit our clientele'. Others state that they do not put on Aboriginal bands because they do not want the rowdy, drunken blackfella crowd these bands attract. They mention the cost of extra security, the potential cost of damage to property, and the risk of police intervention which can jeopardize their licence to serve alcohol. In this context, it was quite an achievement by CAAMA Music to convince the Todd Tavern to stage the double CD launch, which proceeded without any incidents. A week later, another town gig illustrates the 'too much' and 'mongrel' quality that the Aboriginal musicians and audiences tend to value and cultivate as distinctively theirs.

Todd Tavern, Friday

When I arrive at the Todd Tavern, several hundred Aboriginal people fill up the surrounding area. It is a noticeably larger crowd than at the Ltyentye Apurte and Titjikala bands gig. The performers tonight are the Rising Wind Band from Yuendumu and the Blackshadow Band from Amanturrngu (Mt Liebig), both located north-west of Alice Springs (Map 2). Again, CAAMA Music is the organizer, and Stan and Steve the sound engineers. In contrast to the two bands in the previous gig, only a few of the Rising Wind members came for the afternoon's sound check, while none of the Blackshadow men turned up. The atmosphere outside the pub is rowdy. I see some of the band members involved in arguments. There is some pushing and shoving in the crowds, too, and a fist fight is going on down the pedestrian mall. At the door, people are jostling hard to get in. The security guards refuse many people entrance, but unlike the previous concert, people do not move away when asked and instead start to argue with the guards and each other.

A majority of the people who have come to hear their bands are Warlpiri (Rising Wind Band) and Pintupi-Luritja (Blackshadow Band). With their fairly politically influential networks of families, communities and large populations throughout the Western Desert region, these people, and in particular the Warlpiri, are often perceived as more assertive than many other Aboriginal groups in Central Australia. The assertiveness applies to their interactions both with non-indigenous realms and with other indigenous groups. In his seminal work on Warlpiri people, Meggitt describes a Warlpiri 'ethnocentrism' that 'leads them to patronize other Aborigines in a lordly fashion whenever they meet; but, such is the Walbiri reputation for aggressiveness and fighting ability, the victims generally swallow the sneers in silence' (1962: 35). I suspect that his description would be met with approval by quite a few of the Warlpiri musicians I know. They tend to talk of themselves in similar terms when expressing a Warlpiri pride and strength that they at times associate with their warrior status among desert peoples. They also assert this status in songs, such as 'Warlpiri Warriors' (Rising Wind Band 2000).

The white doormen look increasingly intimidated by the ever noisier crowd and proceed to close one of the two doors. Someone taps my shoulder and a hand waves towards the back of the crowd where Chris, Rising Wind's lead singer, wants my help to get in. I shout to him to try the front bar around the corner where the staff should let performers enter. A moment later, lead guitarist Clifford calls out for my help from another flank of the crowd. I call out the same advice. After some thirty minutes in the now rather aggravated crowd, one of the guards waves at me, the only whitefella in the crush. He stretches out his arm to drag me to the door. I hesitate, not sure how people will react to such a blatant racial prioritization. I have already had my hair pulled and had been elbowed in intentional ways, and I have prior bruising experiences of being targeted as the 'white bitch' at drunken Aboriginal gigs. Some of the Arrernte men up front recognize me, though, and they direct the crowd to make way for me. In a self-conscious attempt to take the edge off my racial free-riding, I grab the hands of a couple of women next to me, tell the guards that they are with me, and we are let in.

The gig room appears very quiet compared to the rowdy noise outside. In the predominantly Aboriginal audience I see Sammy Butcher with family. People approach him to shake his hand throughout the evening, paying their respects to this influential regional musician. Chris and Clifford have also managed to get in and when Clifford comes up and hugs me with a big laugh, I realize that he is fairly drunk. He drags me over to meet his 'oldfellas' and other Yuendumu people. I doubt that he would have made such a public show of me if sober. He is married and I am a woman unaccompanied by a man, and also unknown to some of them.

The Blackshadow Band starts up with their mix of gospel, country and reggae-rock style music while people trickle in from outside. The band was formed in a programme aimed at distracting men from petrol-sniffing and drinking. Several original band members are replaced tonight because their lead guitarist is doing time in prison and the drummer has gone missing. These two replacements are obvious in the rather flat and disorganized performance. By the end of their set, the room has filled up with an increasingly loud crowd. The previous gig's dress code has obviously been circulated. Many women wear new, covered canvas shoes and I see shining white sneakers on many male feet. The fact that the previous concert was free of incidents may also be a reason why twice as many people are admitted tonight.

When it is Rising Wind's turn they muck around on stage for quite some time, frequently yahooing into the microphones and shouting 'we're here now!', 'Rising Wind, yeah!' I saw Clifford drinking solidly during the Blackshadow performance and by now he is very drunk and rather cocky. He keeps ordering Stan and Steve to come up and fix this and that for him. In the end, Stan walks firmly up on stage and talks to him. Clifford then leaves the stage. The other band members look confused. After some more messing about they finally start up a song. It turns into a poor, disjointed performance with several stops and restarts. When the song ends, Chris calls out in Warlpiri for somebody to get 'Scotty', Clifford's pet name. The performance is clearly falling apart and the crowd grows increasingly restless, with drunken and loud arguments erupting around the now packed room.

At the sound-desk, Steve looks defeated and wants to cancel the concert before it gets totally out of hand. Stan looks out over the chaotic room, searchingly. He then makes his way through the crowds and gets hold of Sammy Butcher. He proceeds to the stage, says a few words to Chris, and the Rising Wind Band leaves the stage. Sammy, his younger son and the singer from the Blackshadow Band instead enter the stage and shortly start up a heavy, groovy reggae beat. Within minutes the whole room has turned into a sea of swinging, singing, happy people. After a few songs, men and women start climbing up on stage to dance in the spotlights, lifting up their T-shirts to show their naked, twisting torsos. Swiftly, one of the big-bodied security guards moves up on stage and brusquely pushes the men and women off the edge and into the crowd. He kicks with his workman boots to stop other people climbing the stage. A couple of policemen also turn up inside. They tell me through the noise that the police have been busy throughout the night outside, controlling the tumult and picking up a number of disorderly people. Sammy's three-piece saves the night inside, though, and people have to be persuaded to leave when they finish up about midnight. When I leave an hour later, a large number of Aboriginal people move about restlessly in the streets, I hear loud, aggressive arguments, and see police vans and Aboriginal night patrols circulate.

Repairing musical image, restoring male respect

When I run into Clifford with his wife and children a few days later he does not look directly at me. I make a mild joke about the 'non-gig'. He shakes my hand and says 'I'm alright now' with a subdued gesture. I recognize it as an acknowledgement of his slightly inappropriate behaviour at the gig when showing me off to senior family members.

By now I know what happened on stage when Clifford, a main force of the band, disappeared, which caused the performance to fall apart. Stan first told him to get his act together. He then passed on a message from Clifford's wife who wanted to see him outside. This is why a normally well-organized but now drunken and therefore fairly impulsive Clifford left the stage as the performance was about to start. Outside, he had an argument with his wife that attracted the police. When identifying Clifford they discovered that he had an outstanding warrant in his name and he was put in the police lock-up.

The damage done by the Rising Wind Band's drunken behaviour and professional failure to perform required some subsequent repair work by the musicians. Looking at which relationships the men principally work to restore after a failed event can elucidate how they construe their sense of male and blackfella worth and respect in the particular socio-musical setting of regional whitefella towns. One of the relationships potentially damaged is that between the event organizer, in this case CAAMA Music, and the venue operators. Another involves the relationship between the venue operator/ staff and the musicians. A third relationship affected is the one between the organizer and the musicians, and a fourth, between the musicians and the audience. In this particular gig a fifth relationship is endangered: that between the band members and the CAAMA studio men, Stan and Steve. They were in charge of the practical proceedings of the gig, and have, more importantly, been intimately involved in shaping these musicians' work and reputation in the recording studio.

To begin with the relationship between the musicians and the studio men, the first time they meet after the gig is a few weeks later when the Rising Wind is lined up for a live broadcast from the music studio. A few hours before the broadcast, the band members walk into the studio area. Their heads are bowed and the way they move is even more deferential than the normal blackfella etiquette demands. Stan is in the control room setting up for the event. He sees them but does not acknowledge them with a greeting. The band members stand quietly outside the studio, waiting for Stan or Steve to initiate communication. They have to wait for almost two hours. Just before the broadcast starts, Stan tells them in a few restrained words that by being drunks they will lose friends, and they just about lost him at the Todd Tavern. With Stan now having initiated an exchange, Clifford and Chris nod and state that it will not happen again. This is more or less the only verbal exchange between the band members and the studio men during the night. During the broadcast, the band members behave in a noticeably orderly, timid and polite way, and they are highly attentive and responsive to Steve and Stan's gestures. In short, they bend over backwards to demonstrate their ability to work congenially and professionally with the studio men.

After the broadcast, Clifford and Chris talk to me about recording a new album. They are doing more gospel this time, they say with a sincere and matter-of-fact attitude, as if the album deal is sealed and the studio booked. In other circumstances I would probably interpret this kind of talk as part of the 'healthy competition' in which musicians around the studio position themselves through similar kinds of assertions. In this particular situation, however, when their relationship with the studio men is precarious, it is perhaps better understood as a gesture similar to Scotty's handshake with me earlier – a gesture in the process of redemption and of mending relationship, in this case with the studio men. To talk of a new album as if the recordings are already in progress, while no plans for such a venture have been made on the part of the studio and for which there are no songs written, is to establish in the present a future time and place where these relationships are both restored and further developed.[5]

Their gospel ambitions indicate to me that the band members are also in the process of repairing a bruised image as respected musicians and men at home in Yuendumu. They are, in other words, working to restore their relationship with their most important audience. Drunken behaviour is not in itself uncommon or considered inappropriate, in general, in Aboriginal Central Australia. To drink, often excessively, is, in fact, a more or less expected part of male behaviour and sociability at town gigs, which resonates with longstanding practices and male imagery also in global country, rock and reggae music cultures. A merry and drunken Aboriginal crowd is, in other words, not much perturbed by a band not getting through a performance, and, in my experience, people do not to react much to equipment, or even musicians, falling off the stage in a drunken performance situation. As long as some musicians carry on the night of dancing and fun, people tend not to complain.

On the other hand, and as discussed in the previous chapter, to continuously perform competently in a variety of settings is crucial to the musicians' accumulation of respect as adult Aboriginal men and as worthy representatives of their people and communities. The restitution involved in the relationship between musicians and audiences therefore principally rests with the musicians, and in the main, it concerns their self-respect and self-imagery. The talk about playing more gospel indicates such attempts to repair a dented musical and male self-image. I discussed in previous chapters how gospel is regarded as a more mature, morally responsible and respectable practice in many Aboriginal Central Australian settings, compared with, for instance, rock and reggae music practices. This does not mean that individual gospel musicians necessarily live and behave the way they or the churches preach, that is, as sober, responsible, monogamous family men. I have seen country-gospel musicians walk drunk off stage, too, and I have no reason to assume that their extra-marital activities differ much from those of rock musicians. The one man can also be both a gospel and a rock musician. To publicly declare an alignment with gospel practices and sociability is nevertheless to more overtly demonstrate one's aspiration and commitment to change one's 'bad ways', such as drunken and promiscuous behaviour. For established rock musicians who have messed up a town performance, and at least temporarily have caused damage to their musician and male standing, a stated aspiration to do more gospel music can, in other words, be to express intentions for redemption within their immediate and broader Aboriginal social circles.

None of the Rising Wind members, or any other regional musicians I have seen in similar circumstances, seem concerned with repairing their image as performers to non-indigenous venue operators or staff, or with restoring interpersonal and male respect in relation to them. Just as non-indigenous venue operators tend to expect Aboriginal crowds to behave unpredictably or in disorderly ways, blackfellas tend to expect whitefellas in general to view them in negative ways. The musicians seldom expect non-indigenous venue operators or staff to recognize them as particular bands with a name and a distinct musical profile, or as artists from a certain language group and community. Even fewer expect non-indigenous venue staff to recognize them as individual persons in their own right. Hence, from the musicians' point of view, there are no relations here to repair.

From the point of view of the non-indigenous pub staff and guards, both gigs described were framed by a recent knife attack by an Aboriginal man on one of the hotel's guards. The doormen were, therefore, more tense than usual and were not prepared to take any risks, they told me. There had also been a lot of 'blackfella fighting and anger' outside the pub in the past few weeks, and the staff connected this and the rowdy concert with rumours about the arrival of new drugs in town, as well as with some 'family payback business' going on at the moment. I do not question that such a threatening scenario can create an atmosphere in which the guards and staff are easily provoked to intervene when people act in unruly ways, like when dancers climbed the stage. However, the fact that this scenario is so readily construed in terms of causal connection of rather isolated incidents and disparate and rather vague phenomena can provide an example of how the binary system of indigenous and non-indigenous identification operates.

To disentangle these connections it can first be noted that interracial violence such as the knife attack is rare in Alice Springs. Most violent crimes occur among Aboriginal people. Secondly, the illegal drug scene is not principally an Aboriginal domain in this town. The rock concert situation probably partly facilitates this association, though, as rock cultures, like many other musical cultures, have long been linked to, and attacked for promoting, excessive drug taking, drinking and deviant and rebellious behaviour worldwide (Shapiro 1999). Thirdly, Aboriginal 'family business' and 'payback business', that is, conflicts and revenge actions within and between groups of kin, rarely directly affect unrelated people. These vernacular concepts are used for many different practices and values by Aboriginal and non-Aboriginal local speakers. It nevertheless connotes something very particular Aboriginal, albeit ambiguous and mystified, for many non-indigenous locals who rarely engage with Aboriginal life worlds. In their use, the term often becomes a way to explain (away) conflicts and violence among Aboriginal people as somehow part of their sociocultural makeup, rather than as ongoing consequences of historical relations shaped by deep material and sociopolitical inequality and involving both non-indigenous and indigenous people. The concepts of 'family/ payback business' thus become operative in reproducing an undifferentiated definition of Aborigines as largely unintelligible 'others' – fundamentally different from an 'us', and in this case threatening the normative order of the non-Aboriginal 'us'.

Aboriginal and non-Aboriginal people have always shared town space in Alice Springs, and relations of power and influence among them continue to change in various ways in different town sectors, areas of decision-making and activities. Yet, people continue to resort to the historically established separation between Aboriginal and non-Aboriginal domains and forms of identifying, especially in highly charged situations. The separateness lends itself to reducing the 'other' into one-dimensional categories of alikes, rather than recognizing the rich diversity of persons and experiences in such a perceived category. The threatening typecast imagery of an Aboriginal 'other' construed from causal associations between a knife attack, illegal drugs and violent 'family/payback business' can explain why the sturdy, non-indigenous security guards seem blind to the obvious fact that the red-eyed and barefoot Aboriginal aunties, wives and grandmothers they turn away hardly pose any threat to them.

Turning to the organizer-venue relationship, CAAMA Music stood as a guarantor for these Aboriginal gigs' proceeding in an orderly manner. If musicians fail to deliver or a gig gets out of hand, CAAMA loses credibility. Because most venues already are wary of staging Aboriginal acts, it also impacts negatively on the whole performance situation for these acts in town. I noted that the Todd Tavern did not stage any Aboriginal community bands for a long time after the rowdy Rising Wind/Blackstorm gig, and neither did any other commercial town venue. Most participating blackfellas (and myself), though, thought of the concert as a rather normal town gig happening, with a few people ending up in the lock-up and others with hangovers and a few bruises. When the musicians mess up town performances because they are drunk or gigs end up a rowdy chaos, I find that they are to various degrees aware of the consequences for the organizers and for the blackfella performance situation in town. Such more impersonal responsibilities do not seem to shape their actions much, though. They tend to identify more with, and value, the 'too much' Aboriginal modes of being present in town. It seems, then, that the engagements with whitefellas in an elevated mainstream musical realm that the musicians hold up as desirable in their talk about town gigs are only rarely realized.

Mediating contradictions

To understand the contradiction between bush musicians' portrayals of performances in non-indigenous regional towns as valuable and rewarding engagements with non-indigenous people and professional music realms, and how such gigs are actually organized, carried out and evaluated by the same musicians, I return to the analytical model of intercultural mediation outlined in Chapter 1. This approach begins from a view of the world of one person or group as always implicating the world of others, and it proceeds to analyse the reproduction and transformation of sociocultural subjects and distinctions by prioritizing interexistence, intersubjectivity and degrees of mutual influences (e.g. Hinkson and Smith 2005; Merlan 1998; Sider 2006; Sullivan 2006). It means that any sets of sociocultural practices, ideas, forms of identification and beliefs are conceptualized as emerging over time in direct and indirect social interactions and a layering of experience. As such, forms of difference are understood as always already culturally mediated, instead of as existing before they come into an interaction or relationship.

When the above approach is applied to musical events in a regional Australian town, we can recognize how non-indigenous-dominated orders and norms historically have defined the appropriate and inappropriate, the accepted and reprehensible, and the normative 'us' and divergent racial and cultural 'other'. At the same time, Aboriginal people have always insisted on being present here on their own terms, and they continue to cultivate certain forms of 'too much' sociability and belonging that may disturb town orders as well as cause tensions between different Aboriginal parties. Aboriginal people also continue to contradict their own imageries of how they engage with non-Aboriginal people and domains. An intercultural stance can foreground how these orders and forms of presence and imagery emerge in ongoing historical processes of complex interactions and multidirectional influences, both real and imagined, and always in partial and incomplete ways.

The notion of a 'too much' blackfella quality points to how perceptions of meaningful racial, cultural and social boundaries mask, and are recreated in, ambivalent intercultural processes. One can obviously only be 'too much blackfella' in relation to, and in interaction with, some non-blackfella others. A main question to ask, I suggest, is what uses this 'too much' quality may serve for Aboriginal people. In Cowlishaw's study of race relations in a south-eastern Australian town, she notes how unruly and excessive blackfella ways of being present often are desirable and gratifying experiences for Aboriginal people (2004). Aboriginal forms of defiance of non-indigenous orders, including violence and rowdy behaviours, and non-indigenous disciplining and complaints about such ways of being present, demonstrate to her how members of these two 'warring' parties use each other, and are dependent on each other, to create the moralities of meaningful and purposeful everyday life. Cowlishaw suggests that this can explain why people do not want to abandon racial divisions even when they realize that these are full of inequalities and pain.

Aspects of the self-defined 'too much' blackfella ways I have described may indeed, in some situations and for some individuals, be a form of resisting and defying unequal racial orders. In this setting, however, I find the binary framing of non-indigenous and indigenous relations in terms of dominance and resistance too limiting for understanding the complexity of experience. It not least casts contemporary indigenous lives as primarily formed in opposition to non-indigenous orders, which makes it difficult to account for a reality where people self-identify and experience others in ambivalent and multilayered ways, both within and between the perceived categories of indigenous and non-indigenous.

In the desert region, Aboriginal people make up a larger proportion of the population than in the town Cowlishaw describes. To a certain extent, Aboriginal desert people can develop their sense of social selves not only in interaction with non-Aboriginal orders, but also within Aboriginal-dominated spaces where distinct and differentiated non-Western orientations and practices are co-present. Aboriginal ways of being co-present, whether defined as 'too much' or simply 'our ways' in relation to non-Aboriginal ways, are here also, and at times more, about enacting and negotiating forms of Aboriginal difference, inequalities, authority and power – gendered, age-related, economic, moral or based on ancestral knowledge. Such Aboriginal modes of managing relations and authority are reproduced and modified in regional intercultural dynamics, which also mediate broader and shifting ideas and policy aspirations, such as the maintenance of 'Aboriginal culture' and social inclusion.

The fact that aspects of the 'too much' blackfella ways confirm non-Aboriginal stereotypes does not elude Aboriginal people. I discuss in the next chapter how the musicians may 'play' with both negative and romanticized stereotypes of Aborigines, as well as with their own stereotypical perceptions of whitefellas. In analytical terms of intercultural mediation, I understand these gestures not primarily as forms of defiance and resistance, but as creative ways to communicate perceived and actual differences and commonalities which are variably desired, denied and asserted. In the existential sense that all humans seek to maintain integrity and dignity as individuals and groups in co-presence with not-self others, I also hear the talking-up of town gigs as taking control in a marginalized and limiting life situation. It can be seen as demonstration of people's ability to switch between worlds they claim as their own and those spaces considered worlds of others.

The conceptual frame of intercultural mediation can, in these ways, make clearer how, in the making and expression of meaningful racial and cultural distinction, Aboriginal and non-Aboriginal people continue to depend on each other, both across, between and within those groupings. As Weiner notes, it is not always possible to even distinguish between 'difference' emerging within a perceived cultural group, and 'difference' emerging between two such perceived entities (2006: 17). The boundaries and the perceptions of bounded cultures are themselves emerging and reproduced in interactions shaped by mutual and divergent expectations, interests and influences.

This approach brings into focus the incomplete nature of ideas and ideals that the desert men mobilize in their efforts to make meaningful and coherent sense of themselves and others. Their talking-up of town gigs into imagined rewarding non-Aboriginal places of plenty emerges as socially productive as it serves a purpose in Aboriginal sociality and places. It is in these places that the imagery of participating in, and to some degree mastering, a non-Aboriginal socio-musical sphere can be rewarded with increased real Aboriginal male and musician status, even when such participation is not realized as imagined. It may contradict the men's portrayal of town gigs as productive for relationships with mainstream non-Aboriginal domains, but it does not make those ideas less powerful in the men's crafting of their self-perceptions as worthy musicians and men of particular Aboriginal groups and places. In the next chapter, I continue to investigate such interculturally crafted manhood and indigeneity when desert musicians go on tour beyond their home region.

7

Touring blackfellas

Late on an October afternoon, two four-wheel-drive vehicles with trailers fully loaded with instruments, sound equipment and rolled-up swags leave Alice Springs.[1] Eight Aboriginal musicians, roadies and I are going north, leaving the desert for a month-long tour. The plan is to drive the 1,500 km north to tropical Darwin for a big Aboriginal concert. The journey will continue to Broome on the north-western coast of Western Australia, where a number of other artists will meet up and perform at the indigenous Stompem Ground festival. After the festival, the crew from Alice Springs are to be joined by two Central Australian acts, the Teenage Band from Lajamanu community and Pitjantjatjara man Frank Yamma. Frank will also bring non-Aboriginal band members from Melbourne. These two acts are to embark on a 'Bush Tour' with gigs in townships and Aboriginal communities on the way back to the NT and Central Australia. Returning to Alice Springs four weeks and more than 7,000 km later, most of the plan has been accomplished, despite practical and personal dramas that more than once threatened to put an abrupt end to the whole venture.

This chapter explores the ordering dynamics for the blackfella and male ways of identifying that emerge as the heterogeneous group of Aboriginal musicians and men from Central Australia engages with people, places and music practices beyond their home region. During this venture, like in other touring projects I have followed, two broader intercultural dynamics appear. The more prominent dynamic highlights blackfella differentiation and unity. The other key dynamic, which I discuss in the second half of the chapter, concerns interactions between indigenous and non-indigenous people, ideas and socio-musical conventions.

To organize a blackfella tour

The planning of the touring venture begins in the CAAMA Music studio about five weeks before the departure, when the Aboriginal studio employees Stan and Steve see an opportunity emerge from a number of musical, financial and personal circumstances. Several artists on the CAAMA Music label are performing during the week-long Stompem Ground festival in Broome, and CAAMA Music has also secured part-funding for a 'Bush Tour' of Aboriginal communities with the Teenage Band and Frank Yamma. Frank is on the Stompem Ground bill, too. In addition, the legendary Warumpi Band will give their final performances in Darwin and at the Stompem Ground before their formal break-up, and studio manager Stan is their bass player. A CAAMA film team will document the Warumpi Band's finale, and the CAAMA management group is due in Broome for a national indigenous media meeting. With all these artists and people related to CAAMA converging on Broome, and money for a Bush Tour, all is in place for a high-profile promotion of CAAMA Music at this time, and for rejuvenating the somewhat neglected fan base in the north-west region for Frank and the Teenage Band. CAAMA subsequently arranges a special showcase concert with their artists in Broome, and the ticket sale is to contribute to the Bush Tour. Frank's Melbourne-based manager, Simon, is contacted to organize Frank's band there. He is also put in charge of the Bush Tour budget and for booking tour venues. The studio men are responsible for organizing the rest of the musicians, roadies, sound equipment and vehicles.

The studio is chaotic the day before the planned departure. The CAAMA Music vehicle still needs to be serviced and Stan is still chasing Herman, the sound-service provider, for the PA for the Bush Tour (i.e. Public Address system; the basic sound system for stage performances). The final approval of the funding for the venture is not in hand either. The preliminary approved $10,000 budget relies on the men staying in shared, low-cost accommodation, the two Bush Tour acts performing most nights of the tour, and the door takings exceeding the costs for venues. At this stage, though, only four gigs are preliminarily in place. The upstairs manager appears in the studio area several times during the day, asking for confirmation that more gigs are booked before she gives the final go-ahead. Stan assures her that they can easily pick up gigs along the way. 'That's how us blackfella musos' do it all the time,' he tells her calmly.

When trying to get the numerous technical and practical aspects of a tour together, Stan and Steve are, thus, working with many uncertainties, while also chased by a string of people who want them to confirm details on everything from dates and places to technical and financial matters, all of which keeps changing with every hour. In the commotion, they ignore the constantly ringing studio phones. Only people who make their way to the studio and are lucky enough to catch them therefore have any idea of what the current plan is. This means that Frank's manager in Melbourne cannot find out if the tour is definitely happening, while he is under pressure to confirm and budget for more tour venues and verify the itinerary for the Melbourne musicians.

At the end of the day the plan is to have the vehicles packed late that night, ready to go early next day. Next morning, nothing is packed. Stan turns up in a tracksuit, clearly having just woken up. The PA needed to be fixed and he and Herman worked on it till early in the morning, with a few details still left to be sorted out. Steve is at home, having promised his wife to put up a wall in their house before he leaves. The CAAMA vehicle is still at the workshop. Posters for the tour need to be collected from the printers, too. The rest of the crew turns up at the back of the studio and we watch Stan and Steve come and go for hours. None of the men is convinced that they actually will leave today, which does not seem to faze them much. After lunch, however, the vehicle is ready to pick up, the PA works, and in a last-minute rush, the crew is equipped with a mobile phone. The men pack the gear tightly into the trailer and vehicles and a few hours later we roll north.

On the road

After a couple of hours on the road, a certain calm settles in with the realization that the whole venture is, in fact, in motion. Steve feeds the cassette player with bashed-up tapes from the glove box – classic Aboriginal country music or European pop – and the tape played the most, on this first day of the journey, is a live recording from an Aboriginal regional music festival. The men know many of the musicians and they comment on styles of playing, how particular songs turn out and add stories about drunken or drug-induced dramas and sexual adventures that went on at the time. They weave this in with stories from other tours and festivals. It is the kind of talk that constantly surrounds the music work in the studio, band rehearsals and when desert musicians gather for musical events, and which connects them to a wider world of music making and male experiences beyond their everyday settings. By reconstructing such events, the men now create an air of excited expectation about the upcoming weeks – a sense of free flight where anything can happen, and a realization that they are going to be part of the 'real' thing, which is both the energizing thrill of it all and a source of some trepidation.

After a few hours' sleep by the roadside in our swags we reach the small town of Katherine the next morning. The men are supposed to drop off posters for the concert at the Katherine Hotel that is booked for the end of the Bush Tour.[2] Nobody shows any sign of taking the task on. I get a begging glance from Steve. When they are about to give it a miss, I take the posters, walk over to the pub and get hold of the non-indigenous manager. He knows nothing about the concert but takes the posters. Back in the car I inform the men that the concert is news to the hotel. Nobody seems concerned or surprised.

PHOTO 7 *Bush Tour accommodation.*

The men just chuckle and say defiantly that the town will know 'soon enough', when the bands and their blackfella supporters 'hit' the place. Somebody adds that they (whitefella town people) never say no to blackfella money, anyway. As discussed in the previous chapter, the blackfella musicians tend not to expect whitefellas in regional towns to register their presence or musical activities much unless they are 'in their face' – too many and 'too much' blackfella to ignore. They also recognize that their gigs are lucrative for publicans, just as the Aboriginal population, to a great extent, sustains the non-indigenous small-town businesses across this remote region.

As in relation to gigs in Alice Springs, the Aboriginal crew also show limited or no interest in making use of the promotional posters for the Bush Tour during the trip. They tend to trust the local blackfella radio stations and networks to spread the word about performances. As around the studio, the men moreover tend to approach the details of the touring plan, such as set dates and times for particular gigs, more as possibilities than as facts. Circumstances change, and posters that lock in their movements narrow the space for each man and the whole touring party to improvise and adapt to new situations as they see fit.

Precisely such a new situation appears about an hour south of Darwin when the fifth gear suddenly slips out with a loud bang in the studio vehicle. Oil is seeping out of the gearbox, which is obviously finished. To me, this seems to be the end of the tour. No main vehicle, no tour. In five minutes, however, Steve has figured out that an old mate with a workshop in Darwin could change the gearbox in a day. On a very noisy fourth gear we reach the workshop before closing time. While Steve consults his friend, Stan is on the mobile to the CAAMA manager. She tells him to cancel the whole venture. There is no money for a new gearbox or for a replacement vehicle, or for flying the musicians to Broome. Stan assures her calmly that they will fix it and hangs up with a 'see ya' in Broome!' No second-hand dealer we find open has a gearbox for the car model, though. Steve now shakes his head in defeat. A few quiet moments later they come up with a new idea. They call back to CAAMA and get hold of the financial manager just as he is about to leave for the day. After some investigation he confirms that the vehicle is actually still covered by a dealer's warranty. The men just have to find the accredited workshop in Darwin.

We make our way noisily to Darwin city and stop at a main-street motel with a 'vacancies' sign. After some confusion, because no clear agreements have been made on how costs are going to be handled or what and how the roadies are getting paid, Stan pays and allocates the men to shared rooms. The men have been talking about a shower since waking up by the road this morning, and there has been a fair deal of bantering about gulping down cold beers and checking out the pretty girls in Darwin. This is what the rest of the men are concentrating on for the rest of the night, while Stan takes off to rehearse with the Warumpi Band. Next morning, he and Steve disappear early. When they are back they inform us that it will take a week to fix the car, but they have chased up a big rental camper-van that will get them to Broome and back.

During the following weeks on the road the more or less accepted uncertainty and unpredictability that shaped the departure is to be a main mode of operation of the blackfella touring party. So is the creative improvisation in solving whatever practical problems come before them, as demonstrated in the car trouble. The collective drinking late into the nights that began in Darwin will be repeated throughout the trip, and the reluctance to deal with non-indigenous realms, as in relation to the mooted performance at the Katherine Hotel, will be another characteristic feature of the blackfella modus operandi, which I return to later in the chapter. I first explore some intra-blackfella dynamics that emerge as the tour proceeds, for which I backtrack to the first day of the journey.

Narrating blackfella men in other blackfella places

Travelling north from Alice Springs, the men keep commenting on the country we pass through, connecting it with their own and other known Aboriginal families and individuals. Some of them grew up in places along the way and belong to language and kinship groups that are traditional landholders of these areas. They also share memories of performances in Aboriginal communities along the road. When we stop for breaks, the men in the two vehicles continue this exchange of names, knowledge and experiences of places we have passed. The exchanges are not conversations as such, where the men engage with what others say. It is more like a sequence of statements in which they make their contributions to re-enforcing the vast desert and savannah country as a known and relevant blackfella social and musical realm.

When we get closer to Darwin, and even more so when travelling west and leaving the NT, the comments on the country we pass through gradually run out. The blackfella socio-geographical realm becomes an increasingly unknown and 'other' space, open to the men's imaginations and often fearful stories or complaints. On the second afternoon in Darwin, for example, the men bring back food to the motel room. While eating they swap Aboriginal Darwin stories that they have heard. One is about 'alley cats'. These unreliable feline, implicitly feminine creatures are supposed to live in alleys 'out there in the Nightcliff area, 'ey! And they follow single men around!' Another story is about 'this big woman. She's a ghost. True! She sits in the back seat of cars, only with single men, but when you look back she's not there. You only see her in the back mirror. She's supposed to have thrown herself from a rock out there in Nightcliff, killing herself over a man, they reckon.'[3] The men make faces and draw up their shoulders as if hit by chilly air.

Lyndon tells me later that night that he does not like Darwin. The others have also started to complain by now. They do not like the humid tropical heat or, due in part to an incident that I return to, the motel. Lyndon's added complaint is about 'the stories in this place, you know. I don't like them. Not my kind of thing. I don't like being here!' The further away from known country and people the men travel, the more common these kinds of statements about feeling uneasy as blackfellas in other blackfella places become, and the more the men tend to close ranks as a group.

One way in which they negotiate their understandings of themselves in foreign blackfella places is, as we saw, through narrating themselves into blackfella stories in those places. The motel-room stories are obviously about themselves. They are now, in effect, single men and therefore perceived as exposed to sexual temptations and social dangers, here dressed up as predatory, yearning and somewhat revengeful female figures. In telling such stories, the men put into play their own blackfella norms of social control and related notions of appropriate male and sexual behaviours, including aspects of Christian models for morally virtuous male behaviours, where the sacred status of monogamy within marriage looms large. They also include norms that draw on ancestral belief systems for organizing kin relations, where the formation of appropriate sexual relationships is between men and women of particular kin categories, and not others. These norms shape models of adult manhood where Aboriginal men earn respect by being fair, authoritative and responsible in relation to their wives, children and younger men. They may be shamed and shame their families if they disrespect such interactional norms. All these ideas are co-productive as the men narrate themselves in other blackfella places. Stories such as those shared in the motel room can operate as self-imposed warning signs for the men that promote greater self-control and sexual discipline. At the same time, the stories demarcate the interlocutors as blackfella outsiders who lack inside knowledge of the blackfella dynamics in the place they are in, which accentuate the potential dangers of acting indiscreetly because they cannot foresee the consequences.

On tour, these modes for identifying as indigenous men are also constantly negotiated through imagery of global musical cultures, where hard drinking, drugs, sexual adventures and non-conformity to mainstream norms are commonly accepted, expected and valued masculine behaviours. The tension between these models for masculine behaviour is a constant feature of the men's activities during the tour, as illustrated by the stay in Darwin.

Blackfella musicians in other places

The last night in Darwin, the crew team up with the male Aboriginal film crew from Alice Springs and party into the early morning hours. Mostly a non-drinker, Stan tries to keep out of it, but as we sit and talk in one of the rooms, the other men constantly come asking for his help in the drunken dramas out in the street. A few of the men are pursuing a couple of very drunk local women. A couple of the others turn up to hide in the motel room, deeply shamed over their fellow men's behaviour. 'You have to be fucking careful, man! This is not our place, we're fucking desert rats, we don't belong here!' one of them cringes, crouching on the floor with his arms over his head. He declares that he cannot continue the tour, the group is now shamed. Soon thereafter another man storms in, panicking over having lost the keys to the touring van, followed by another crew member who begs Stan to come and sort things out with those drunken, now sick, women. When Stan drives the women home, a second man declares that he has had enough already of this life on the road. 'I am a married man, sis'!' he wails, drunk and stoned. 'I have a six months old baby! There are things I can't do anymore, I have responsibilities!' he says and shakes his head in defeat.

A younger man instead craves for the freedom of being out of the blackfella regimes at home. He recounts the strict disciplines he has to endure from the senior men in Central Australia. To prove his point he pulls up his shirt to expose a broad scar on his lower back. 'You know how hard mulga is, bros'? It's fucking hurtful, man!' he challenges them.[4] 'I want to get out of it, bros', out on the road, become a pro,' he declares glumly. He saw the sound check with the Warumpi Band the previous afternoon and describes how professional and respected they are, how they stay in the best hotels and are paid well. He states that from now on he will turn down his 'oldfellas' when they tell him to play for them. They treat him poorly and never pay him.

The older men nod and say that with his talent he can go a long way with his music. But they scold him for complaining about the oldfellas. 'Listen bros', one of them says sternly, 'you shouldn't disrespect your grandparents! We are all brought up older than we are. I had to do stuff a twenty-one-year old should when I was sixteen. Got a lot of hidings, too, we all did! You just take it, and get on with your life!' By bringing a junior man back in line, the senior men here reinforce some basic Aboriginal values from home, where younger men are expected to show respect for men older than themselves, and where senior men exercise authority and responsibility in relation to junior ones. This hierarchy of male respect is reinforced within the Aboriginal group throughout the tour. The youngest member is at times 'bossed around' by the older men, who may order him to run errands for them or point him to the most uncomfortable place to sleep. At the same time, they 'look after' him by making sure that he is fed (he came on the tour without money) and that he does not drink too much.

The men's stories from the nights in Darwin will be repeated during the tour and long after the return to Alice Springs, their theatrical imitation of each other becoming ever more exaggerated and funny. There is one of them, so drunk and stoned that he stands as a paralysed 'scruffy blackfella' in the midst of the teeming, smart inner-city clubbing crowd. There is the bar where they are about to be thrown out, and there is the strip club, and the rock club with a live band. These nights become the happy memories from the trip for them, before any serious work started and the weariness began to show. Over time, the repeated re-enactments of these nights sediment a self-ironic narrative of a mob of 'desert rats' hitting the 'big town' and being out of place in an innocent, hilarious way – a narrative that becomes important for articulating male bonding and prowess in the touring party. As in the drunken situations in Darwin, individual men may disagree with aspects of less restricted behaviours and may try to keep it somewhat under control by referring to their everyday Aboriginal norms for responsible male behaviours. All of them nevertheless tend to accept the fact that when they are on tour away from home, many restrictions are negotiable and many of them no doubt want to take advantage of the more permissible conditions.

Back home in Central Australia, the self-narrative will later create a bond between the men who were part of this touring adventure. When told to others, the selectively narrated 'wild' blackfellas on tour (they never bring up the boredom, exhaustion and non-eventful times that make up a considerable part of touring) will also enhance their status as more experienced and street-wise men and musicians. A further elevating aspect of touring experiences concerns the assertion of blackfella musical brotherhood imagery.

Blackfella musical brotherhood imagery

When at home in Central Australia, the Aboriginal musicians mostly describe their touring experiences in positive terms. It is a more advanced version of the talk about town gigs, as described in the previous chapter, in that touring narratives elevate the narrator further and therefore tend to leave both community music events and town gigs in some kind of backwater of ordinariness. Apart from being perceived as valuable occasions for professional interactions in a non-indigenous realm, touring narratives also often emphasize interactions with other indigenous musicians and musical styles. The musicians mention how great it is to meet up with other famous or less well-known blackfella artists, how they end up in impromptu performances with them, and how inspiring it is to hear and see a wide range of Aboriginal styles of music and performing. Talk about appreciative local blackfella audiences in other places is also common, and how important this feedback is for their motivation and development as Aboriginal musicians.

The musicians, in these ways, commonly evoke an imagery of tours and music festivals as loci for producing and consolidating what Slobin calls an 'affinity interculture' (1993: 68), through a mutual learning from direct contact between artists. Festivals, Slobin suggests, 'can create a musical world without frontiers, one that seems to exist across, or somehow suspend above, national lines' (69). The Aboriginal musicians' touring narratives suggest a blackfella version of such an affinity intra-culture: a distinct, idealized blackfella socio-musical brotherhood without frontiers. However, on most occasions when I have followed Central Australian musicians on tours, there is little direct evidence of them cultivating such a musical black brotherhood. The Warumpi concert in Darwin can show how the men seldom seek to establish blackfella bonds even across regional lines.

The Warumpi Band's second to last performance of a twenty-year-long career is part of a concert with well-established Aboriginal bands from the Top End. It is held in the outdoor amphitheatre in the tropical Darwin Botanic Gardens, where a couple of thousand people have gathered for the event. Here are indigenous scruffy 'bushies' and dressed up 'townies', as well as non-indigenous dread-locked 'ferals' and modestly dressed, middle-class families. People dance in front of the stage and when the locally popular Wildwater Band finishes up, they receive enthusiastic applause and whistling.

The Saltwater Band from Galiwinku in Arnhem Land is on next. Alluding to the water-related names of the Top End bands, the Central Australian men joke about being the 'no water mob' when we move up the grassy slope to get a good view of the stage. The Saltwater Band is a highly respected act in the Top End and they have toured both interstate and overseas. They perform with dancers in red hip-cloths, ornamental feathers, and bodies and faces painted in ancestral patterns, while the six instrumentalists and singers are dressed in the more mainstream ways. Their songs are of the prevalent Top End style of smooth, reggae-island music sung in Aboriginal languages, interspersed with ancestral song styles and accompanied by *bilma* (clap sticks) and *yidaki* (didjeridu).

The crew from Central Australia are not that impressed with this island-style music. They make a few disinterested and rather negative comments about blackfella Top End music in general and soon lose interest in the performance altogether. Stan has fallen asleep and wakes up just as the Saltwater Band leaves the stage. He stands up and strolls leisurely down the slope. Minutes later, he enters the stage with the rest of the Warumpi Band. Large crowds of screaming and whistling people now stream down the slope to the stage.

Lead singer George shouts a hoarse 'Hello!' and the crowd responds with a massive howl. He is in his usual stage gear – slim-fitting black jeans patched with Aboriginal flags, and a vest in the Aboriginal flag pattern. The only other remaining original band member is non-indigenous guitarist and singer Neil. Nowadays, Stan is the only Central Australian in this famous Central Australian Aboriginal rock act. All five men perform in rather ordinary pants or jeans, shirts or T-shirts, and they are in their element tonight, performing the most loved Warumpi numbers while the Central Australian film team is shooting them from all angles on stage. A middle-aged Aboriginal woman beside me in front of the stage cannot stop laughing all through the performance. Tears are running down her face from being moved and happy by the music. Other Aboriginal men and women respond in similarly emotional ways, and both indigenous and non-indigenous men and women lose themselves in joyful dancing. When the band walks off stage, the crowds screams, whistles, stomps and shouts until the band returns for an encore. They end with a captivating version of 'My Island Home', a country-rock ballad that has become a kind of indigenous

PHOTO 8 *Warumpi Band on stage.*

national Australian anthem. An Aboriginal man, overflowing with emotions, grabs my shoulders and rocks me for a good minute while repeatedly crying 'Was that *good*, or *what!*'.

Most Central Australian musicians I meet place the Warumpi Band in another, higher league of music making than their own. At the same time, the band was just like them when they started out: a bunch of bush community guys who were passionate about making music, built up a repertoire of locally grounded original songs and through their continuous performing around the desert region came to be perceived as representing their people, language and community (Papunya). Many desert musicians participated directly in the making of the Warumpi Band, too, as fellow local musicians, audiences, relatives and members of the regional blackfella sociality that shaped the band's early music and career. They can, therefore, identify closely with the band and its music, and can see them as a realistic model for their own music making taking off into another league.

When the Papunya members retired in the mid-1980s, the Warumpi Band proceeded to make their fame outside of Central Australia with indigenous and non-indigenous musicians from elsewhere. For many desert musicians, Warumpi then became, almost, like any other Aboriginal band from elsewhere – grounded and meaningful in other musical, male and social relatedness. This is evident in the Darwin performance, where people of all kinds of origins respond in intimate and passionate ways to the band and their music.

Hence, the Central Australian crew's attitudes to the Warumpi Band's performance are partly informed by a historical intimacy, and partly by a degree of detachment because the band is no longer embedded in Central Australian blackfella worlds. The men's immediate identification with the band is, moreover, framed by Stan's involvement with it, and is coloured by their relationships with him. While these different levels and qualities of identifications are put into play within the male group, it is, in tonight's line-up, with the Warumpi Band's performance that they can claim a special relatedness to as the 'no water mob' from the desert. Before the performance ends, I see them disappear backstage where they join the jostle of musicians, managers, stage crew, camera men, fans and groupies. Looking closer, however, they do not engage much with these people. Instead, they soon find the Aboriginal men in the Alice Springs film crew and they all leave for a night on the town.

What emerges, then, is a group of blackfella Central Australian musicians and men in a place away from home who gather and feed off the energy of devoted fans of a band that is widely perceived and promoted as a legendary Aboriginal rock band from a desert community. While the band has long been a mixed non-indigenous and indigenous band based elsewhere, the Warumpi performance becomes a means for the men from the desert to reinforce their own particular blackfella exclusivity. Here, as in other places during this tour, and as I have observed when following other Central Australian musicians on tours, they do not show much interest in interacting directly with other indigenous music workers, or in exchanging musical experiences and styles with them. The stories they tell about these events nevertheless tend to emphasize precisely such interactions, exchanges and shared experiences. Other ways of contradicting their rhetoric of a productive blackfella musical and social affinity 'without frontiers' emerge as the men perform in fairly dense Aboriginal social settings during the Bush Tour.

Too much blackfella 'Others'

It is mid-morning when the touring party drives into the small, remote township of Halls Creek in the north-west Kimberley region (see Map 1). The Central Australian crew has now been joined by Frank, his Melbourne manager and non-indigenous musicians, and the second Bush Tour act, the Teenage Band, who turns up later in their own vehicle. During the hot and humid day, the Aboriginal men more or less stay put at the community hall where they are to perform tonight. The Melbourne men and I move out more to explore the place, find a shower and bring back food for all to share. Throughout the day, groups of curious Aboriginal kids hang around the men, and when the men rehearse a few songs in the afternoon, adult Aboriginal men and women are also attracted to the hall. The Melbourne men strike up conversations with these locals. The Central Australian men and these people acknowledge each other with nods but keep a kind of mutually respectful distance. When the Melbourne men propose a beer before the concert, none of the Aboriginal crew comes along to the pub.

By sunset, a large, rowdy all-Aboriginal crowd has gathered outside the hall. Many men and women are very drunk, some have brought babies, and a large number of children run around making lots of noise. Inside, the Central Australian men stay out of sight of the people who are pushing against doors and windows, eager to get in. To avoid aggravating the increasingly impatient crowds, the men open the doors early. Droves of children push their way in. They then try to push their way out again. Many of the adults eager to enter also turn around and push through the crowd at the door to get back out. A number of drunken men and women do not want to pay the five-dollar entrance fee and argue their case in increasingly aggressive and drunken manners. Many more try to squeeze their way in without paying or arguing at all.

Frank's band starts up and people are up dancing immediately. Many more are now crushing to get in, effectively blocking the entrance. I go over to help the Central Australian crew at the door, but soon find myself alone when they retreat to watch the commotion from the opposite wall. Simon steps in to help. A wild fight between a man and a woman erupts inside the hall and I see at least two brawls going on outside. A couple of enraged men try to climb in over the people who block the entrance, shouting that they are brothers of the woman in the fight inside. Simon now calls the police on his mobile phone. In the turmoil at the door I miss Frank's performance but I do note the Teenage Band starting up, because the pressure and rage at the entrance increases considerably. A couple of policemen arrive but soon stand back when people take little note of their attempts to bring some order to the chaos. A few moments later, the Night Patrol arrives, the local Aboriginal community law and order team. The Aboriginal patrol men soon identify some key men and women and talk to them with stern calm. In a few moments, the crowd has moved away from the door and fights are dissolved, at least momentarily. We can now let a steady stream of people in, and the hall is soon packed. People start climbing the stage, women lifting up their shirts and dancing, wriggling their breasts before the audience who respond with howls and laughter. With more and more people up on stage, amplifiers and microphone stands fall over and the Teenage Band members are forced backward. They never stop playing, though, and just wait patiently for the locals to give them the microphones back.

After the last song, we turn the main lights back on and the hall empties quickly. Several women stop outside, signing to the musicians to come over. The musicians largely ignore them. A couple of people also stay around to talk to some of the desert men who they know as distant relatives. The desert men keep these interactions polite and brief and begin to pack the vehicles, pretending a departure to make people leave. When the stage is packed, the men gather in the kitchen and recount how crazy it was at the door. 'It's fucking hard to handle people out of your own place! You don't know them, bros! Don't know how to talk to them! You're a stranger in their country!' one of them says.

During the tour, the desert men's reserved, cautious and held-back way of being present and performing when in other blackfella places was, not surprisingly, most obvious in confrontational and drunken situations such as this one. The men are certainly experienced in performing for rowdy, drunken and fighting Aboriginal crowds like these at home, and at times they get involved in fights or intervene to bring a reasonable order to the event. In Halls Creek, however, where they lack knowledge of local Aboriginal authority and kin relations, such interferences are potentially dangerous. Especially in drunken situations, their actions could easily prompt locals to physically put the desert men in their proper blackfella place. That is, as visitors in others' country they are expected to show respect in relation to local men and women, no matter how they behave.

The men's wary manners and their retreat to their own mob when in other indigenous places are not limited to drunken and volatile situations, though. Later on the tour, they perform in Beswick Aboriginal community, an hour from Katherine (see Map 2).[5] The community provides us with two comfortable houses, and apart from performing on the first night, the men mostly stay put in one of the houses and watch television, play cards, eat and sleep. When our hosts invite us to go fishing and swimming in nearby waterholes, the desert men are very hesitant to join, while the Melbourne men and I happily come along. We are invited to stay until the next performance north of Katherine a few days later. The houses are provided for free, which is great for the tour budget. Early on the second morning, however, we are woken up to hurriedly pack the cars and we soon take off without a goodbye to anybody. On the road when we start to wake up, the Melbourne men question the sudden departure. They enjoyed the peaceful and comfortable break in the bush community and cannot see the point of leaving just to stay in a 'boring' town. Besides the budgetary consequences, Simon is most upset about leaving without explanations or thanks to his old friend Tom, our main Aboriginal host. He raised the money to pay for the Beswick performance and made sure our stay was pleasant. When Simon wants an explanation for our departure, somebody finally mumbles that they are out of tobacco.

However, the indigenous men do not seem too sure why we are leaving either, and they do not seem to care. They are happy to stay in Katherine town where there is a wider variety of ways to kill time, and where they may run into relatives and friends. They check in at a motel and the Aboriginal crew then pretty much keep together, separate from the Melbourne men, in the motel rooms, walking the streets for food and drinking at the pub. In this whitefella-dominated town, the blackfella 'ownership' of the place is less all-embracing and direct than in Aboriginal Beswick. It is obvious that the men feel more at ease when they do not have to worry so much about their movements as Aboriginal men in other more markedly Aboriginal places. At the same time, they are increasingly restricted by being blackfellas in whitefella ordered spaces.

Blackfellas in whitefella places

Hanging out in the motel in Darwin at the beginning of the tour, the desert men decide to try out the small motel pool. When the Aboriginal men move into the small area, the non-indigenous motel guests at the pool soon gather their towels, bottles of sunscreen, wet bathers, books, radio, sunglasses and water bottles, and leave. One of the musicians takes a dip, with his clothes on. 'I forgot to bring my beach gear', he smirks with a feminine hand gesture. I take it that he is referring to all the 'gear' the non-indigenous guests brought for their pool visit.

Very soon, a motel employee appears and the men go quiet. She asks if they are guests at the motel. Steve says a simple 'yep'. Nobody looks at her. The woman asks for proof. The men look to each other for the keycard. They finally find it and show it to her without a word. A few minutes after she is gone the men return to their rooms. 'Fucking racist mob, this place,' one of the men concludes. 'Guess she thought we would wash off and dirty the water, ey?' another one says harshly. The first man now suggests that 'the cunt' in reception is certain to be 'a poofter', he must be 'with his little voice'. He does an exaggerated imitation of the man's (to me rather normal) service manners and the men chuckle.

The incident is fairly typical of the Aboriginal men's engagements with non-indigenous-dominated spaces on the tour. Here, like when they enter coffee shops, restaurants, shops and so forth, their presence is variably noted by non-indigenous people with curiosity, suspicion and at times intervention. The men also more or less expect that their legitimate presence in those spaces will be questioned and interfered with because they are Aboriginal. Not surprisingly, therefore, the men rarely sit down in food establishments or use motel facilities outside their rooms. Frank is an exception to this, perhaps because he prefers that his manager Simon keeps his money for him and pays for his meals. The other Central Australian men mainly buy take-away meals or supermarket food which they eat and drink by the car, in their motel rooms, or elsewhere away from the direct gaze of whitefellas.

Non-indigenous aspects of the places we visit are not the subject of any of the multilayered story-telling the men engage in to negotiate their presence in 'other' blackfella realms either. While that narration is open to complex and imaginative personal and shared interpretations, their interactions with non-Aborigines are mostly articulated in the form of complaints and rather one-dimensional typecasting that reinforce homogenized notions of whitefella ways of acting and thinking. The Aboriginal men also commonly associate non-indigenous manners with feminized or less masculine modes of conduct, as indicated by the feminine hand gesture over non-indigenous pool guests' gear and by the mocking of the male receptionist's service manners as gay. By mocking such manners, the Aboriginal men also emphasize and demarcate their own valued 'mongrel', somewhat crude 'too much' and rather direct 'no bullshit' masculine demeanour.

The men's commentary or complaints about non-indigenous practices are mainly made in the privacy of their own group, and they rarely 'talk back' in situations when they are approached as potential suspects for breaching non-indigenous codes of conduct. In this, they not only give voice to a long history of non-indigenous subjugation of Aboriginal people. By airing their grievances, and at times humiliation and rage, in the exclusive company of 'their own', they also buttress a shared sense of blackfella and male integrity and masculine worth, as distinct from a homogenized, effeminate whitefella other. The covert frustrations may, however, erupt in situations other than the ones that primarily caused them, especially when the men are drunk. In a Broome café, for example, Frank turns up for breakfast still drunk from the night before. He soon begins to accuse a German tourist in rather crude, aggressive ways for staring at him. 'I'm no fucking animal in a fucking zoo,' he growls at the rather taken-aback tourist, who, in my view, does not stare. It was, however, impossible not to notice Frank's extravagant entrance when he greeted me loudly by singing a few lines before sitting down with a big laugh. He now tells the man in a few more crude lines that blackfellas, in fact, can eat with fork and knife.

The pattern emerging during this and other tours I have followed, then, is that the Aboriginal men tend to limit their interactions with whitefellas in general to a detached minimum. However, on the two-week-long Bush Tour, they have to engage directly with Frank's Melbourne non-indigenous musicians and manager. By looking at the interactional dynamics in this touring party, I explore some of the ways in which the men articulate their mutual understanding of each other, and simultaneously of themselves as indigenous and non-indigenous men and musicians.

Tensions and alterations

The morning the Bush Tour party is to take off from Broome is messy. The Central Australian men are hungover and hard to get out of bed. Stan is furious with them for not getting their act together and helping to pack the van. The Melbourne men mainly observe the situation. The Teenage Band and their Lajamanu entourage drive around and keep an eye on what happens around the touring van. They told Stan yesterday that their bass player had taken off to Lajamanu to tend to 'family trouble'.

Stan wants to be at small, largely Aboriginal township of Fitzroy Crossing, 400 km east, by the early afternoon to get the PA set up and tested before their performance tonight. Well after lunchtime they are still in Broome. I have to travel separately and meet up with them the morning after at the roadhouse in Halls Creek, 300 km east of Fitzroy Crossing. When they arrive, the men look wasted and the tensions between them are obvious. Simon shakes his head and sets out to find the town office to get the keys to the hall where they are to perform. One of the Melbourne musicians puts a scouting hand above his eyes, gazes out over the rather dreary-looking township and asks jokingly where one could get a latte and a hot croissant in this place. Nobody cares to smile and he is off to find a shower.

When Stan pays for petrol, the rest of the crew gather in the shade behind the roadhouse. They tell me they have not eaten, showered or slept since the day before yesterday. They arrived in Fitzroy Crossing about at sunset and later performed for a small crowd of Aboriginal locals. Most of them wanted to stay in Fitzroy Crossing to eat, clean up and sleep in. Stan decided that the van was leaving. So they did. Steve seems convinced that Stan has had enough and will take off back to Alice Springs any minute. When he looks around the corner the van is gone. The men look shocked. After a swarm of explanations for Stan being 'stressed out', they admit that he did a lot of the work yesterday, but to leave them stranded is an overreaction, they agree. They consider the practical consequences of his departure. Somebody mentions that his stuff is in the van, someone else wonder how they will get paid now. Steve is not pleased with having to take over the full responsibility for this CAAMA venture. He suggests that they cut down the performances to a minimum and try to get home as quick as possible. The others agree. They then realize that they cannot fit into the one remaining vehicle. A lot of the stage gear is in the van, too. Steve says that they have to cancel the whole tour. Nobody contradicts him and they all seem to accept this radical change of plans.

From where I stand I can see that Stan has just driven over to the community hall and is unloading the stage gear. I point this out. The men look over, shrug their shoulders and we all walk over to the hall. The tour is on again. Most of us help to get the gear out. Nobody speaks. Later, Stan tells me his version of events. From before leaving Broome he basically had to do everything, he says. He packed the van, drove it to Fitzroy Crossing, unloaded the van, set up the stage and sound gear, both sound-engineered and played bass during the performance, then packed up and got the equipment into the van. The others, hungover and tired, did not lift a finger to make it happen. He did not ask for help either. He should not have to, he says; they could all see what needed to be done. During the day in Halls Creek conflicts flare up between him and some of the others who he accuses of not pulling their weight. He charges Simon in similar terms, which Simon rejects loudly by listing what he has done over the last couple of weeks to make this tour work. This is the only open conflict I see during the tour between an indigenous and non-indigenous member of the touring party.

Before the Halls Creek concert begins, the Teenage Band takes Stan and Steve to the side and announces that they are driving back to Lajamanu after the gig. Someone passed away and they have to attend funeral ceremonies. They will join up again as soon as they can, they say. Next morning we continue the 400 km to Kununurra. Stan drops the men and gear off by the outdoor stage where the next performance is booked in. He then takes off to return the rental van and pick up the CAAMA vehicle in Darwin.

Hence, in less than twenty-four hours, the tour has been on, off and on again, and the circumstances have changed radically. The popular Teenage Band is the big local draw-card for the Bush Tour. A main idea was to combine this regionally well-established and popular rock-reggae act with Frank's recent cosmopolitan fusion music, and Stan was to play bass for Frank because he knows Frank's recent music well. The now sudden one-band tour requires flexible musicians. Replacing Stan on bass, country guitarist Lyndon has to learn Frank's more eclectic music, which he does to a workable degree after just a few rehearsals. To please the taste of local Aboriginal audiences, Frank also has to revive some of his old rock guitar and country repertoire. He does so with ease. The Melbourne musicians, however, are not familiar with Frank's old numbers. As experienced and professional musicians, they would no doubt be able to play these songs as well as other old rock and country covers. Nonetheless, some of the desert men step in as Frank's backing band for those parts of the performances, to ensure the performance will appeal and adapt to their blackfella community audiences. If the crowds do not respond, for instance, the desert men know how to shorten and change to more suitable songs, and if there are tensions in the crowds, the desert men can better read the moods to defuse the situation musically if needed.

Nobody knows when, or even if, the Teenage Band or Stan will turn up again. The Central Australian men seem to accept this without discussion or questions. The Melbourne men are less relaxed about the ongoing

PHOTO 9 *Setting up the stage in Kununurra.*

uncertainties and constant changes. This highlights the different ways the indigenous and non-indigenous tour members operate.

Blackfella modus operandi

The allocation of tasks and hierarchies of decision making within the Central Australian touring party is rarely formalized, verbalized or agreed on. However, some patterns are pretty much established before they leave Alice Springs. Stan is the senior sound engineer and studio manager, a musician with years of experience of performing in a national music scene, and he is the oldest man in the Aboriginal male group. The Central Australian crew, therefore, basically expect him to make the decisions about any activities and do not say much about his decisions. It does not necessarily mean that they have the same agenda as Stan. He, for instance, expects full commitment from them all in the musical activities. To him, the whole tour *is* 'musical activities' and he perceives the men to be on the job from the time they leave home, including the Melbourne men. Others in the Central Australian crew prefer to see time outside performances as being 'off work'. Some also tend to see themselves only as musicians and therefore not expected to set up and pack stage gear.

As he does around the studio, Stan often makes decisions according to the situation, people and opportunities before him at any time on the tour, while keeping to the overall plan, and he does not always communicate his most immediate 'plans' to many others. A lot of the time the other men, therefore, do not have a clear idea of when, where and how gigs are to take place exactly, or what their precise roles in those gigs are. They may not know at what particular time the vehicles are leaving, staying, or where exactly they are heading. Similar to most tours with Central Australian musicians I have followed, there is seldom any question from the Aboriginal men about such details. Instead, they stay around each other most of the time to keep up with what *actually* happens, not relying on what somebody said yesterday or a moment ago. If somebody is missing when it is time to perform because he has not kept up with what goes on, it seldom creates much stress among these musicians. With the multi-instrumental skills, someone else just steps in and does the job. To be able to 'go with the flow' and appear confident and relaxed about one's performance on and off stage within the male groupings in different settings and when circumstances change emerge as valued, smooth male behaviour in the Central Australian blackfella touring party.

The other blackfella party on the tour, the Teenage Band, is even more flexible and less concerned with set agendas. They basically follow their own agenda with friends and family from Lajamanu, while touching base with Stan and Steve to be informed and to let them know when something changes on the band's part. Organizational detail is largely redundant information for these men, as it is for most bush musicians I have met. Gigs usually start in the hours after sunset and it is never difficult to figure out where it is taking place in a community or township. They usually check just before a gig starts what the particular deal for the night is and then carry out their stage performances, adapting to the particular audiences and venues as they play. The fact that they suddenly abandon the tour after two performances is not seen as a problem by them. Talking to band leader Alfred months later, he tells me that it would have been great to perform in all the places, but he does not express any concerns for upsetting the organization of the tour or leaving other musicians stranded. He, like most desert musicians I meet, takes more or less for granted that if they fail to show up, other musicians will stand ready and pull off a performance in order not to let local Aboriginal crowds down. That is, even if the men in the Teenage Band certainly proudly perceive their own band and music as distinct and unique, they do not see themselves as irreplaceable in a stage line-up. The ways in which they operate are even more adaptable to actual, immediate situations, and they pay even less attention to pre-scheduled agendas than the Central Australian crew.

When the non-indigenous Melbourne musicians join these groupings for the Bush Tour, some differences in modus operandi soon become apparent.

Meetings of modus operandi

All the Melbourne men have prior experiences over many years of working with Aboriginal Australian musicians and with ethnically mixed bands, in the NT and in south-eastern cities. These men, however, work mainly within performance and touring conventions of urban-based, professional music scenes. Here, tour itineraries with hours, dates and places listed for sound checks, performances, checking in and out of accommodation, and departure and arrivals are standard features. In these conventions, musicians are usually fairly specialized and irreplaceable instrumentalists or singers who are, therefore, updated on changes of plans without having to ask. They can organize their own time around this schedule, independent of other participants.

Accordingly, Simon has handed the Melbourne musicians a preliminary schedule with times and places for activities at the Stompem Ground and the Bush Tour. Stepping out of the plane in Broome, the Melbourne men encounter the first of many subsequent departures from this schedule. They are met by a national television crew and are informed that they are going directly to the Stompem Ground venue to perform for a back-up shoot for the live national broadcast of the festival.[6] The musicians are, therefore, instructed to wear the same clothes on stage for the actual performance next night. Casually dressed for hours on planes, the men are not happy about wearing these clothes when performing at a big, nationally broadcast concert. But this is how it is done. The prelude to this incident took place the day before when the television producer asked Stan if it was okay that his team picked up Frank's band at the airport and took them to the venue for a back-up shoot. Stan said that he saw no problems with this. When they ran into each other later in the evening, the producer asked if all was okay. Stan put a thumbs up with a relaxed 'no problems, bros'!' This could easily be interpreted as a confirmation that he had consulted the Melbourne musicians about the arrangement. He had not. In his mind, Stan expected the touring party, including the Melbourne men, to be at work from the moment they left home for this tour.

The men in the Central Australian crew also work in a 'let's do it', impromptu mode of music making, which is discussed as a feature of the studio ethos in Chapter 3. They approach changes as something usual, not as something that has to be discussed, confirmed or communicated in detail. To 'make a fuss' about every new move is basically seen as superfluous. A few days into the Bush Tour it becomes clear that several of the Aboriginal men perceive the Melbourne men as somewhat 'fussy', which refers to the non-Aboriginal men asking for verbal confirmation on what they are doing next and where, and then expecting this plan to be followed. Simon is responsible for the touring budget and understandably wants to discuss any changes, and also to reach some kind of group consensus before a decision is made. His attempts at a participatory approach to decisions produce minimal response among the Aboriginal men. As mentioned, by staying together they know what is happening when and where, and they seldom see a reason to discuss the turn of events much.

In the main blackfella modus operandi for this musical venture, then, the ad hoc, improvised turn of events is the general norm. It is, in fact, the men's ability to constantly reframe their expectations and practices with every new situation and place that makes the music performances and the whole venture alive and pulsating for the Aboriginal men. They largely approach touring as an always-in-the-making flow of events. For the Melbourne men, in contrast, verbal confirmation of when and where vehicles are to leave, when sound checks are to take place and when to meet before a gig are prerequisites for them to 'go with the flow'. They operate more as individual men independent of each other within the group. An agreed-on plan of action is a way to tune such a group of individuals into a shared project and to reduce the risk of upsets. The constant changes of plans without explanations or consultations upset their sense of a smooth operation.

One consequence of the discrepancy in modus operandi is that the Melbourne men may be late or not around when the touring crew is leaving or when other activities are on, which can be decided on without further ado. One morning after a performance, they even leave without one of the Melbourne men. He is elsewhere when they are ready to go, which is earlier than he was told the night before. He has to organize a lift with a local to the next tour location a couple of hours away.

Needless to say, these touring musicians, like any group who embark on a joint project, have to deal with their individual ways of operating, and mostly they get on with each other without major dramas. I still wish to focus on the tensions that do appear between the indigenous and non-indigenous men, because it can illuminate the negotiations involved as the men try to make sense of their 'own kind' and the 'other'. One way of working out their differences is to exaggerate their own practices, and to more or less jokingly mock that of the 'other'. This game of mutual typecasting becomes a kind of sideshow of the tour.

Exaggerating blackfellas and whitefellas

As an aspect of his professional musicianship, one of the Melbourne men is rather meticulous in how he prepares himself before performing. In order to read and follow the other musicians he wants to be in a certain place on the stage, and he carefully places his things around this position. He jots down on a piece of paper any changes in the way they play particular pieces of music, and he is inquisitive about the Aboriginal musicians' techniques and ways of playing particular songs. As a seasoned performer he wears earplugs on stage to avoid the common occupational health hazard for musicians: impaired hearing. Experienced in touring, he takes precautions against wearing himself out by weeks on the road by using earplugs also to sleep well, and he eats healthily and only occasionally participates in the Aboriginal men's drinking long into the nights. These habits seem rather similar to those of other professional musicians I know who also care about details and prepare themselves and their equipment thoroughly in order to relax, improvise and deliver a strong performance.

This can be compared to the valued 'mongrel' and 'too much' masculine regimes in which the Aboriginal musicians tend to operate. Here, men are not expected to seem to worry much about things like loud noise, impaired hearing, lack of sleep, or eating regularly and healthily. The Aboriginal men are consequently rather worn out early on during the tour, while the Melbourne musicians are in good shape for most of the tour. In the music work, the Aboriginal musicians definitely care about the condition of the instruments and the quality of sound when they perform. But they tend to pick up and play the instruments available without worrying about many rituals before performing. They are, in a way, always ready, and move with whatever happens when it happens.

As the days pass, I notice how some of the Aboriginal men begin to embellish a seemingly overly careless attitude to the music work. It looks to me as if they are out to prove to the Melbourne musicians that they do not need a lot of preparation before performing. That is, they show that they are skilled enough to improvise and pick up whatever musical challenge comes before them. They do not respond much when the Melbourne musicians want

PHOTO 10 *Frank Yamma in sound check.*

to pin down the exact way they are playing either, which may be explained by the fact that the Aboriginal men seldom play a song in exactly the same way twice. Some of the Aboriginal men also begin to exaggerate their crude language, eating habits and other behaviours in the presence of the Melbourne men. On one occasion when we are travelling in the van, for instance, one of the Melbourne men cuts up fruit on a plate that he passes around. Frank grabs a piece but the others just look at the neat fruit arrangement. Soon thereafter, Lyndon opens the cooler and grabs a piece of the fried meat that we cooked in the motel yesterday. He rips into it with his teeth, chews with loud smacking sounds and satisfied grunts. When he is done, he rubs his greasy hands together as if he truly enjoys the feel of it, and laughs mockingly.

When the Melbourne men are not present, the desert men also begin to comment on the non-indigenous men's habits. The remarks are often made in passing and in a joking manner, and should not necessarily be seen as expressions of deeply felt sentiments or personal opinions about particular persons. The comments do, however, reaffirm some typecast notions of whitefella manners in general that are fairly widespread among the Aboriginal musicians I have met in Central Australia. Framed by such notions, the careful preparation of stage performances or fruits on a platter appears as somewhat effeminate. Tearing into a solid piece of meat with your hands and teeth is, in some respects, to talk back to such manners. It can at the same time be interpreted as parodying a stereotypical imagery of blackfella masculine strength and energy, but also of somewhat 'primitive' manners, both of which are part of the ambivalent 'mongrel' qualities that the Aboriginal men identify with.

The Melbourne men also begin to comment on their Aboriginal travel companions in their absence, and at times jokingly imitate their crude language and 'too much' habits. One of them increasingly shakes his head over the fact that the men in the Aboriginal crew rarely overtly question Stan's decisions or express opinions of their own. Again, these gestures should not be overstated, and while they involve some ridiculing of the 'other' there is no sense of malice.

On one level, I interpret these gestures as assertions of one's own ways of approaching music and life matters. On another level, I take them to involve a great deal of self-mockery when the men exaggerate their own demeanour. The fruit and meat incident, for instance, works just as much to communicate to the other party that one is aware of the typecast perceptions of one's own kind. That is, by exaggerating their respective actual and perceived whitefella and blackfella manners, the men can be seen as communicating to the other party that one knows that it might look ridiculous to them (and at times to oneself, too), but this is what 'we' are, so live with it.

The imitation and mocking of each other's manners can also be seen as trying out and playing around with the others' male ways of being. It may, furthermore, be read as a demonstration of competence in the manners of the 'other'. This is to simultaneously disrupt the idea that they are in fact so different, and to show a preference for one's own valued ways of identifying with certain modes of male behaviours. At the same time, it can involve the mocking of one's own male manners.

One morning, for instance, I meet the Melbourne men for breakfast at a small coffee shop. We chat about the mix of minds and manners of the touring party, and agree that the tour will probably become a memorable experience for all involved. One of them proceeds to pour a cup of tea and spurts out with a wry smile, 'well, fuck it, I'm fucking gonna have my fucking breakfast any fucking way I fucking want, fuck it!' He then sips his tea with the small finger sticking out prudishly. By contrasting exaggerated white Anglo tea-drinking manners, in this way, with a defining feature of the blackfella crew's masculinist demeanour – the use of the word 'fuck' for all things and actions – he parodies the typecast habits of his 'own kind' as much as the Aboriginal men's manners. Lyndon's meat eating performance can be seen as a similar mocking of his own 'mongrel' masculine manners, by contrasting himself to the typecast whitefella manner that the neat fruit platter represents. To borrow from Taussig's (1993) discussions of the significance of mimesis as a means to engage with Otherness, the indigenous and non-indigenous musicians' mimetic contestations can be seen as 'a gateway from the Self to the Other' (Harrison 2002: 222), as well as a confrontation with images of oneself. It can be seen as a show of competence in 'steering a course between' as well as with self and others (Jackson 1998: 19).

Most of the mutual commentary is played out with indirect gestures among the men. Despite one of the desert men's prediction that it is only a matter of time before the Melbourne men are put in their 'proper place' by one of the more senior Aboriginal men, open confrontation is not necessary in this particular touring venture. From the Aboriginal crew's point of view, this tour is a blackfella project in which the whitefella musicians do not decide the turn of events and where they are not essential for the core, male blackfella sociability. The Aboriginal men certainly talk with respect and admiration of the Melbourne musicians' skills and professionalism, and they do not see them as overly 'square' whitefellas. But to put it starkly, if the Melbourne men are not happy and even choose to leave, it would not disrupt the situation much for the Aboriginal men. It is basically the same as if Aboriginal musicians were to leave; the Melbourne men can always be replaced by Aboriginal musicians and the song list can simply be changed to suit these men's skills and tastes.

Open endings

The finale of the Bush Tour is staged in the beer garden at the Katherine Hotel. Stan returned to the group a few days before, and when he and Steve are setting up the stage, the Teenage Band drives into town, keen to perform. The concert turns out to be one of the best stage experiences of the whole journey. Frank has never really stopped drinking since the day before, but he and the Melbourne men seem to revel in their musical skills. They are rewarded with passionate responses from the several hundred Aboriginal people who fill the beer garden to its limits. The Teenage Band men are likewise in a brilliant mood and clearly enjoy themselves on stage, never letting the tempo down, and giving their all to satisfy the wildly dancing crowds. When Frank's band is playing, the Teenage Band men are up on the dance floor, and when they take over on stage, Frank's band members are sweating it out on the floor to support their touring colleagues, too.

When the crowds have left, the men gather around the stage, drinking, laughing and hugging each other. Stan takes a drunk Frank aside for a word. Frank then makes an honest attempt to deliver a kind of speech, thanking them all for making the tour worthwhile and successful. The others applaud, yell in agreement that they definitely have to do this again. Someone suggests that the Bush Tour should become an annual event. They all shout and clap their approval, while everybody knows that it will never happen, and is perhaps glad to leave it at that. Caught up in a shared sense of satisfaction by having accomplished this joint venture, and a great deal of relief that they will soon be back in their respective homes and musical scenes, the men end on a conciliatory note of mutual acceptance of their differences.

The diversity of intercultural engagements that I have discussed in this chapter and in the previous ones enables the mobilization and mediation of many divergent, resonating and overlapping modes of male, musical and sociocultural identifications. The musicians we have followed on this tour, like other touring musicians, will return home with experiences that change the way they see themselves and how other people see them and relate to them. For the desert men, touring ventures beyond their home region generate, in these ways, transformed male and socio-musical locations through which these men can act, identify and are recognized as they return home.

8

Changing Aboriginal men and musicians

The detailed ethnography of four different Aboriginal socio-musical settings in previous chapters presents music making as a rewarding arena for exploring how Australian Aboriginal men make sense of themselves and others as they draw on, recombine, ignore and create differentiated modes of being male and Aboriginal. I have pointed to how the particular mediating dynamic of each of the settings explored involves the affirmation of already established models for being men, musicians and indigenous, and a simultaneous blurring of social and musical distinctions, all of which are shown to be co-productive in the making of contemporary Aboriginal men and musicians.

Mediations

The Aboriginal men we followed in the touring venture in the previous chapter, like any musicians who go on tour, return home with experiences that change the way they see themselves and how other people see them and relate to them. The Lajamanu Teenage Band members, for instance, can return home to their remote Aboriginal community and Warlpiri sociality and tell stories of being part of the famous Aboriginal Stompem Ground festival in Broome. In doing so, they narrate themselves into a broader national blackfella professional musical brotherhood, which can improve their musical and male standing in the Aboriginal realm that their home community is part of. In their stage performances, they also made their local blackfella social and cultural experiences heard in a larger imagined and actual Aboriginal realm.

Some of the Teenage Band men's wives and countrymen came along to Broome. The band could, therefore, receive direct support and appreciation from their home 'mob', who they, in the main, direct their music toward, and whose response counts the most for the musicians' evaluation of their performances. In the process, the band and this audience mutually reinforce a shared Warlpiri form of identification, and the band members simultaneously reinforce their particular male and musician status at home and buttress their capacity to represent their people and community. The men will talk about their performances in the Aboriginal community of Fitzroy Crossing and in the non-indigenous town of Katherine, and words about these gigs will resonate through regional indigenous networks, all of which reinforce their Warlpiri, musician and male status at home as well as across their Aboriginal region. In these away-from-home places, the band and their music come to represent and (re)connect dispersed countrymen/women and ways of living as Warlpiri. Maybe their music, and especially their community song 'Lajamanu', will move 'lost' Warlpiri to stop drinking and come back home to their people and country. The gig in Katherine can be narrated in terms of non-indigenous recognition, too, adding further to the band's status as elevated from that of fellow Lajamanu and other bush musicians who mainly play in the hinterland blackfella music circuit.

By participating in the tour, the men in the Teenage Band have, moreover, reinforced their male bonds and musical standing with the professional, blackfella male space of the CAAMA Music studio. The fact that they were included in a CAAMA touring venture had already boosted the band's credibility and reputation among fellow musicians and people across the region. By turning up and performing well, the band proved their continued commitment and capacity as musicians. They did have to leave for 'sorry business', but traditional business is a wholly valid reason for a no-show in this Aboriginal music scene, and it did not put a dent in their standing with the studio.

On their part, Stan and Steve from the music studio come back home as more experienced and confident in organizing and seeing an interstate touring venture through. 'I felt like I could've gone on tour with Deep Purple right after, that's the kind of high I was on!' Stan described his state of mind at the time. Narratives about the tour soon begin to circulate as part of the blackfella male studio sociality, reaffirming and strengthening the studio men's male and professional positions among the bush, town and out-of-town musicians around the studio. In contrast to many other possible projects circulating in the studio sociality, this venture made the transition from talk to action. It is, therefore, an occasion when the 'healthy competition' among the men takes a tangible form, and when musicians' studio visits and show of commitment in this space may pay off for real. In the process, the studio men's positions as mediators of male and musical recognition are reasserted as they more or less decide who will participate, and these decisions will change relative male and musician recognition and reputation around the studio and beyond.

For CAAMA, the Bush Tour venture was not a successful project in financial terms. The studio men also ran this project as they run the studio: a more or less exclusively male and blackfella activity that the management, whitefellas and women have limited access to. After the event, a few senior female CAAMA employees ask me what the men were really up to during the tour. Their questions imply that when out of control of management or women, the studio men and musicians will work as little as possible and instead indulge in the 'slack and black' forms of male and blackfella qualities of the studio that can frustrate the management. When the requested time sheets for the tour are delivered, though, there is only the odd day when the men had not been travelling between venues or performing. With time, the performances in Broome and the Bush Tour become feathers in the hat for CAAMA Music in that they gave the record label and its artists exposure in the wider northern region and among the Aboriginal people the association aims to service and represent. The studio men did, therefore, earn some belated credibility with the management.

An exploration of the Melbourne musicians' everyday lives is outside the scope of my research. From less in-depth experiences I still argue that the touring experience reshaped their socio-musical position at home, too. For instance, next time I run into one of the musicians at a gig in Melbourne, it seems that the tour has become a somewhat romanticized memory for him. 'It was unreal! It's like a whole other world out there with those guys! Simpler!' he says, not so much to me as to his fellow non-indigenous Melbourne musicians who stand around us and who have not been on tour with Aboriginal musicians from remote Australia. They nod as he says that he would jump at a chance to do it again. By connecting him with Aboriginal people in Central Australia, the Bush Tour experience seems to earn the man important points in an urban south-eastern music scene. Here, as outlined in Chapter 1, Central Australia is often associated with 'real', 'traditional' and 'authentic' Aboriginal people. Regardless of whether these qualities are valued as something in the past or in the present, they are now mostly cherished in wider Australia, and beyond. The main point I wish to argue, however, is that the touring experiences are transformed, as well as transformative, when mediated by norms, values and practices in the musicians' home settings, be they towns, the studio, bush communities or big cities.

Similarly, when indigenous desert musicians return from studio recording sessions, they are endowed with an altered male and musician confidence and status in their day-to-day socio-musical settings. Their participation in the blackfella and male dynamics of professionalism and 'healthy competition' at the studio may also alter their male and musician status in this setting itself.

Like the Teenage Band, or the bands playing at the Todd Tavern mentioned in Chapter 6, the musicians may be rewarded by being included in music events and tours that the studio organizes. Bush and town musicians' diverse musical and life experiences and orientations, and their different male and musical ideals and aspirations, at the same time confer upon the studio its particular blackfella and male ethos. These men's presence and work in the studio underpin the rationale for CAAMA Music's existence as a means for Aboriginal self-representations, and become an all-important factor when CAAMA competes for public grants by emphasizing its status as a community-based and representative Aboriginal corporation.

The dynamics of the hinterland Aboriginal community music circuit explored in Chapter 5 connect, too, to that of the other settings explored. The musician status and male respect bush musicians earn through establishing a reputation and representative role in the Aboriginal community circuit often engender the musical and male confidence and aspirations for 'hitting town', 'going to CAAMA' to record, and interstate touring. Chapters 6 and 7 explained how the musicians' talk about such activities is in itself important in construing an elevated sense of self as man and musician among fellow men, musicians and other people. To establish a reputation in the hinterland music scene may also work the other way. The studio men or other festival organizers may hear about or come across musicians who have made a name for themselves out bush, and may subsequently contact them for a recording project or performance. This is how the Benning Brothers that we saw in Chapter 1 came to appear at Womadelaide.

Blackfella gigs in whitefella-dominated towns fold into the particular dynamics for producing male and Aboriginal forms of identification in the studio, in bush communities, in towns and on interstate tours, too. Town gigs are associated with imagined and real non-indigenous and inter-indigenous recognition, both of which are means for boosting musicians' self-imagery, their male and musician position among fellow regional musicians, and for how they are perceived across the Aboriginal desert region.

Framing my explorations of the interplay of observed activities and the men's articulated thoughts and lived experiences analytically with the concept of intercultural mediation, I have set out to detail how the mundane day-to-day engagement of ideas, practices and values from a range of sources and different sociocultural formations involve an embedding of layers upon layers of experience. As aspects of these experiences come to shape the men's actions and experience in subsequent interactions and socio-musical circumstances, there is an inevitable process of displacement and reformulation. Direct experience, imagery and varying values are, in this way, co-implicated in the ongoing formation of ambivalent and multifaceted, but distinctively blackfella and male 'mongrel', ways of existing and doing things.

Mongrel music and Aboriginal men

As Thomas (1991: 185) argues in relation to intercultural engagements in the Pacific, elements of differing belief systems are acted upon and reformulated by the parties as they interact and as sociopolitical circumstances change. There will be misinterpretations, subversive and ironic reproductions, and partial appropriations, all of which will gradually mutate and change with subsequent interactions. In the social world of Aboriginal music making in Central Australia, too, practices, meanings, attitudes, rhetoric and norms for male indigenous manners are continuously interculturally mediated and transformed. Similar to the colonial engagements Thomas describes, these layered entanglements and mutations are construed to express qualitative difference and in oppositional practice to that of non-indigenous others. As I have demonstrated among the desert men and musicians, indigenous difference and practice are constantly construed in relation and opposition to indigenous others, too.

The theme of 'otherness' has reappeared throughout the book, just as the capitalized 'Other' has loomed large in the anthropological discipline's core concerns with human diversity and social and cultural difference. Approached as relational from the outset, collective and individual identity formation necessarily involve the attribution of meaning to experienced and perceived similarities and differences between 'self' and 'other', 'us' and 'them', whether such difference concerns belief systems, cultural forms, moral values, gender, race, ethnicity, class or other registers of identification (e.g. Otto and Driessen 2000). Such conceptions of self and other are co-productive in a dialogic and always interdependent mirroring process. That is, when one thinks of somebody else as 'other', one automatically thinks of oneself as not an 'other', and vice versa. How we conceive of the 'other' therefore helps form our conception of 'self', as distinctive social beings. I have explored the details of how such indigenous and non-indigenous otherness and sameness are actively made and remade through each other in the daily reiteration of ideas and practice, and how, as the 'other' is created with certain and changing characteristics, the 'self' is transformed (Benhabib 2002). We have seen how the indigenous desert musicians variously desire and dismiss, fear and admire, non-indigenous and indigenous others. As they interact directly or indirectly with such others, they also expand the repertoire from which they draw in the making of themselves. The negotiation of one's own sense of self through the other, in this way, permits an ambivalent play of difference in which multiple, partial and overlapping forms of identifying may be absorbed into the one, coherent experience of self.

In my outline of the 'persistent othering' between indigenous and non-indigenous people, practices and domains in Central Australia in Chapter 1,

I emphasized how the particular ways in which difference is defined, and the specific meanings attributed to 'sameness' and 'otherness', must be understood as emerging from ongoing histories and changing constellations of relationships over time and in different places (e.g. Mitchell 2000; Stoler 1995). In this view, representations of selfhood and otherness become ongoing 'historical outcomes of connected peoples' (Coronil 1996: 56), which challenges more limited views of indigenous and non-indigenous Australians in terms of already formed distinct or opposed cultural forms and traits. I think that my ethnographic explorations make clear how the making and remaking of Aboriginal men and music is better understood as a continuum of intercultural engagements and relations, which, in essence, are processes of mediation.

The described proliferating 'mongrel' forms of identifying are also meant to challenge privileged notions of worthy, 'real' and 'authentic' Aboriginality. Despite the fact that indigenous people's lives and expressions are as heterogeneous, ambivalent and constantly changing as any other social realities, they are still to a large extent evaluated in academic, legal, political, nationalistic and popular terms that take the 'traditional' as a main point of reference. The substance of such 'traditional' qualities is defined in as many ways as the different purposes for which they are put to use, and indigenous persons and groups are under constant pressure to prove and perform forms of relationship and identification in these evasive and ultimately impossible 'traditional' models of existence.

As authoritative producers of knowledge and representations of indigenous peoples, anthropologists and other scholars in the field continue to contribute to the privileging of the 'traditional' in their preoccupation with documenting and interpreting ancestral bodies of knowledge and values, and how such features persist in the present. At the same time, anthropologists have long acknowledged that traditionalist frameworks of interpretation are increasingly at odds with the contemporary indigenous lives they encounter (Attwood and Arnold 1992; Cowlishaw 1986, 1992; Lattas 1993; Morton 1998; Thiele 1991). Concurring with developments in critical social and cultural theory more generally, it has been convincingly argued that notions of 'tradition' are inadequate as tools for understanding changing dynamics of internal politics and agency within and between indigenous settings, or for describing and analysing the cultural processes in which indigenous life worlds are formed and transformed (Austin-Broos 2001; Cowlishaw 2001; Merlan 1998, 2005; Taylor et al. 2005). Considering the debates and insights generated about the diversity and complexity of historical and contemporary indigenous peoples' experience and life orientations, it is not only peculiar how a great deal of anthropological and other research in indigenous Australia continue to focus on continuities (i.e. traditions) and remote-living, non-urban (i.e. traditionally oriented) people and practices. It is also misrepresenting and detrimental to both indigenous peoples and the discipline of anthropology, as the former can increasingly rarely recognize themselves in descriptions or public debates drawing on research in the latter, which, in turn, is increasingly rarely perceived as producing relevant knowledge about contemporary indigenous life worlds.

Popular, non-ancestral music activities are ordinary, regular and ubiquitous phenomena of indigenous people's contemporary lives all over Australia, as they are in indigenous populations elsewhere (Diamond 2001; Neuenfeldt 1991; Samuels 2004). One reason these socially productive and deeply cultural practices are largely ignored by anthropologists may be that they are seen as too mundane or too obvious. Perhaps they are viewed as too much associated with Western practices to be a subject for serious anthropological inquiry. That is, they are 'too much' 'mongrel' and ambiguous cultural forms, and not enough associated with what is taken to be distinctively Aboriginal as defined in terms of privileged traditionalist perspectives.

After hanging out with Aboriginal desert musicians in all kinds of settings and situations, I argue that it is precisely because these expressive forms are so obvious and mundane that they merit special attention. It is precisely through such ever-present, everyday phenomena that we can better understand what is most indicative of Aboriginal personal and social relations, moralities and aspirations. It is through attending to these and other forms of overtly (inter) culturally messy practice that we can begin to account for the multifaceted and place-specific ways in which indigenous people experience, act and identify in their contemporary lives. My use of the concept of intercultural mediation is an attempt to expand the ways in which we can theorize ethnographic explorations of cultural engagements and entanglements in the production of distinctively indigenous experience as profoundly meaningful and coherent. As an analytical concept, mediation can be a tool for capturing how meanings and practices can be transferred and at the same time inevitably transformed. It can provide a conceptual means to connect concrete everyday practice and relations with more abstract levels of human existence, and with flows of global imagery and conventions – the processes at the core of the practices and the social worlds through which 'mongrel' music, male and indigenous ways of being continue to be made.

Notes

Preface

1 My use of the terms for indigenous people in the book varies and is loosely informed by the musicians' usage. I use 'indigenous' as the most encompassing term, denoting both Australian mainland and Torres Strait Islander peoples, and 'Aboriginal' for mainland people. I use both 'non-Aboriginal' and 'non-indigenous' for all other people, practices and domains. 'Blackfella' is the everyday term the musicians use for themselves, and its other half, 'whitefella', is similarly used for non-indigenous people and things, and I use both. I use 'black' and 'white' as the musicians use them – as abbreviations of blackfellas and whitefellas. I use the more politically loaded capitalized 'Black' in relation to indigenous and Black rights rhetoric. Central Australian Aboriginal people mainly identify by language/ancestral affiliations, such as Warlpiri, Arrernte, Luritja, Pitjantjatjara or Warumungu, which I use when marking out where a person comes from. I use the self-identifying terms that indigenous peoples use in other Australia regions, such as Koori in parts of Victoria and New South Wales, and Yolngu in northern Northern Territory (NT).

Chapter 1

1 This means that they cannot be identified as proper Aboriginal cattle workers either, which is another, albeit somewhat dated rural form of Aboriginal male representation. In dominant national perceptions, though, this was never so much a 'true' Aboriginal image as a powerful non-indigenous masculine imagery, with a legacy in depictions of hard-working, resilient European men at the Australian colonial frontiers (e.g. Moore 1998; Murrie 1998).

2 Semiotic theory has not least provided an analytical base in strands of cultural and communication studies, and in the study of artistic expressions as systems of 'languages' or 'texts' (Barthes 1984, 1988; Gilroy, Grossberg and McRobbie 2000; Hall 1992; Hebdige 1979; Williams 1985).

3 For ancestral genres of music and dance in Australian Aboriginal societies, see, for example, Barwick, Marett and Tunstill (1995), Brock (1989), Clunies Ross, Donaldson and Wild (1987), Elkin (1956), Magowan (2007), Marett (2005), Moyle (1979, 1986) and Strehlow (1971).

4 For an exception, see Beckett's work in small-town Australia (1958).

5 The resistance approach is probably best understood in the emergence of popular music as a field of research with focus on music in terms of subcultures and countercultures. For overviews of popular music theory and research, see Hesmondhalgh and Negus (2002), Kaemmer (1993), Longhurst (1995) and Negus (1996). Studies of Black music have also been influenced by dominant notions of Black as a category of organized struggle and of positive identification that arose in the 1960s' Black Power movement in the United States. For recent theorizing of music and race, see Radano and Bohlman (2000) and Wade (2000).

6 One young woman in Alice Springs, Jacinta Castles, should be mentioned as a potential exception. Brought up in a progressive Warlpiri-Irish family, she used to perform with a local hip-hop act and then moved into other artistic activities, such as theatre production, television hosting and being an assistant art curator. At the time of writing in 2014, she is making a return to music as a career, besides her television work.

7 The main body of modern masculinity theory emerged as 'men's studies' in North America during the 1970s and 1980s (e.g. Brod 1987; Carrigan, Connell and Lee 1985; Connell 1995; Kimmel 1987; Messner and Sabo 1990), followed by a 'second wave' in the 1990s (e.g. Brod and Kaufman 1994; Cornwall and Lindisfarne 1994; Kimmel 1996; Klein 1993; Messner 1992; Messner and Sabo 1994; Segal 1990).

8 The concepts of hegemonic and subordinate masculinity have been criticized as too static and as implying monolithic understandings of power (Worth 2002), and thus of limited use for analysing the ambiguous, overlapping, multiple and alternative models of masculinity that people draw on in different times, places and situations as they locate themselves in appropriate or strategic ways. In Connell's definition, though, hegemonic and subordinated masculinity are, in fact, seen as embodying historically and situationally specific and mobile relations that are open for contestation (1995: 77).

9 Contemporary Aboriginal male practice and positions are also side themes in works on Aboriginal women's changing roles in gender relations, which first emerged as part of feminist and women studies (e.g. Bell 2002; Brock 1989; Gale 1974, 1983; Hamilton 1980, 1981).

10 As Povinelli notes, 'The majority of white Australians understood sacred acts of bestiality, ritual masturbation, same sex, and group sex as incommensurate with a modern civil society's understanding of sex and intimacy as a private, normatively monogamous heterosexual affair' (2002: 136).

11 For a collection of these types of images of Central Australian Aboriginal peoples, see the beautiful publication of Baldwin Spencer's photographs (Batty, Allen and Morton 2005).

12 For photographs of early adoptions of Christian appearance by Aboriginal locals, see Aboriginal preacher Blind Moses with wife Sophia in the 1920s in Hill (2002: plate 2). Aboriginal men's adoptions of cattle worker appearance have appeared on images for as long as Aboriginal people have been present in the rural industries. More often than not, the intention of these images has, in fact, been to show 'traditional' phenomena, but the men have obviously turned up to ceremonies as they wish, adding a cattle worker hat or dressed in full cattle worker gear, as in Meggitt (1962: opposite 79). Tonkinson observes briefly how, in Aboriginal Jigalong, the 'emulation of the "cowboy" image is every young man's aim, so broad buckles, big hats, riding boots, and tight blue jeans are popular' (1974: 59), as were cowboy comics, movies and country and western music.

13 Also see Hunt (1986). Moore (1998), moreover, questions depictions of colonial males as fiercely heterosexual. He suspects that in the kind of single-sex white rural settings of colonial and post-colonial Australia, male-to-male sex was probably commonplace.

14 Hamilton (1972), for instance, refers to Pitjantjatjara and Yankunytjatjara women describing how senior tribal men gave selected women to white men as reciprocal acts in order to secure rights to food in the earlier decades of non-indigenous settlement in Central Australia.

15 A main example of how Indigenous musicians may 'authenticate' their profile and material is the widespread incorporation of the didjeridu, a blow-trumpet traditionally used only in Aboriginal societies in northern Northern Territory and north-western Australia, but that has become a potent and globally recognized marker of authentic, traditional Australian Aboriginality (Neuenfeldt 1993a, 1994a, 1997, 1998c). Other examples of 'neo-authentication' and cultural assertion are musicians who previously used their English names but began to add their Aboriginal names on album sleeves in the 1980s, and musicians who increasingly perform with ancestral body decorations. Processes of re-authentication and a renaissance of traditional features in popular music are also evident in indigenous populations elsewhere, such as the 'modern jojk' among Scandinavian Saami (Jones-Bamman 2001).

16 Yothu Yindi's ethnically mixed membership is sometimes mentioned but rarely analysed in the many scholarly texts on the band (for instance, Hayward and Neuenfeldt 1998; Magowan 1994; Mitchell 1996: 173ff; Muecke 1990; Neuenfeldt 1998b; Nicol 1998; Shoemaker 1994).

17 The band was re-booked only after an indigenous organizer contacted the artistic director of Womad in London and promised protest actions if any local indigenous acts were dropped (Hollinsworth 1996).

18 *Adelaide Advertiser*, February 17, 2001.

19 Clifford Brown's 'Coniston' is not in commercial release.

20 It refers to the administrative region of the Central Land Council, an elected statutory body established in 1974 to represent and support Aboriginal people in land claims and in negotiations with miners and non-Aboriginal landowners in the region. The CLC area covers 775,963 sq km, out of which 381,792 sq km is Aboriginal land (www.clc.org.au).

21 The terms 'Aboriginal bush towns' or 'Aboriginal towns' are also in use, to avoid confusion with the meanings of 'community' that refer to a set of social relations. The prefixes 'Aboriginal' or 'bush' are also meant to distinguish these Aboriginal-dominated and restricted places from open, non-indigenous Australian towns (Stanley 1989). The statistical term for all the mentioned types of settlements is 'discrete' indigenous communities – 'those that comprise largely, or only Aboriginal and Torres Strait Islander people' (HREOC 2004).

22 For example, 'Kintorelakutu' by the Warumpi Band (1985), 'Ghan to the Alice' by Herbie Laughton (1999) and the North Tanami Band's album *The Travelling Warlpiri* (1995), named from the band's touring experiences.

23 As in 'Highway to Nowhere' by Blackstorm (1998).

24 Listen, for instance, to the compilation *Wama Wanti – Drink Little Bit* (Various 1988b).

25 The town is named after Alice Todd, the wife of the Superintendent of Telegraphs overseeing the construction of the overland telegraph line, and after the permanent spring by the old telegraph station north of the present-day township.

26 In the 2011 Census, 19 per cent of the 27,000 town residents were born overseas, and 26 per cent reported that both parents were born overseas.

27 For a feminist view of this form of ideal masculinity, see Lake (1999: 31).

Chapter 2

1 These features also characterize local appropriations of Christian hymns elsewhere, as described, for instance, in Hawai'i (Stillman 1996).

2 For examples of desert country-gospel, listen to the Kintore Gospel Band and Mount Liebig Band (ca 1988), the Country Wranglers (1999) and Trevor Adamson (1997).

3 Hermannsburg was the home of Albert Namatjira, the first famous Australian Aboriginal painter in the late 1930s. He and other local painters were instrumental in bringing country music to the mission, using part of their artwork earnings to buy gramophones and country records.

4 Isaac Yamma's released two albums with the Pitjantjatjara Country Band (1983, 1987) tracks on *Desert Songs 1* and *2* (Various 1982, 1983) and *Papal Concert in Alice Springs* (Various 1988a).

5 Many other oldfella country music men have greatly influenced, mentored and inspired music making in their particular sub-region, language group and communities. It is a risky business to try to name them all because the list could never be complete and may offend those not mentioned. Many have also passed away. I want to emphasize, though, that the musicians I have worked with frequently pay respect to these locally influential predecessors.

6 For John Williamson's 'hyper-Australian style' and early collaboration with Warren, see Smith (2005: 119).

7 The first, nationally recognized indigenous Australian reggae band was No Fixed Address, formed at the Centre for Aboriginal Studies in Music in Adelaide at the time Bob Marley performed in that city. NFA's influence was boosted by their appearance in the 1981 film *Wrong Side of the Road*, a rather unique production in that it featured the working conditions for indigenous musicians at the time (Lawe Davies 1993).

8 Both songs by the Blackshadow Band (2001).

9 Jimmy Langdon (1999).

10 Sammy Butcher does not appear on the 1987 recordings.

11 Statistics from the Australian Bureau of Statistics 2011 Census.

12 For ceremonial practices in Aboriginal Central Australia, see Bell (2002), Berndt and Berndt (1996), Elkin (1974), Meggitt (1962), Munn (1970) and Myers (1986, 1995).

13 For the fundamental connection between ancestral knowledge and music performance in Central Australia, see Elkin (1956), Ellis and Barwick (1989), Moyle (1979, 1986), Strehlow (1971) and Wild (1987).

14 Statistics from the Australian Bureau of Statistics 2011 Census and the 2014 Regional Population Growth, Australia, 2012–13, Cat. No. 3218.0.

15 'Koori' is a common term of self-designation among Aboriginal people in south-eastern coastal and urban regions.

Chapter 3

1 The nineteen so-called 'town camps' in Alice Springs are Aboriginal housing associations built on special leases and serviced by an Aboriginal organization, not the municipal council. For more, see Ottosson (2014).

2 The described life of the studio has now changed after several reconstructions of CAAMA Music, new staff and a reorganization of the spaces they occupy in the building. I still mostly use present tense in my descriptions, in order to better communicate the sociability and the personalities that generated the studio world at the time.

3 When I refer the matter to Stan, he tells me to put the man in contact with a Warlpiri country and blues musician knowledgeable in ancestral music genres. 'But he doesn't play didj?' I ask confused. Stan shrugs his shoulders. 'Can't be *that* hard. He's a muso, he'll pull it off,' he says.

4 This is a rare strain of music in Aboriginal Central Australia and is mainly heard among middle-aged Yuendumu musicians. I traced it back to non-indigenous Peter Bartlett, a self-confessed 'drop-out hippie' who arrived in Yuendumu in the 1970s and started a guitar club, introducing the local Aboriginal men to the music of black American Delta blues men.

5 See, for example, Becker on jazz musicians (1963), Cohen on Liverpool rock bands (1991) and Frith and Horne on bohemian artistic notions in popular music (1987). So-called independent studios and labels ('indies'), which CAAMA Music presents itself as an independent studio and recording label, or an 'indie', which also usually indicates aspirations to stay outside or to rebel against the practices of a mainstream, profit-driven music industry (Bannister 2002; Frith 1996; Mathieson 2000).

6 CAAMA Music promotes itself as producing 'Aboriginal Music for the World' and its record label as representing the 'Sound of Aboriginal Australia'.

7 The recordings were released in a cassette version (Ikuntji Gospel Band 2003).

Chapter 4

1 The increased interest in indigenous country was triggered by a celebrated television documentary, 'Buried Country', on the rich history of Australian indigenous country music, accompanied by a book (Walker 2000) and a CD (Various 2000).

2 As it turned out, CAAMA Music did not send anybody to Tamworth. Warren and Lyndon went there as part of the Herbie Laughton and Gus Williams (see Chapter 2) entourage, and Lyndon performed some of his own material as part of their performances.

3 Stubbe notes similar systematic differences between styles of interactions in a comparison of conversational speech by New Zealand Maori (indigenous people) and Pakeha (people of European descent) (1998). She shows that in Maori interactions among Maori, a lack of verbal feedback and long silences are recognized 'as having several causes, meanings and values in interpersonal relations, in comparison with the negative interpretation often placed upon silence by Pakehas' (271). Pakehas more often 'provides a more or less continuous stream of talk' (269), with frequent verbal feedbacks in their intra-interactions. She notes, too, how Maori make greater use of non-verbal rather than verbal feedback in many contexts.

4 For a detailed, ethnographic description and discussion of the practices and sensibilities of country music in the United States, see Fox (2004).

5 The ways in which language and bodily practices operate to create male and masculinist cultures and spaces are discussed not only in studies of popular music making (e.g. Cohen 1991; Finnegan 1989; Frith and McRobbie 1990; Reynolds and Press 1995; Walser 1993), but also in other arenas of highly gendered practices, such as sports (Messner 1992; Messner and Sabo 1990, 1994), school fraternities (Lyman 1987), prisons (Sabo, Kupers and London 2001) and body building (Klein 1993), to mention a few. Also see Johnson and Meinhof (1997) on language and masculinities.

6 I was not excluded from the sexualized commentary, which after some time was also made (I assume selectively) in my presence.

7 I did not participate in CAAMA management or section meetings. My knowledge of workplace rules and management policies, and how those were communicated and understood by individuals in the building, is based on conversations with current and former employees, board members and management people.

8 The movements of studio gear should be understood as part of socio-musical relations of informal exchanges of both things and work in which the studio and a number of external people have been engaged over the years. Many CAAMA Music events and projects would have been difficult to accomplish if formal rules of ownership, fees for hiring equipment and monetary compensation for work had been enforced.

Chapter 5

1 Lajamanu is located in the North Tanami desert (see Map 2) and has a predominantly Warlpiri population of approximately 600. It began as the Hooker Creek Aboriginal Reserve in 1948, a state assimilation centre built on the ancestral country of Gurindji people, who are northern neighbours of Warlpiri people. The first Warlpiri people were moved here in 1949 and the main contingent in 1952 from Yuendumu Aboriginal Reserve (est. in 1946) (Wild 1987). The Warlpiri were reluctant to settle on other people's country and staged walk-backs to Yuendumu on three occasions between 1952 and 1965. However, by the 1970s, Warlpiri and Gurindji people conducted joint ceremonies at Hooker Creek and they made a joint, successful land claim over the larger area in which no boundaries were drawn between their respective traditional territories (Peterson and Langton 1983).

2 This style of dancing involves shaking one's buttocks rapidly while twisting one's upper body in slower and sexually suggestive movements, with hands moving up and down along the body or held up above the head. The dance is encouraged from the time Aboriginal children can stand up, and a great deal of effort is invested in developing personal styles.

3 The man has passed away and I replace his name with *Kumunjayi*, which means 'no name' in Warlpiri. It is used for a deceased person, or for names of persons and things that are the same as, or similar to, the name of the deceased, until taboos on using his name are lifted.

4 The Lajamanu Teenage Band was formed in the early 1990s by half-brothers Alfred Rose and Kenneth Martin, and the then teenage boys performed in the Aboriginal community circuit for some years before recording an album (Lajamanu Teenage Band 1995). After winning the Battle of the Bands at the high-profile Barunga Festival in 1996, they released more albums (1998, 1999, 2002, 2006) and attracted wider attention. They performed at nationally noted festivals and featured twice in the prestigious *Rolling Stone* magazine. I suspect that Kenneth was quoted accurately as saying: 'We're young and good looking. We're sexy boys. ... The girls, they go crazy for us' (*Rolling Stone Magazine*, July 1997: 40). The success obviously boosted the men's confidence and they aimed for an international career, a goal still to be attained.

The Rising Wind Band was formed in Yuendumu in 1989 (then named Desert Mulga). Lead guitarist Clifford Brown and singer/guitarist Chris Gallagher have been the leading forces as the band played in Aboriginal communities and regional towns and festivals throughout the 1990s. Their first recordings in the early 1990s were aborted when the drummer never returned after a smoke break, and they later released two albums (Rising Wind Band 2000, 2004).

5 Of course, not all musicians end up as respected senior community leaders or representatives for their people and country. As mentioned in Chapter 2, local stardom may instead lead to heavy drinking, big-headed behaviour and sleeping with the wrong women, all of which can lead to trouble with both Western and ancestral laws, and to violence and premature death.

6 *Kumunjayi* Patterson and Gus Williams were also devoted, practising Christians (Baptist and Lutheran, respectively), which further boosted their social and moral status, and shaped their personal commitment to work for the improvement of their people. Both men were recognized also as gospel musicians in the region.

Chapter 6

1 Meintjes discusses similar movements between the imagined and the experienced in the construction of 'a specific version of blackness' among Zulu musicians (2003: 241). Their talk about an idealized overseas and international success is mapped onto the musicians' lived conditions at home as a kind of limiting backwater of global modernism.

2 The Ltyentye Apurte Band was formed in 1994 and is known for its distinct style of edgy rock, which centres on lead guitarist Chris' creative playing. He and rhythm guitarist Justin wrote the band's first original song (in English), 'Arrernte Tribe', about the history of their people. After performing in desert communities for a few years, their community's arts coordinator began acting as the band's manager, and the art centre part-funded the recording of their album. The Titjikala Desert Oaks Band was formed in the 1980s as part of the first wave of regional Aboriginal artists that recorded with CAAMA (1989). When their lead singer committed suicide in the late 1980s, the band 'just collapsed', as lead guitarist Terry explained to me. They later re-formed as the Titjikala Band and returned to the CAAMA studio to record in 1999. The release was delayed for more than a year when their drummer committed suicide.

3 For the complex causes, effects and roles of alcohol in indigenous settings, see Brady (1988, 1995, 2008), Saggers and Gray (1998) and Sansom (1980).

4 Some examples are the North Tanami Band's 'Ngamarlangu' ('Mother and Child') (1990), 'Wama Kuru Wanti' ('Leave the Grog Alone') with Titjikala Desert Oaks Band (1989), 'Who's Gonna Wipe Their Tears' with Danny Plain (Various 1988b), or 'She's Coming Back' with the Areyonga Desert Tigers (1988).

5 Two years later, the Rising Wind Band released a new album (2004). It featured only one gospel song, which supports my argument that their stated gospel ambitions were more a means to repair image than realizing a socio-musical redirection.

Chapter 7

1 A swag is a portable bush bed usually consisting of a mattress in a sturdy canvas cover and is rolled up when not in use. It is a common item where people spend lots of time in the bush.

2 A 'hotel' in small-town Australia often means a pub. 'Motels' provide accommodation.

3 Nightcliff is a Darwin beach suburb where many Aboriginal people have lived. The now demolished Nightcliff Hotel was an (in)famous performance space for Aboriginal bands in the 1970s and 1980s, as well as a known Aboriginal drinking spot.

4 Mulga is a hardwood tree in the desert region.

5 The Teenage Band has returned home for a funeral and is not part of the group here.

6 This is an Australian Broadcasting Corporation crew, not the CAAMA film team.

References

Akenson, J. E. (2003), 'Australia, the United States and Authenticity', in
P. Hayward (ed.), *Outback and Urban: Australian Country Music, Vol. 1*,
187–206, Gympie, QLD: Australian Institute of Country Music.

Altman, J. (2007), *Inquiry into Australia's Indigenous Arts and Craft Sector*, Topical
Issue No. 4, Canberra: CAEPR, Australian National University.

Anderson, C. and Dussart, F. (1988), 'Dreamings in Acrylic: Western Desert
Art', in P. Sutton (ed.), *Dreamings: The Art of Aboriginal Australia*, 89–142,
Ringwood, VIC: Viking, Penguin Books.

Appadurai, A. (1991), 'Global Ethnoscapes: Notes and Queries for a Transnational
Anthropology', in R. Fox (ed.), *Recapturing Anthropology: Working in the
Present*, 191–210, Santa Fe: School of American Research Press.

Askew, K. M. (2002), *Performing the Nation: Swahili Music and Cultural Politics in
Tanzania*, Chicago, IL: The University of Chicago Press.

Atkinson, J. (2002), *Trauma Trails, Recreating Song Lines: The Trans-Generational
Effects of Trauma in Indigenous Australia*, North Melbourne, VIC: Spinifex
Press.

Attwood, B. and Arnold, J., eds (1992), *Power, Knowledge and Aborigines*,
Melbourne: La Trobe University Press.

Attwood, B. and Markus, A. (1999), *The Struggle for Aboriginal Rights:
A Documentary History*, Sydney, NSW: Allen & Unwin.

Austin-Broos, D. (2001), 'Whose Ethics? Which Cultural Contract? Imagining
Arrernte Traditions Today', *Oceania* 71(3): 189–200.

Austin, T. (1992), *Simply the Survival of the Fittest: Aboriginal Administration in
South Australia's Northern Territory 1863-1910*, Darwin: Historical Society of
the Northern Territory.

Austin, T. (1997), *Never Trust a Government Man: Northern Territory Aboriginal
Policy 1911-1939*, Darwin: Northern Territory University Press.

Back, L. (1994), 'The "White Negro" Revisited. Race and Masculinities in South
London', in A. Cornwall and N. Lindisfarne (eds), *Dislocating Masculinity:
Comparative Ethnographies*, 172–83, London: Routledge.

Bannister, M. (2002), 'Anchor Us: Pakeha Masculinities, Cultural Identity and Indie
Guitar Rock in New Zealand', in K. Kärki, R. Leydon and H. Terho (eds), *Looking
Back, Looking Ahead: Popular Music Studies 20 Years Later*, 230–47, Turku:
IASPM-Norden.

Barber, K. and Waterman, C. (1995), 'Traversing the Global and the Local: Fújì
Music and Praise Poetry in the Production of Contemporary Yorùbá Popular
Culture', in D. Miller (ed.), *Worlds Apart: Modernity through the Prism of the
Local*, 240–62, London: Routledge.

Barthes, R. (1984), *Image, Music, Text*, London: Fontana Paperbacks.

Barthes, R. (1988), *The Semiotic Challenge*, New York: Hill and Wang.

Barwick, L., Marett, L. and Tunstill, G. (1995), 'The Essence of Singing and the Substance of Song', *Oceania Monograph 46*, Sydney, NSW: University of Sydney.

Batty, P. (2003), *Governing Cultural Difference: The Incorporation of the Aboriginal Subject into the Mechanisms of Government with Reference to the Development of Aboriginal Radio and Television in Central Australia*, PhD Thesis, Adelaide: University of South Australia.

Batty, P., Allen, L. and Morton, J., eds (2005), *The Photographs of Baldwin Spencer*, Melbourne: Miegunyah Press, Museum Victoria.

Bayton, M. (1990), 'How Women Become Musicians', in S. Frith and A. Goodwin (eds), *On Record*, 238–57, New York: Pantheon.

Beal, B. and Peterson, R. A. (2001), 'Alternative Country: Origins, Music, World-View, Fans, and Taste in Genre Formation', *Popular Music and Society* 25(1–2): 233–49.

Becker, H. (1963), *Outsiders: Studies in the Sociology of Deviance*, New York: The Free Press.

Beckett, J. (1958), 'Aborigines Make Music', *Quadrant* 2(4): 32–42.

Beckett, J. (1985), 'Colonialism in a Welfare State: The Case of Australian Aborigines', in C. Schrire and C. Gordon (eds), *The Future of Former Foragers in Australia and Southern Africa*, 7–24, Cambridge, MA: Cultural Survival Inc.

Beckett, J., ed. (1988a), *Past and Present: The Construction of Aboriginality*, Canberra: Aboriginal Studies Press.

Beckett, J. (1988b), 'The Past in the Present; The Present in the Past: Constructing a National Aboriginality', in J. Beckett (ed.), *Past and Present: The Construction of Aboriginality*, 191–217, Canberra: Aboriginal Studies Press.

Beckett, J. (1988c), 'Aboriginality, Citizenship and Nation State', *Social Analysis* (24): 3–18.

Bederman, G. (1995), *Manliness and Civilization: A Cultural History of Gender and Race in the United States 1880-1917*, Chicago, IL: The University of Chicago Press.

Bell, D. (1998), *Ngarrindjeri Wurruwarrin: A World that Is, Was, and Will Be*, North Melbourne, VIC: Spinifex Press.

Bell, D. (2002), *Daughters of the Dreaming*, 3rd edn, North Melbourne, VIC: Spinifex Press.

Benhabib, S. (2002), *The Claims of Culture: Equality and Diversity in the Global Era*, Princeton: Princeton University Press.

Bennett, T., Buckridge, P., Carter D. and Mercer, C., eds (1992), *Celebrating the Nation: A Critical Study of Australia's Bicentenary*, Sydney, NSW: Allen & Unwin.

Berndt, R. M. (1962), *An Adjustment Movement in Arnhem Land, Northern Territory of Australia*, Paris: Mouton.

Berndt, R. and Berndt, C. (1996), *The World of the First Australians: Aboriginal Traditional Life: Past and Present*, 5th edn, Canberra: Aboriginal Studies Press.

Bhabha, H. (1994), *The Location of Culture*, London: Routledge.

Bilby, K. (1999), '"Roots Explosion": Indigenization and Cosmopolitanism in Contemporary Surinamese Popular Music', *Ethnomusicology* 43(2): 256–96.

Blacking, J. (1973), *How Musical is Man?*, Seattle: University of Washington Press.

Bolger, A. (1991), *Aboriginal Women and Violence*, Darwin, NT: ANU North Australia Research Unit.

Booker, C. (2000), *'I Will Wear No Chain!': A Social History of African American Males*, Westport: Praeger.

Born, G. and Hesmondhalgh, D., eds (2000), *Western Music and its Others: Difference, Representation, and Appropriation in Music*, Berkeley, CA: University of California Press.

Brady, M. (1988), *Where the Beer Truck Stopped: Drinking in a Northern Australian Town*, Darwin, NT: ANU North Australia Research Unit.

Brady, M. (1995), *Giving Away the Grog: Aboriginal Accounts of Drinking and Not Drinking*, Canberra: Australian Institute for Aboriginal and Torres Strait Islander Studies.

Brady, M. (2008), *First Taste: How Indigenous Australians Learned About Grog*, Canberra: Alcohol Education and Rehabilitation Foundation.

Breen, M., ed. (1989), *Our Place, Our Music: Aboriginal Music: Australian Popular Music in Perspective*, Canberra: Aboriginal Studies Press.

Brock, P., ed. (1989), *Women Rites and Sites: Aboriginal Women's Ritual Knowledge*, St Leonards, NSW: Allen & Unwin.

Brod, H., ed. (1987), *The Making of Masculinities*, New York: Routledge.

Brod, H. and Kaufman, M., eds (1994), *Theorizing Masculinities*, London: Sage Publications.

Brunton, M. (1987), 'Musical Structure as a Reflection of the Process of Acculturation among Detribalised Aboriginal People in S.E. Australia', *Miscellanea Musicologica* 12: 246–58.

Burbank, V. (1994), *Fighting Women: Anger and Aggression in Aboriginal Australia*, Berkeley, CA: University of California Press.

Butler, J. (1990), *Gender Trouble: Feminism and the Subversion of Identity*, New York: Routledge.

Butler, J. (1993), *Bodies that Matter: On the Discursive Limits of 'Sex'*, New York: Routledge.

Butler, J. (1997a), *Excitable Speech: A Politics of the Performative*, New York: Routledge.

Butler, J. (1997b), *The Psychic Life of Power*, Stanford: Stanford University Press.

Carby, H. (1998), *Race Men*, Cambridge, MA: Harvard University Press.

Carrigan, T., Connell, B. and Lee, J. (1985), 'Towards a New Sociology of Masculinity', *Theory and Society* 14(5): 551–604.

Carter, J. (1988), 'Am I too Black to Go with You?', in I. Keen (ed.), *Being Black: Aboriginal Cultures in 'Settled' Australia*, 65–76, Canberra: Aboriginal Studies Press.

Casey, E. (1996), 'How to Get from Space to Place in a Fairly Short Stretch of Time', in S. Feld and K. H. Basso (eds), *Senses of Place*, 13–52, Santa Fe: School of American Research Press.

Castles, J. (1998), 'Tjungaringanyi: Aboriginal Rock (1971-91)', in P. Hayward (ed.), *Sound Alliances: Indigenous Peoples, Cultural Politics and Popular Music in the Pacific*, 11–25, London: Cassell.

Chatwin, B. (1987), *The Songlines*, New York: Viking.

Clarke, B. (2003), *Wisdom Man: Banjo Clarke as Told to Camilla Chance*, Camberwell, VIC: Viking.

Clatterbaugh, K. (1990), *Contemporary Perspectives on Masculinity*, Boulder: Westview Press.

Clendinnen, I. (2003), *Dancing with Strangers*, Melbourne: The Text Publishing Company.

Clunies Ross, M., Donaldson T. and Wild, S., eds (1987), *Songs of Aboriginal Australia*, Sydney, NSW: University of Sydney.

Cohen, S. (1991), *Rock Culture in Liverpool: Popular Music in the Making*, Oxford: Oxford University Press.

Collins, J. and Richards, P. (1989), 'Popular Music in West Africa', in S. Frith (ed.), *World Music, Politics and Social Change*, 12–46, Manchester: Manchester University Press.

Conklin, B. (1997), 'Body Paint, Feathers, and VCRs: Aesthetics and Authenticity in Amazonian Activism', *American Ethnologist* 24(4): 711–37.

Connell, B. (1995), *Masculinities*, Cambridge: Polity Press.

Connell, B. (2000), *The Men and the Boys*, Berkeley, CA: University of California Press.

Coombe, R. (1997), 'The Properties of Culture and the Possession of Identity: Postcolonial Struggle and the Legal Imagination', in B. Ziff and P. V. Rao (eds), *Borrowed Power: Essays on Cultural Appropriation*, 74–96, New Brunswick, NJ: Rutgers University Press.

Corn, A. (1999), *Dreamtime Wisdom – Modern Time Vision: The Aboriginal Acculturation of Popular Muisc in Arnhem Land, Australia*, Darwin, NT: ANU North Australia Research Unit.

Cornell, S. and Hartmann, D. (1998), *Ethnicity and Race: Making Identities in a Changing World*, Thousand Oaks, CA: Pine Forge Press.

Cornwall, A. and Lindisfarne, N., eds (1994), *Dislocating Masculinity: Comparative Ethnographies*, London: Routledge.

Coronil, F. (1996), 'Beyond Occidentalism: Toward Nonimperial Geohistorical Categories', *Cultural Anthropology* 11(1): 51–87.

Cowlishaw, G. (1986), 'Aborigines and Anthropologists', *Australian Aboriginal Studies* 1: 2–12.

Cowlishaw, G. (1992), 'Studying Aborigines: Changing Canons in Anthropology and History', *Journal of Australian Studies* 35: 20–31.

Cowlishaw, G. (1998), 'Erasing Culture and Race: Practising "Self-determination"', *Oceania* 68(3): 145–69.

Cowlishaw, G. (2001), '"Old Contempt and New Solicitude": Race Relations and Australian Ethnography', *Oceania* 71(3): 169–87.

Cowlishaw, G. (2004), *Blackfellas, Whitefellas and the Hidden Injuries of Race*, Carlton, VIC: Blackwell Publishing.

Creswell, T. and Fabinyi, M. (1999), *The Real Thing 1957-Now: Adventures in Australian Rock & Roll*, Sydney: Random House Australia.

Cribbin, J. (1984), *The Killing Times: The Coniston massacre 1928*, Sydney: Fontana/Collins.

Davis, R. (1998), *Epochal Bodies and Gendered Time: Engagement and Transformation in Saibaian (Torres Strait) Masculinity*, PhD Thesis, Canberra: Australian National University.

Diamond, B. (2001), 'Re-Placing Performance: A Case Study of the Yukon Music Scene in the Canadian North', *Journal of Intercultural Studies* 22(2): 211–24.

Dodson, M. (2003), 'The End in the Beginning: Re(de)finding Aboriginality', in M. Grossman (ed.), *Blacklines. Contemporary Critical Writing by Indigenous Australians*, 25–42, Melbourne, VIC: Melbourne University Press.

Donovan, P. (1988), *Alice Springs: Its History and the People Who Made It*, Alice Springs: Alice Springs Town Council.

du Bois, W. E. B. (1982 [1903]), *The Souls of Black Folks*, New York: New American Library.

Dunbar-Hall, P (1997), 'Site as Song – Song as site: Constructions of Meaning in an Aboriginal Rock Song', *Perfect Beat* 3(3): 58–76.

Dunbar-Hall, P. and Gibson, C. (2004), *Deadly Sounds, Deadly Places: Contemporary Aboriginal Music in Australia*, Sydney: University of New South Wales Press.

Dyck, N., ed. (1985), *Indigenous Peoples and the Nation-State: 'Fourth world' Politics in Canada, Australia and Norway*, St. John's, NL: Memorial University of Newfoundland.

Edensor, T. (2002), *National Identity, Popular Culture and Everyday Life*, Oxford: Berg.

Elkin, A. P. (1956), 'Aboriginal Music', *Canon* 10(4): 112–15.

Elkin, A. P. (1974), *The Australian Aborigines*, 5th edn, Sydney: Angus & Robertson.

Ellis, C. (1985), *Aboriginal Music: Education for Living*, St Lucia, QLD: University of Queensland Press.

Ellis, C. (1994), '"Country Music", "Gospel Music" and "Music"', in D. Horton (ed.), *The Encyclopedia of Aboriginal Australia, Vol.1*, Canberra: Aboriginal Studies Press.

Ellis, C. and Barwick, L. (1989), 'Antikirinja Women's Song Knowledge 1963–72', in P. Brock (ed.), *Women Rites and Sites. Aboriginal women's cultural knowledge.* St Leonards, NSW: Allen & Unwin.

Erlmann, V. (1999), *Music, Modernity, and the Global Imagination*, New York and Oxford: Oxford University Press.

Feld, S. (1974), 'Linguistic Models in Ethnomusicology, *Ethnomusicology* 18(2): 197–217.

Feld, S. (1994), 'Communication, Music, and Speech about Music', in C. Keil and S. Feld (eds), *Music Grooves*, 77–95, Chicago, IL: The University of Chicago Press.

Feld, S. and Fox, A. (1994), 'Music and Language', *Annual Review of Anthropology* 23: 25–54.

Fine, G. A. (1987), 'One of the Boys: Women in Male Dominated Settings', in M. Kimmel (ed.), *Changing Men: New Directions in Research on Men and Masculinity*, 131–47, Newbury Park, CA: Sage Publications.

Finnegan, R. (1989), *The Hidden Musicians: Music Making in an English Town*, Cambridge: Cambridge University Press.

Fox, A. (2004), *Real Country: Music and Language in Working-Class Culture*, Durham: Duke University Press.

Frith, S. (1996), 'The A&R Men', in C. Gillett and S. Frith (eds), *The Beat Goes On: The Rock File Reader*, 93–108, London: Pluto Press.

Frith, S. and Horne, H. (1987), *Art into Pop*, London: Routledge.

Frith, S. and McRobbie, A. (1990), 'Rock and Sexuality', in S. Frith and A. Goodwin (eds), *On Record*, 371–89, New York: Pantheon.

Furlan, A. (2005), *Songs of Continuity and Change: The Reproduction of Aboriginal Culture through Traditional and Popular Music*, PhD Thesis, Sydney, NSW: University of Sydney.

Gale, F. (1973), *Urban Aborigines*, Canberra: Australian National University Press.

Gale, F., ed. (1974), *Woman's Role in Aboriginal Society*, Canberra: Australian Institute of Aboriginal Studies.

Gale, F., ed. (1983), *We are Bosses Ourselves*, Canberra: Australian Institute of Aboriginal Studies.

Garofalo, R. (1993), 'Black Popular Music: Crossing Over or Going Under?', in T. Bennett, S. Frith, L. Grossberg, J. Shepherd and G. Turner (eds), *Rock and Popular Music: Politics, Policies, Institutions*, 231–48, London: Routledge.

Garton, S. (1998), 'War and Masculinities in Twentieth Century Australia', *Journal of Australian Studies* 56: 68–95.

Gerstin, J. (1998), 'Reputation in a Musical Scene: The Everyday Context of Connections between Music, Identity, and Politics', *Ethnomusicology* 42(3): 385–414.

Gilbert, K. (1994), *Because a White Man'll Never Do It*, Sydney: Angus & Robertson.

Gilroy, P. (1987), *'There Ain't No Black in the Union Jack' : The Cultural Politics of Race and Nation*, Chicago, IL: The University of Chicago Press.

Gilroy, P. (1993), *The Black Atlantic: Modernity and Double Consciousness*, Cambridge, MA: Harvard University Press.

Gilroy, P., Grossberg, L and McRobbie, A., eds (2000), *Without Guarantees: In Honour of Stuart Hall*, London: Verso.

Ginsburg, F. (1991). 'Indigenous Media: Faustian Contract or Global Village?', *Cultural Anthropology* 6: 92–112.

Ginsburg, F. (1994), 'Embedded Aesthetics: Creating a Discursive Space for Indigenous Media', *Cultural Anthropology* 9(3): 365–82.

Glowczewski, B. (1998), '"All One but Different": Aboriginality: National Identity Versus Local Diversification in Australia', in J. Wassman (ed.), *Pacific Answers to Western Hegemony: Cultural Practices of Identity Construction*, 335–54, Oxford: Berg.

Goodwin, C. and Duranti, A. (1992), 'Rethinking Context: An Introduction', in A. Duranti and C. Goodwin (eds), *Rethinking Context: Language as an Interactive Phenomenon*, 1–42, Cambridge: Cambridge University Press.

Gorbman, C. (2000), 'Scoring the Indian: Music in the Liberal Western', in G. Born and D. Hesmondhalgh (eds), *Western Music and its Others: Difference, Representation, and Appropriation in Music*, 234–53, Berkeley, CA: University of California Press.

Hall, R. (1989), *The Black Diggers*, Canberra: Aboriginal Studies Press.

Hall, S. (1992), 'Cultural Studies and its Theoretical Legacies', in L. Grossberg, C. Nelson and P. Treichler (eds), *Cultural Studies*, 277–94, New York: Routledge.

Hamilton, A. (1972), 'Blacks and Whites: The Relationships of Change', *Arena* 30: 34–48.

Hamilton, A. (1980), 'Dual Social Systems: Technology, Labour and Women Secret Rites in the Eastern Western Desert of Australia', *Oceania* 50: 4–19.

Hamilton, A. (1981), 'A Complex Strategical Situation: Gender and Power in Aboriginal Australia', in N. Grieve and P. Grimshaw (eds), *Australian Women: Feminist Perspectives*, 69–85, Melbourne: Oxford University Press.

Hannerz, U. (1996), *Transnational Connections: Culture, People, Places*, London: Routledge.

Hanson, A. (1989), 'The Making of the Maori: Culture Invention and its Logic', *American Anthropologist* 91: 890–902.

Harrison, S. (2002), 'The Politics of Resemblance: Ethnicity, Trademarks, Head-Hunting', *Journal of the Royal Anthropological Institute* 8: 211–32.

Hayward, P., ed. (1992), *From Pop to Punk to Postmodernism: Popular Music and Australian Culture from the 1960s to the 1990s*, North Sydney, NSW: Allen & Unwin.

Hayward, P. (1998a), 'Safe, Exotic and Somewhere Else: Yothu Yindi, "Treaty" and the Mediation of Aboriginality', in P. Hayward (ed.), *Sound Alliances: Indigenous Peoples, Cultural Politics and Popular Music in the Pacific*, 190–98, London: Cassell.

Hayward, P., ed. (1998b), *Sound Alliances: Indigenous Peoples, Cultural Politics and Popular Music in the Pacific*, London: Cassell.

Hayward, P. and Neuenfeldt, K. (1998), 'Yothu Yindi: Context and Significance', in P. Hayward (ed.), *Sound Alliances: Indigenous Peoples, Cultural Politics and Popular Music in the Pacific*, 175–80, London: Cassell.

Hebdige, D. (1979), *Subculture: The Meaning of Style*, London: Methuen.

Heelas, P., Lash, S. and Morris, P., eds (1996), *Detraditionalization: Critical Reflections on Authority and Identity*, Cambridge, MA: Blackwell Publishers.

Heppell, M. and Wigley, J. J. (1981), *Black Out in Alice: A History of the Establishment and Development of Town Camps in Alice Springs*, Canberra: Australian National University Press.

Hesmondhalgh, D. and Negus, K., eds (2002), *Popular Music Studies*, London: Arnold.

Hill, B. (2002), *Broken Song: T.G.H. Strehlow and Aboriginal Possession*, Sydney: Knopf/Random House Australia.

Hinkson, M. (2004), 'What's in a Dedication? On Being a Warlpiri DJ', *Australian Journal of Anthropology* 15(2): 143–62.

Hinkson, M. (1996), 'The Circus Comes to Yuendumu, Again', *Arena Magazine* 25(October–November): 36–39.

Hinkson, M. and Smith, B. (2005), 'Introduction: Conceptual Moves Towards an Intercultural Analysis', *Oceania* 75(3): 157–66.

Hollinsworth, D. (1996), '"Narna Tarkendi" Indigenous Performing Arts Opening Cultural Doors', *Australian-Canadian Studies* 14(1 and 2): 55–68.

HREOC (2004), *A Statistical Overview of Aboriginal and Torres Strait Islander Peoples in Australia*, Sydney: Australian Human Rights and Equal Opportunities Commission.

HREOC (2009), *Social Justice Report 2008*, Sydney: Australian Human Rights Commission.

Hunt, S. (1986), *Spinifex and Hessian: Women in North-West Australia, 1860-1900*, Nedlands, WA: University of Western Australia Press.

Hunter, T. W. (2000), '"Sexual Pantomimes," the Blues Aesthetic, and Black Women in the New South', in R. Radano and P. V. Bohlman (eds), *Music and the Racial Imagination*, 145–64, Chicago, IL: The University of Chicago Press.

IAD (2002), *Central Australian Aboriginal Languages: Current Distribution*, Alice Springs: Institute for Aboriginal Development.

Jackson, A., ed. (1989), *Anthropology at Home*, London: Tavistock Publications.

Jackson, J. (1989), 'Is there a Way to Talk about Making Culture without Making Enemies?', *Dialectical Anthropology* 14: 127–43.

Jackson, M. (1998), *Minima Ethnographica. Intersubjectivity and the Anthropological Project*, Chicago, IL: The University of Chicago Press.

Jamison, A. and Eyerman, R. (1998) *Music and Social Movements*, Cambridge: Cambridge University Press.

Jennett, C. (1987), 'Incorporation or Independence? The Struggle for Aboriginal Equality', in C. Jennett and R. Stewart (eds), *Three Worlds of Inequality.* 57–93, South Melbourne: Macmillan.

Johnson, S. and Meinhof, U. H., eds (1997), *Language and Masculinity*, Oxford: Blackwell Publishers.

Jones, P. (1992), 'The Boomerang's Erratic Flight: The Mutability of Ethnographic Objects', *Journal of Australian Studies*, 35: 59–71.

Jones-Bamman, R. (2001), 'From "I'm a Lapp" to "I am Saami": Popular Music and Changing Images of Indigenous Ethnicity in Scandinavia', *Journal of Intercultural Studies* 22(2): 189–210.

Kaemmer, J. (1993), *Music in Human Life: Anthropological Perspectives on Music*, Austin: University of Texas Press.

Kane, J. (1997), 'Racialism and Democracy: The Legacy of White Australia', in G. Stokes (ed.), *The Politics of Identity in Australia*, 117–31, Cambridge: Cambridge University Press.

Kanitkar, H. (1994), '"Real True Boys": Moulding the Cadets of Imperialism', in A. Cornwall and N. Lindisfarne (eds), *Dislocating Masculinity: Comparative Ethnographies*, 184–96, London: Routledge.

Keeffe, K. (1988), 'Aboriginality: Resistance and Persistence', *Australian Aboriginal Studies* (1): 67–81.

Keen, I. (1988), 'Introduction', in I. Keen (ed.), *Being Black: Aboriginal Cultures in 'Settled' Australia*, 1–26, Canberra: Aboriginal Studies Press.

Keillor, E. (1995), 'The Emergence of Postcolonial Musical Expressions of Aboriginal Peoples within Canada', *Cultural Studies* 9(1): 106–24.

Kibby, M. and Neuenfeldt, K. (1998), 'Sound, Cinema and Aboriginality', in R. Coyle (ed.), *Screen Scores*, 66–77, North Ryde, NSW: Australian Film, Television and Radio School.

Kimmel, M. (1987), *Changing Men: New Directions in Research in Men and Masculinity*, Newbury Park, CA: Sage Publications.

Kimmel, M. (1994), 'Masculinity as Homophobia: Fear, Shame, and Silence in the Construction of Gender Identity', in H. Brod and M. Kaufman (eds), *Theorizing Masculinities*, 119–41, Thousand Oaks, CA: Sage Publications.

Kimmel, M. (1996), *Manhood in America: A Cultural History*, New York: The Free Press.

Klein, A. (1993), *Little Big Men: Bodybuilding Subculture and Gender Construction*, Albany: State University of New York Press.

Kondos, V. and Cowlishaw, G. (1995), 'Introduction: Conditions of Possibility', *Australian Journal of Anthropology* 6(1–2): 1–14.

Kowal, E. (2008), 'The Politics of the Gap: Indigenous Australians, Liberal Multiculturalism, and the End of the Self-Determination Era', *American Anthropologist* 110(3): 338–48.

Kurtzer, S. (2003), 'Wandering Girl: Who Defines "Authenticity" in Aboriginal Literature?', in M. Grossman (ed.), *Blacklines: Contemporary Critical Writing by Indigenous Australians*, 181–8, Melbourne, VIC: Melbourne University Press.

Lake, M. (1999), *Getting Equal: The History of Australian Feminism*, St Leonards, NSW: Allen & Unwin.

Langton, M. (1993a), *'Well I heard it on the radio and I saw it on the television ...'*, North Sydney: Australian Film Commission.

Langton, M. (1993b), 'Rum, Seduction and Death: "Aboriginality" and Alcohol', *Oceania* 63(3): 195–206.

Langton, M. (2003), 'Aboriginal Art and Film: The Politics of Representation', in M. Grossman (ed.), *Blacklines: Contemporary Critical Writing by Indigenous Australians*, 109–124, Melbourne, VIC: Melbourne University Press.

Larbalestier, J. (1988), '"... For the Betterment of these People": The Bleakley Report and Aboriginal Workers', *Social Analysis* 24: 19–33.

Latta, D. (1991), *Australian Country Music*, Sydney: Random House Australia.

Lattas, A. (1992), 'Primitivism, Nationalism and Individualism in Australian Popular Culture', in B. Attwood and J. Arnold (eds), *Power, Knowledge and Aborigines*, 45–58, Bundoora: La Trobe University Press.

Lattas, A. (1993), 'Essentialism, Memory and Resistance: Aboriginality and the Politics of Authenticity, *Oceania* 6(3): 183–94.

Laughren, M., Hoogenraad, R., Hale, K. and Granites, R. J. (1996), *A Learner's Guide to Warlpiri: Wangkamirlipa Warlpirilki*, Alice Springs: IAD Press.

Lawe Davies, C. (1993), 'Aboriginal Rock Music: Space and Place', in T. Bennett, S. Frith, L. Grossberg, J. Shepherd and G. Turner (eds), *Rock and Popular Music: Politics, Policies, Institutions*, 249–65, London: Routledge.

Lévi-Strauss, C. (1966), *The Savage Mind*, Chicago, IL: University of Chicago Press.

Levin, M. D., ed. (1993), *Ethnicity and Aboriginality: Case Studies in Ethnonationalism*, Toronto: University of Toronto Press.

Liberman, K. (1985), *Understanding Interaction in Central Australia: An Ethnomethodological Study of Australian Aboriginal People*, London: Routledge and Kegan Paul.

Long, J. (1964), 'Papunya: Westernization in an Aboriginal Community', in M. Reay (ed.), *Aborigines Now*, 72–82, Sydney: Angus and Robertson.

Longhurst, B. (1995), *Popular Music and Society*, Cambridge: Polity Press.

Lyman, P. (1987), 'The Fraternal Bond as a Joking Relationship', in M. Kimmel (ed.), *Changing Men: New Directions in Research on Men and Masculinity*, 148–63, Newbury Park, CA: Sage Publications.

Mac an Ghaill, M. (1994), 'The Making of Black English Masculinities', in H. Brod and M. Kaufman (eds), *Theorizing Masculinities*, 183–99, London: Sage Publications.

Macdonald, G. (1988), 'A Wiradjuri Fight Story', in I. Keen (ed.), *Being Black: Aboriginal Cultures in 'Settled' Australia*, 179–99, Canberra: Aboriginal Studies Press.

Magowan, F. (1994), '"The Land is Our Märr (Essence), It Stays Forever": The Yothu Yindi Relationship in Australian Aboriginal Traditional and Popular Musics', in M. Stokes (ed.), *Ethnicity, Identity and Music: The Musical Construction of Place*, 135–55, Oxford: Berg.

Magowan, F. (2007), *Melodies of Mourning: Music and Emotion in Northern Australia*, Crawley: University of Western Australia Press.

Majors, R. and Manchini Billson, J. (1992), *Cool Pose: The Dilemmas of Black Manhood in America*, New York: Touchstone.

Marett, A. (2005), *Songs, Dreamings, and Ghosts: The Wangga of North Australia*, Middleton: Wesleyan University Press.

Markus, A. (1990), *Governing Savages*, Sydney, NSW: Allen & Unwin.

Mathieson, C. (2000), *The Sell-In: How the Music Business Seduced Alternative Rock*, St Leonards, NSW: Allen & Unwin.

McCoy, B. (2008), *Holding Men: Kanyirninpa and the Health of Young Aboriginal Men*, Canberrra: Aboriginal Studies Press.

McClary, S. (1991), *Feminine Endings: Music, Gender and Sexuality*, Minneapolis: University of Minneapolis Press.

McGrath, A. (1984), '"Black Velvet": Aboriginal Women and their Relations with White Men in the Northern Territory 1910-1940', in K. Daniels (ed.), *So Much Hard Work: Women and Prostitution in Australian History*, 233–97, Sydney: Fontana/Collins.

Meggitt, M. (1962), *Desert People*, Sydney: Angus & Robertson Publishers.

Meintjes, L. (2003), *Sound of Africa! Making Music Zulu in a South African Studio*, Durham: Duke University Press.

Memmot, P., Stacy, R., Chambers, C. and Keys, C. (2001), *Violence in Indigenous Communities*, Canberra: Crime Prevention Branch, Attorney General's Department.

Merlan, F. (1988), 'Gender in Aboriginal Social Life: A Review', in R. M. Berndt and R. Tonkinson (eds), *Social Anthropology and Australian Aboriginal Studies*, 15–76, Canberra: Aboriginal Studies Press.

Merlan, F. (1991), 'Women, Productive Roles, and Monetisation of the "Service Mode" in Aboriginal Australia: Perspectives from Katherine, Northern Territory', *Australian Journal of Anthropology* 2(3): 259–92.

Merlan, F. (1998), *Caging the Rainbow: Places, Politics, and Aborigines in a North Australian Town*, Honolulu: University of Hawai'i Press.

Merlan, F. (2005), 'Explorations Towards Intercultural Accounts of Socio-Cultural Reproduction and Change, *Oceania* 75(3): 167–82.

Mertz, E. (1985), 'Beyond Symbolic Anthropology: Introducing Semiotic Mediation', in E. Mertz and R. Parmentier (eds), *Semiotic Mediation: Sociocultural and Psychological Perspectives*, 1–19, Orlando, FL: Academic Press Inc.

Mertz, E. and Parmentier, R., eds (1985), *Semiotic Mediation: Sociocultural and Psychological Perspectives*, Orlando, FL: Academic Press Inc.

Messner, M. (1992), *Power at Play: Sports and the Problem of Masculinity*, Boston: Beacon Press.

Messner, M. and Sabo, D., eds (1990), *Sport, Men, and the Gender Order: Critical Feminist Perspectives*, Champaign, IL: Human Kinetics Books.

Messner, M. and Sabo, D. (1994), *Sex, Violence and Power in Sports: Rethinking Masculinity*, Freedom, CA: The Crossing Press.

Michaels, E. (1985), 'Constraints on Knowledge in an Economy of Oral Information', *Current Anthropology* 26(4): 505–10.

Michaels, E. (1986), *The Aboriginal Invention of Television in Central Australia*, Canberra: Australian Institute of Aboriginal Studies.

Mitchell, T. (1988), *Colonising Egypt*, Berkeley, CA: University of California Press.

Mitchell, T. (1993), 'Treaty Now! Indigenous Music and Music Television in Australia', *Media, Culture and Society* 15: 299–308.

Mitchell, T. (1996), *Popular Music and Local Identity: Rock, Pop and Rap in Europe and Oceania*, London: Leicester University Press.

Mitchell, T. (2000), 'The Stage of Modernity', in T. Mitchell (ed.), *Questions of Modernity*, 1–34, Minneapolis: University of Minnesota Press.

Molnar, H. and Meadows. M. (2001), *Songlines and Satellites: Indigenous Communications in Australia, the South Pacific and Canada*, Sydney: Pluto Press.

Moore, C. (1998), 'Colonial Manhood and Masculinities', *Journal of Australian Studies* 56: 35–50.

Morphy, H. (1991), *Ancestral Connections: Art and an Aboriginal System of Knowledge*, Chicago, IL: The University of Chicago Press.

Morphy, H. (1996), 'Aboriginal Art in a Global Context', *Australian Journal of Anthropology* 7(3): 211–39.

Morris, B. (1988), 'The Politics of Identity: From Aborigines to the First Australian', in J. Beckett (ed.) *Past and Present: The Construction of Aboriginality*, 63–85, Canberra: Aboriginal Studies Press.

Morris, B. (1989), *Domesticating Resistance*, London: Berg.

Morrissey, P. (2003), 'Aboriginality and Corporatism', in M. Grossman (ed.), *Blacklines. Contemporary Critical Writing by Indigenous Australians*, 52–59, Melbourne, VIC: Melbourne University Press.

Morton, J. (1998), 'Essentially Black, Essentially Australian, Essentially Opposed: Australian Anthropology and its Uses of Aboriginal Identity', in J. Wassman (ed.), *Pacific Answers to Western Hegemony: Cultural Practices of Identity Construction*, 355–84, Oxford: Berg.

Mountford, C. P. (1948), *Brown Men and Red Sand: Journeyings into Wild Australia*, Melbourne: Robertson and Mullens.

Mountford, C. P. (1965), *Ayers Rock, Its People, Their Beliefs and Their Art*, Sydney: Angus and Robertson.

Moyle, R. (1979), *Songs of the Pintupi: Musical Life in a Central Australian Society*, Canberra: AIAS.

Moyle, R. (1986), *Alyawarra Music: Songs and Society in a Central Australian Community*, Canberra: AIAS.

Muecke, S. (1990), 'Yolngu Culture in the Age of MTV', *Independent Media (UK)*, 92(October).

Mundine, D. (2000), 'Millennia Indigenna', in V. Baxter and K. Gallasch (eds), *Australia's Indigenous Arts*, Strawberry Hills, NSW: Australia Council.

Munn, N. (1970), 'The Transformation of Subjects into Objects in Warlbiri and Pitjantjatjara Myth', in R. Berndt (ed.), *Australian Aboriginal Anthropology*, 141–63, Nedlands: University of Western Australia Press.

Murray, N. (1993), *Sing for Me, Countryman*, Rydalmere: Hodder & Stoughton Australia.

Murrie, L. (1998), 'The Australian Legend: Writing Australian Masculinity/Writing "Australian" Masculine', *Journal of Australian Studies* 56: 68–77.

Myers, F. (1985), 'Illusion and Reality: Aboriginal Self-Determination in Central Australia', in C. Schrire and R. Gordon (eds), *The Future of Former Foragers in Australia and Southern Africa*, 109–21, Cambridge, MA: Cultural Survival.

Myers, F. (1986), *Pintupi Country, Pintupi Self: Sentiment, Place, and Politics among Western Desert Aborigines*, Berkeley, CA: University of California Press.

Myers, F. (1995), 'Representing Culture: The Production of Discourses for Aboriginal Acrylic Paintings', in G. E. Marcus and F. Myers (eds), *The Traffic in Culture: Refiguring Art and Anthropology*, 55–95, Berkeley, CA: University of California Press.

Myers, F. (2002), *Painting Culture: The Making of an Aboriginal High Art*, Durham: Duke University Press.

Nagel, J. (1996), *American Indian Ethnic Renewal: Red Power and the Resurgence of Identity and Culture*, New York: Oxford University Press.

Negus, K. (1996), *Popular Music Theory*, Cambridge: Polity Press.

Negus, K. and Pickering, M. (2002), 'Creativity and Musical Experience', in D. Hesmondhalgh and K. Negus (eds), *Popular Music Studies*, 178–90, London: Arnold.

Neuenfeldt, K. (1991), 'To Sing a Song of Otherness: Anthros, Ethno-Pop and the Mediation of 'Public Problems', *Canadian Ethnic Studies* 23(3): 92–118.

Neuenfeldt, K. (1993a), 'The Didjeridu and the Overdub: Technologising and Transposing Aural Images of Aboriginality', *Perfect Beat* 1(2): 60–77.

Neuenfeldt, K. (1993b), 'Yothu Yindi and Ganma: The Cultural Transposition of Aboriginal Agenda through Metaphor and Music', *Journal of Australian Studies* 38: 1–11.

Neuenfeldt, K. (1994a), 'The Essentialistic, the Exotic, the Equivocal and the Absurd: The Cultural Production and Use of the Didjeridu in World Music', *Perfect Beat* 2(1): 88–104.

Neuenfeldt, K. (1994b), *Sounding Silences: Ethnogenesis, Ethno-Pop Music and Indigenous Peoples*, PhD Thesis, Perth: Curtin University of Technology.

Neuenfeldt, K. (1996), 'Songs of Survival: Ethno-Pop Music as Ethnographic Indigenous Media, *Australian-Canadian Studies* 14(1 and 2): 15–31.

Neuenfeldt, K., ed. (1997), *The Didjeridu: From Arnhem Land to Internet*, Sydney: John Libbey & Company.

Neuenfeldt, K. (1998a), 'Sounding Silences: The Inclusion of Indigenous Popular Music in Australian Education Curricula', *Discourse: Studies in the Cultural Politics of Education* 19(2): 201–18.

Neuenfeldt, K. (1998b), 'Yothu Yindi: Agendas and Aspirations', in P. Hayward (ed.), *Sound Alliances: Indigenous Peoples, Cultural Politics and Popular Music in the Pacific*, 199–208, London: Cassell.

Neuenfeldt, K. (1998c), 'The Quest for a "Magical Island": The Convergence of the Didjeridu, Aboriginal Culture, Healing and Cultural Politics in New Age Discourse', *Social Analysis* 42(2): 73–102.

Neuenfeldt, K. (2001), 'Cultural Politics and a Music Recording Project: Producing "Strike Em!" Contemporary Voices from the Torres Strait', *Journal of Intercultural Studies* 22(2): 133–45.

Nicol, L. (1998), 'Culture, Custom and Collaboration: The Production of Yothu Yindi's "Treaty" Videos', in P. Hayward (ed.), *Sound Alliances: Indigenous People, Cultural Politics and Popular Music in the Pacific*, 181–89, London: Cassell.

Nicoll, F. (2001), *From Diggers to Drag Queens: Configurations of Australian National Identity*, Annandale: Pluto Press.

Otto, T. and Driessen, H. (2000), 'Protean Perplexities: An Introduction', in T. Otto and H. Driessen (eds), *Perplexities of Identification: Anthropological Studies in Cultural Differentiation and the Use of Resources*, 8–26, Aarhus: Aarhus University Press.

Ottosson, Å. (1988), *Drömtidslandet: Möten med Natur och Människor i Australien*, Stockholm: Norstedts.

Ottosson, Å. (2012), 'The Intercultural Crafting of *Real* Aboriginal Country and Manhood in Central Australia', *Australian Journal of Anthropology* 23(2): 179–96.

Ottosson, Å. (2014), 'To Know One's Place: Belonging and Differentiation in Alice Springs Town', *Anthropological Forum* 24(2): 115–35.

Ottosson, Å. (2016), 'Holding On to Country: Musical Moorings for Desired Masculinities in Aboriginal Australia', in D. Pecknold and K. McCusker (eds), *Country Boys and Redneck Women: New Essays in Gender and Country Music*, Jackson, MS: University Press of Mississippi.

Parry, S. and Austin, T. (1998), 'Making Connections or Causing Disconnections', in T. Austin and S. Parry (eds), *Connection and Disconnection: Encounters Between Settlers and Indigenous People in the Northern Territory*, 1–26. Darwin: Northern Territory University.

Peirce, C. (1974), *Collected Papers, Vols. I and II*, Cambridge, MA: Harvard University Press.

Peterson, N. and Langton, M., eds (1983), *Aborigines, Land and Land Rights*, Canberra: Australian Institute of Aboriginal Studies.

Peterson, R. A. (1997), *Creating Country Music: Fabricating Authenticity*, Chicago, IL: University of Chicago Press.

Povinelli, E. (2002), *The Cunning of Recognition: Indigenous Alterities and the Making of Australian Multiculturalism*, Durham: Duke University Press.

Pringle, H. (1997), 'The Making of an Australian Civic Identity: The Bodies of Men and the Memory of War', in G. Stokes (ed.), *The Politics of Identity in Australia*, 92–104, Cambridge: Cambridge University Press.

Prins, H. (1997), 'The Paradox of Primitivism: Native Rights and the Problem of Imagery in "Cultural Survival"', *Visual Anthropology* 9: 243–66.

Radano, R. and Bohlman, P., eds (2000), *Music and the Racial Imagination*, Chicago, IL: The University of Chicago Press.

Reynolds, H. (2000), *Black Pioneers: How Aboriginal and Islander People Helped Building Australia*, Ringwood, VIC: Penguin Books.

Reynolds, S. and Press, J. (1995), *The Sex Revolts: Gender, Rebellion, and Rock'n'roll*, Cambridge, MA: Harvard University Press.

Rowse, T. (1988), 'From Houses to Households? The Aboriginal Development Commission and Economic Adaptation by Alice Springs Town Campers', *Aborigines and the State in Australia, Special Issue. Social Analysis* 24: 50–65.

Rowse, T. (1998), *White Flour, White Power: From Rations to Citizenship in Central Australia*, Cambridge: Cambridge University Press.

Rowse, T. (2002), *Indigenous Futures: Choice and Development for Aboriginal and Islander Australia*, Sydney: University of New South Wales Press.

Rutherford, J. (1980), 'Aboriginal Rights Give Way to Alcoa at Portland', *Legal Service Bulletin* 5(6): 316–17.

Ryan, R. (2003), 'Gumleaves or Paper Roses? Indigenous and Introduced Traits in the Koori/Goori Country Music Tradition', in P. Hayward (ed.), *Outback and Urban: Australian Country Music, Vol.1*, Gympie, QLD: Australian Institute of Country Music.

Sabo, D., Kupers, T. and London, W., eds (2001), *Prison Masculinities*, Philadelphia: Temple University Press.

Saggers, S. and Gray, D. (1998), *Dealing with Alcohol: Indigenous Usage in Australia, New Zealand and Canada*, Cambridge: Cambridge University Press.

Samuels, D. (2004), *Putting a Song on Top of It: Expressions and Identity on the San Carlos Apache Reservation*, Tucson: The University of Arizona Press.

Sansom, B. (1980), *The Camp at Wallaby Cross*, Canberra: Australian Institute of Aboriginal Studies.

Saussure, F. (1959), *Course in General Linguistics*, New York: Philosophical Library.

Scott, J. (1985), *Weapons of the Weak: Everyday Forms of Resistance*, New Haven, CT: Yale University Press.

Scott, J. (1990), *Domination and the Arts of Resistance: Hidden Transcripts*, New Haven, CT: Yale University Press.

Segal, L. (1990), *Slow Motion: Changing Men, Changing Masculinities*, London: Virago.

Shapiro, H. (1999), *Waiting for the Man: The Story of Drugs and Popular Music*, London: Helter Skelter Publishing.

Shoemaker, A. (1994), 'The Politics of Yothu Yindi', in K. Darian-Smith (ed.), *Working Papers in Australian Studies*, 88–96, London: Institute of Commonwealth Studies.

Sider, G. (2006), 'The Walls Came Tumbling Up: The Production of Culture, Class and Native American Societies', *Australian Journal of Anthropology* 17(3): 276–90.

Slobin, M. (1993), *Subcultural Sounds: Micromusics of the West*, Hanover: Wesleyan University Press.

Smith, G. (2005), *Singing Australia: A History of Folk and Country Music*, North Melbourne: Pluto Press Australia.

Spencer, B. and Gillen, F. (1899), *Native Tribes of Central Australia*, London: Macmillan.

Spencer, B. and Gillen, F. (1904), *Northern Tribes of Central Australia*, London: Macmillan.

Spivak, G. C. (1996), *The Spivak Reader*, New York: Routledge.

Stanley, O. (1989), 'The Changing Roles for Aboriginal Bush Towns', in P. Loveday and A. Webb (eds), *Small Towns in Northern Australia*, 156–64, Darwin, NT: ANU North Australia Research Unit.

Stanner, W. E. H. (1968), *After the Dreaming*, Crows Nest, NSW: Australian Broadcasting Corporation.

Stillman, A. K. (1996), 'Beyond Bibliography: Interpreting Hawaian-Language Protestant Hymn Imprints', *Ethnomusicology* 40(3): 469–88.

Stokes, M., ed. (1994), *Ethnicity, Identity and Music: The Musical Construction of Place*, Oxford: Berg.

Stokes, M. (2000), 'East, West, and Arabesk', in G. Born and D. Hesmondhalgh (eds), *Western Music and its Others*, 213–33, Berkeley, CA: University of California Press.

Stoler, A. L. (1995), *Race and the Education of Desire: Foucault's History of Sexuality and the Colonial Order of Things*, Durham: Duke University Press.

Strehlow, T. D. G. (1971), *Songs of Central Australia*, Sydney: Angus & Robertson.

Stubbe, M. (1998), 'Are You Listening? Cultural Influences on the Use of Supportive Verbal Feedback in Conversation', *Journal of Pragmatics* 29: 257–89.

Sullivan, P. (2006), 'Introduction: Culture Without Cultures – The Culture Effect', *Australian Journal of Anthropology* 17(3): 253–64.

Sutton, P. (1992), 'Aboriginal Art, the Nation State, Suburbia', *Artlink* 12(3): 6–8.

Sutton, P. (2009), *The Politics of Suffering: Indigenous Australia and the End of Liberal Consensus*, Carlton, VIC: Melbourne University Press.

Taussig, M. (1993), *Mimesis and Alterity: A Particular History of the Senses*, New York: Routledge.

Taylor, J. (2009), 'Social Engineering and Indigenous Settlement: Policy and Demography in Remote Australia, *Australian Aboriginal Studies* 1: 4–15.

Taylor, J. and Bell, M. (1994), *The Mobility Status of Indigenous Australia*, Discussion Paper 78, Canberra: Australian National University, CAEPR.

Taylor, L., Ward, G., Henderson, G., Davis, R. and Wallis, L., eds (2005), *The Power of Knowledge, the Resonance of Tradition*, Canberra: Aboriginal Studies Press.

Thiele, S., ed. (1991), 'Reconsidering Aboriginality', *Australian Journal of Anthropology* 2(2) Special Issue.

Thomas, N. (1991), *Entangled Objects: Exchange, Material Culture, and Colonialism in the Pacific*, Cambridge, MA: Harvard University Press.

Thomas, N. (1994), *Colonialism's Culture: Anthropology, Travel and Government*, Cambridge: Polity Press.

Tonkinson, R. (1974), *The Jigalong Mob: Aboriginal Victors of the Desert Crusade*, Menlo Park, CA: Cummings Publishing Company.

Tonkinson, R. (1998), 'National Identity: Australia after Mabo', in J. Wassman (ed.), *Pacific Answers to Western Hegemony: Cultural Practices of Identity Construction*, 287–310, Oxford: Berg.

Torgovnick, M. (1990), *Gone Primitive: Savage Intellects, Modern Lives*, Chicago, IL: The University of Chicago Press.

Trigger, D. (1992), *Whitefella Comin': Aboriginal Responses to Colonialism in Northern Australia*, Cambridge: Cambridge University Press.

Tunstill, G. (1989), 'An Overview of the Centre for Aboriginal Studies in Music 1988', *Australian Aboriginal Studies* 1: 29–30.

Turino, T. (1999), 'Signs of Imagination, Identity, and Experience: A Peircian Semiotic Theory for Music', *Ethnomusicology* 43(2): 221–55.

Turner, T. (2002), 'Representation, Politics, and Cultural Imagination in Indigenous Video', in F. D. Ginsburg, L. Abu-Lughod and B. Larkin (eds), *Media Worlds. Anthropology on New Terrain*, 75–89, Berkeley, CA: University of California Press.

von Sturmer, J. (1981), 'Talking with Aborigines', *Australian Institute of Aboriginal Studies Newsletter New Series* 15: 1–19.

von Sturmer, J. (1989), 'Aborigines, Representation, Necrophilia', *Art & Text* 32: 127–39.

Wade, P. (2000), *Music, Race and Nation: Musica Tropical in Colombia*, Chicago, IL: The University of Chicago Press.

Wade, P. (2002), *Race, Nature and Culture: An Anthropological Perspective*, London: Pluto Press.

Walker, C. (2000), *Buried Country: The Story of Aboriginal Country Music*, Annandale: Pluto Press.

Walser, R. (1993), *Running with the Devil: Power, Gender, and Madness in Heavy Metal Music*, Hanover: Wesleyan University Press.

Waterman, C. (2000), 'Race Music: Bo Chatmon, "Corrine Corrina," and the Excluded Middle', in R. Radano and P. V. Bohlman (eds), *Music and the Racial Imagination*, 167–205, Chicago, IL: The University of Chicago Press

Weiner, J. (2006), 'Eliciting Customary Law', *Asia Pacific Journal of Anthropology* 7(1): 15–25.

Wells, J. (1998), 'Welfare Colonialists: Contexts and Encounters on Government Settlements', in T. Austin and S. Parry (eds), *Connection and Disconnection:*

Encounters Between Settlers and Indigenous People in the Northern Territory, 275–297, Darwin: Northern Territory University.

Whidden, L. (1984), 'How Can You Dance to Beethoven? Native People and Country Music', *Canadian University Music Review* 5: 87–103.

Whiteley, S. and Hawkins, S., eds (1997), *Sexing the Groove: Popular Music and Gender*, London: Routledge.

Whiteoak, J. (2003), 'The Frontiers: Early Cowboy Music in Australian Popular Music', in P. Hayward (ed.), *Outback and Urban: Australian Country Music, Vol.1*, 1–28, Gympie, QLD: Australian Institute of Country Music.

Wild, S. (1987), 'Recreating the Jukurrpa: Adaptation and Innovation of Songs and Ceremonies in Warlpiri Society', in M. Clunies Ross, T. Donaldson and S. A. Wild (eds), *Songs of Aboriginal Australia*, 97–120, Sydney, NSW: University of Sydney.

Williams, R. (1985), *Keywords: A Vocabulary of Culture and Society*, New York: Oxford University Press.

Willis, J. (1997), *Romance, Ritual and Risk: Pitjantjatjara Masculinity in the Era of AIDS*, PhD Thesis, Brisbane: University of Queensland.

Willis, J. (2003a), 'Heteronormativity and the Deflection of Male Same-Sex Attraction among the Pitjantjatjara People of Australia's Western Desert', *Culture, Health & Sexuality* 5(2): 137–51.

Willis, J. (2003b), 'Condoms are for Whitefellas: Barriers to Pitjantjatjara Men's Use of Safe Sex Technologies', *Culture, Health & Sexuality* 5(3): 203–17.

Wilson, R. (1997), *Bringing Them Home: Report of the National Enquiry into the Separation of Aboriginal and Torres Strait Islander Children from their Families*, Sydney: Sterling Press.

Wong, D. (2000), 'The Asian American Body in Performance', in R. Radano and P. V. Bohlman (eds), *Music and the Racial Imagination*, 57–94, Chicago, IL: The University of Chicago Press.

Worth, H. (2002), '"Tits is just an Accessory"; Masculinity and Femininity in the Lives of Maori and Pacific Queens', in H. Worth, A. Paris and L. Allen (eds), *The Life of Brian*, 117–38, Dunedin, NZ: University of Otago Press.

Yarwood, A. T. (1962), 'The "White Australia" Policy', *Historical Studies* 10(39): 257–69.

Young, E. and Doohan, K. (1989), *Mobility for Survival: A Process Analysis of Aboriginal Population Movement in Central Australia*, Darwin: ANU North Australia Unit.

Yuval-Davis, N. (2006), 'Belonging and the Politics of Belonging', *Patterns of Prejudice* 40(3): 197–214.

Discography

Adamson, Trevor (1997), *Waltzing Matilda*, CAAMA Music.
Alberts, Andy (1998), *Gunditjmara Land*, Andrew Alberts.
Alberts, Andy (2001), *Close to Home*, Andrew Alberts.
Areyonga Desert Tigers (1988), *Light On*, CAAMA Music.
Blackshadow Band (2001), *Blackshadow Band*, CAAMA Music.
Blackstorm (1998), *Highway to Nowhere*, CAAMA Music.

Butcher, Sammy (2002), *Desert Surf Guitar*, CAAMA Music.

Country Wranglers (1999), *Kintore Gospel*, CAAMA Music.

Ikuntji (Haasts Bluff) Gospel Band (2003), *Ikuntji (Haasts Bluff) Gospel Band*, CAAMA Music.

Kintore Gospel Band and Mt Liebig Band (circa 1988), *Western Desert Gospel*, Imparja Recordings.

Lajamanu Teenage Band (1995), *Echo Voices*, CAAMA Music.

Lajamanu Teenage Band (1998), *Vision*, CAAMA Music.

Lajamanu Teenage Band (1999), *Dreamtime Hero*, CAAMA Music.

Lajamanu Teenage Band (2002), *Warlpiri Woman*, CAAMA Music.

Lajamanu Teenage Band (2006), *Prisoner*, CAAMA Music.

Langdon, Jimmy (1999), *My Spinifex Country*, CAAMA Music.

Laughton, Herbie (1983), *Herbie Laughton*, Imparja Recordings.

Laughton, Herbie (1999), *Country From the Heart*, Pindaroo Music.

Lazy Late Boys (1999), *Freedom Day*, CAAMA Music.

Ltyentye Apurte Band (2001), *It's Our Home - Santa Teresa*, CAAMA Music.

NoKTuRNL (2003), *Time Flies*, Mushroom Records.

North Tanami Band (1990), *Warlpiri, Warlpiri People*, CAAMA Music.

North Tanami Band (1995), *The Travelling Warlpiri*, CAAMA Music.

North Tanami Band (1999), *This Land*, CAAMA Music.

North Tanami Band (2003), *Land is Our Life*, CAAMA Music.

North Tanami Band (2005), *Warlpiri Tribe*, CAAMA Music.

Pukatja Band (1992), *Pukatja Band*, CAAMA Music.

Reid, Lyndon (2002) *Make a Start*, CAAMA Music.

Rising Wind Band (2000), *Living on Yurrampi*, CAAMA Music.

Rising Wind Band (2004), *Clear My Mind*, CAAMA Music.

Titjikala Band (2001), *Tapatjatjaka*, CAAMA Music.

Titjikala Desert Oaks Band (1989), *Titjikala Desert Oaks Band*, CAAMA Music.

Ulpanyali Band (1991), *Ulpanyali Band*, CAAMA Music.

Various (1982), *Desert Songs, Vol. 1*, Imparja Recordings.

Various (1983), *Desert songs, Vol. 2*, Imparja Recordings.

Various (1988a), *Papal Concert*, Imparja Recordings.

Various (1988b), *Wama Wanti - Drink Little Bit*, CAAMA Music.

Various (1990), *Sing Loud Play Strong*, CAAMA Music.

Various (2000), *Buried Country*, Larrikin Records.

Warumpi Band (1985), *Big Name, No Blanket*, Festival Records.

Warumpi Band (1987), *Go Bush!*, Festival Records.

Warumpi Band (1996), *Too Much Humbug*, CAAMA Music.

Williams, Gus (1993), *My Kind of Heaven*, Ntjalka.

Williams, Gus and Country Ebony (1989), *Storm in My Heart*, Ntjalka.

Williams, Gus and Country Ebony (1991), *I'm Not Trying to Forget*, Ntjalka.

Williams, Gus and Country Ebony (1992), *Straight From the Heart*, Ntjalka.

Williams, Gus and Country Ebony (1993), *Southern Cross*, Ntjalka.

Williams, Gus and Country Ebony (1994), *Through the Years*, Hadley.

Williams, Warren H. (1995), *Western Wind*, CAAMA Music.

Williams, Warren H. (1998), *Country Friends and Me*, CAAMA Music.

Williams, Warren H. (2000), *Where My Heart Is*, CAAMA Music.

Williams, Warren H. (2002) *Places in Between*, CAAMA Music.

Williams, Warren H. (2005), *Be Like Home*, CAAMA Music.

Williams, Warren H. (2009), *Looking Out*, Heartland.

Williams, Warren H. and the Warumungu Songmen (2012), *Winanjjara*, ABC Music.

Yamma, Frank (1997), *Solid Eagle*, CAAMA Music.

Yamma, Frank (1999), *Playing with Fire – Warungku Inkanyi*, CAAMA Music.

Yamma, Frank (2006), *Keep up the Pace*, CAAMA Music.

Yamma, Frank (2010), *Countryman*, Wantok/Planet.

Yamma, Frank (2014), *Uncle*, Wantok Musik.

Yamma, Isaac and the Pitjantjatjara Country Band (1983), *First Album*, Imparja Recordings.

Yamma, Isaac and the Pitjantjatjara Country Band (1987), *Second Album*, Imparja Recordings.

Index

Page references in *italics* refer to photos and maps.

Lightning Source UK Ltd.
Milton Keynes UK
UKOW06n0501090516

273849UK00004B/18/P